A Garland Series

RENAISSANCE DRAMA

A COLLECTION OF CRITICAL EDITIONS

edited by
STEPHEN ORGEL
The Johns Hopkins University

An Old-Spelling, Critical Edition of THE HISTORY OF THE TWO MAIDS OF MORE-CLACKE

ALEXANDER S. LIDDIE

GARLAND PUBLISHING, INC.
NEW YORK & LONDON • 1979

All volumes in this series are printed on
acid-free, 250-year-life paper.

Library of Congress Cataloging in Publication Data

Armin, Robert, fl. 1610.
An old-spelling, critical edition of The history of the two maids of More-Clacke.

(Renaissance drama)
Originally presented as the author's thesis, Rutgers University, 1967.
Bibliography: p.
I. Liddie, Alexander S., 1933– II. Title.
III. Title: The history of the two maids of More-Clacke.
IV. Series.
PR2417.H5 1979 822'.3 78-66849
ISBN 0-8240-9742-4

PRINTED IN THE UNITED STATES OF AMERICA

Preface to the Garland Edition

The study of Armin's work is an ongoing process, and at least three scholars have recently published articles relevant to questions raised by my work, which was completed in 1967. The key question dealt with by these scholars is whether or not Armin also wrote a play entitled *The Valiant Welshman*. If we could prove that he did, then we would be safe in saying that the embarrassing stylistic idiosyncrasies of *Two Maids* are due to the nature of the printer's copy and do not represent Armin's polished work. If we could prove that he did not write *Welshman*, then Armin would stand convicted of being a very bad writer indeed. In my Appendix I present the reasons, which I say are "sound but not compelling," for believing that he did write *Welshman*, which is a far more literate play than *Two Maids*. My contention, therefore, that the printer worked from a set of completed but inadequately revised foul papers (what we would today call a "rough draft") is based on the unproven assumption that Armin wrote *Welshman*.

My arguments were endorsed and supplemented by John P. Feather of Oxford in his articles "A Check-List of the Works of Robert Armin" (*The Library* xxvi. 2 (1971), 165-172) and "The Authorship of *The Valiant Welshman*" (as far as I know, still unpublished). Two other writers, however, have challenged Feather's reasoning and have adduced evidence which undermines claims for Armin's authorship. H. F. Lippincott (Bibliographic Problems in the Works of Robert Armin," *The Library* xxx. 4 (1975) 330-333), drawing, in part, upon arguments used by J. G. Tilney-Bassett in his unpublished thesis ("Robert Armin, ?1570-1615," Keble College, Oxford, 1935), argues tellingly against some of my evidence and my conclusion. Lippincott's position is further supported by D. J. Lake's study, "The Canon of Robert Armin's Works: Some Difficulties," N&Q 24 (1977) 117-120. Lake presents a chart to show that in his acknowledged works Armin preferred such usages as "amongst" to "among," "betwixt" to "between," "while" to "whilst," and "ye" to you," whereas the opposite usages appear in Welshman. Lake's is surely the hardest evidence yet to be presented against the case for Armin's authorship, and although the reliability of the kind of evidence he presents is still disputed by bibliographical scholars, I would certainly agree with his conclusion that the case for Armin is "not proven."

I am very grateful to professors Lake, Feather, and Lippincott for their explorations of the question and especially grateful to John Feather and Fred Lippincott for their keeping me informed of their discoveries and for their gracious aid and encouragement. In 1967 I would have said that the odds were three to two in favor of Armin's authorship of The Valiant Welshman; I now think they are about three to one against it. I hope that this edition will stir other scholars to pursue, refine, amend, and correct some of the other arguments, conjectures, guesses, and "facts" proposed in this edition of The History of the Two Maids of More-clacke.

TABLE OF CONTENTS

Page

FOREWORD

The ensuing work is an old-spelling, critical edition of _The History of the two Maids of More-clacke_, a comedy by Robert Armin, who wrote it during the years from 1598 to 1606, a period spanning his employment as a comic actor in Shakespeare's company. The play was first published in 1609 with a prefatory epistle by the author, claiming that it was performed by the Children of the King's Majesty's Revels. There is no evidence of its further performance. There were no further editions until 1880, when Alexander B. Grosart published Armin's collected works; the original quarto was reprinted by Tudor Facsimile Texts in 1913. The play relates the complicated intrigues leading up to the marriages of two daughters of a knight of More-clacke (now called Mort-lake, a suburb some ten or fifteen miles southwest of London); its style is frequently garbled beyond comprehension and almost never lucid, its plot is incredibly labyrinthian, and its characterizations vague. But its style, plot, and characterization are also the vehicles for an extended criticism-by-parody of Shakespeare's major tragedies, especially _Hamlet_. Therefore, all those interested in Shakespeare must be curious to assess the popular entertainer's response to the great dramatist.

THE WORKS OF ROBERT ARMIN

1590 A preface to *A Brief Resolution of the Right Religion*.

1600 *Quips Upon Questions*.

Foole Upon Foole.

1604 "Dedication" to *A True Discourse of the Practices of Elizabeth Caldwell*.

1605 *Foole Upon Foole*, second edition.

1608 *A Nest of Ninnies*.

1609 *The Italian Tailor and his Boy*.

The History of the two Maids of More-clacke.

1615 *The Valiant Welshman*.

1.
AUTHOR

Had all the writings of Robert Armin been among the many of his era that disappeared before we could take their measure, we should not be crucially deprived. Considered as a literary artist only, he made no shaping contribution to English literature. His significance derives almost exclusively from his roles as a comic actor and, perhaps, as a source of comic inventions in the acting company for which Shakespeare wrote. Still, his life and work deserve a niche in our study of the literary, theatrical, and social scene of Shakespearean England. As a goldsmith, actor, singer, student of foolery, pamphleteer, poet, playwright, and acquaintance of Shakespeare, his life and work provide crossing strands for the scholar's net. It has been said that "among two hundred playwrights of the period and two hundred seventy-five actors, scarcely a score combined the creative function with the mimetic art,"[1] and Armin was one of the score. His talent, though limited, was varied, and he probably occupied a place in the popular culture of his day similar to that of an Ed Wynn, Steve Allen, Milton

[1]Felix Schelling, Elizabethan Drama, 1558-1642, II (New York, 1908), 376.

Berle, Zero Mostel, or Jerry Lewis in our own, men who clown, mime, sing, pontificate, and write third-rate fiction, men who are alternately scorned and given grudging admiration by the *literati*, men whose pretensions and lapses of taste are often forgiven because they offer undemanding but craftsmanlike entertainment.

Armin was born approximately four years after Shakespeare, in King's Lynne, Norfolk, East Anglia, *circa* 1568.[2] His burial is recorded in the register of St. Bodolphe Aldgate, November 30, 1615, a few months before Shakespeare's death. His will reveals that despite conventional protestations and bits of other evidence to the contrary he was "fairly well off,"[3] indicating to some extent the success of his career.

The record of that career begins with his apprenticeship to John Lowyson, goldsmith, of London, in 1581, which brought him to London when he was approximately thirteen. He must have had some talent to win such an apprenticeship because "goldsmithing was perhaps the closest to an art form of all Elizabethan trades and demanded taste and a discriminating eye not only in the

[2]Leslie Hotson, *Shakespeare's Motley* (Oxford, 1952), p. 105. Hotson, in turn, is heavily indebted to Emma Marshall Denkinger ("Actors' Names in the Registers of St. Bodolphe Aldgate," *PMLA*, XLI [1926], 91-109). Hotson deduces the date from Armin's signed entry of his apprenticeship, dated 1581, to John Lowyson. The apprenticeship was to last for eleven years, and it was customary for them to end at the age of twenty-four.

[3]Hotson, p. 111.

making of jewelry but in the cosseting of rich customers as well,"[4] so that the boy must have been reasonably well-spoken and soundly educated in grammar school.

We do not know when or whether Armin completed his apprenticeship, since his master died the following year and he was certainly involved in other affairs before 1592. But Hotson[5] has demonstrated exhaustively that his knowledge of the trade is drawn on both in his own writings and in the parts Shakespeare created for him. Very probably the turning point in Armin's life came between 1581 and 1588, for it was during this period that he met Richard Tarleton (d. 1588), the most famous clown of his day and actor for the Queen's Company.

In his <u>Jests</u> Tarleton tells how he adopted Armin as a son to succeed him. Armin had been collecting installment payments on a debt owed his master by a man named Charles, who lived in the same lodging as Tarleton. When the man could no longer pay, Armin left these verses chalked on a wainscot:

> O world, why wilt thou lye?
> Is this Charles the Great! that I deny
> Indeed Charles the Great before,
> But now Charles the lesse, being poore.

When Tarleton came upon and read the verses, he was so pleased that he wrote these beneath them:

[4]Charles S. Felver, <u>Robert Armin, Shakespeare's Fool</u> (Kent, Ohio, 1961), p. 78.

[5]Hotson, pp. 116-128.

A wagge thou art, none can prevent thee;
And thy desert shall content thee.
Let me devine. As I am
My adopted sonne therefore be,
To enjoy my clownes sute after me.[6]

Although the anecdote may be a dramatic fiction (it anticipates the souped-up Hollywood biographies of contemporary entertainers), Denkinger has shown that the parish of St. Bodolphe extra Aldgate, Armin's residence, was "an artistic colony"[7] where such a meeting could have taken place. Though his connection with the goldsmiths from this time on must have been tenuous, the records of his death indicate that he was "ffree of the goldsmiths and a player,"[8] and Felver speculates that he may have been given his "freedom" from the apprenticeship "as a tribute to his fame as an actor."[9]

Presumably, Armin left the trade and began observing and practicing comic routines in the theater, at the same time beginning to make himself known as a pamphleteer, though none of his work is extant. In 1590 he supplied a preface to a pious work entitled A Brief Resolution of the

[6]Richard Tarleton, Tarleton's Jests and News Out of Purgatory, ed. James O. Halliwell-Phillipps (London, 1844), p. 22.

[7]Denkinger, p. 93.

[8]Denkinger, p. 95.

[9]Charles S. Felver, "William Shakespeare and Robert Armin His Fool: A Working Partnership," unpublished doctoral dissertation (University of Michigan, 1955), p. 182.

Right Religion.[10] In 1592 Thomas Nashe groups him with other pamphleteers in Strange Newes: "Hough! Thomas Delone, Phillip Stubb, Robert Armin, &c., your father Elderton is abus'd. Revenge! Revenge on your course paper and want of matter that hath most sacrilegiously contaminated the divine spirit and quintessence of penny a quart."[11]

Though there is little authoritative knowledge of Armin's activities between 1590 and 1599, it seems probable that he was primarily engaged in acting comic parts at Sudely Castle, Gloucestershire, for Lord Chandos' provincial company of players, under the patronage of Giles, and,

[10]Alexander B. Grosart, ed., The Works of Robert Armin, Actor (Manchester, 1880), p. x.

[11]Thomas Nashe, "Strange Newes of the Intercepting Certaine Letters," The Works of Thomas Nashe, ed. R. B. McKerrow, I (London, 1904), 280. There is some scholarly disagreement on Nashe's intention in invoking Armin's name. Felver (Robert Armin, Shakespeare's Fool, p. 10) writes, "Nashe jocosely invokes the wrath of Armin, along with his fellow pamphleteers, against amateur pamphleteers like Harvey." This suggests that Nashe is calling upon Armin as a professional equal to join him in squashing a pretentious upstart. But those familiar with Nashe know that anyone linked with the morally austere Stubb must be, for Nashe, part of a Dunciad. The point seems to be not that Harvey is challenging the good reputation of fellow professionals but that his work challenges or competes only with that of dunces. This interpretation is further supported by Armin's public piety reflected in his previously mentioned preface and in his remarks on tobacco (see Two Maids, XVIII, 57-60, and A Nest of Ninnies, ed. J. P. Collier [London, 1842], p. 49). Furthermore, Harvey's reply to Nashe (in Harvey's Works, II, ed. A. B. Grosart [London, 1884], 280-281) rebukes Nashe for imitating the very men "he desdaineth." Thus Harvey, at least, interprets Nashe's mention of Armin as contemptuous rather than comradely. (For further commentary on the dispute, see George Richard Hibbard, Thomas Nashe [Cambridge, Mass., 1962], p. 218 et passim.)

later, William Brydges (1577-1602).[12] The significant evidence for supposing this connection is Armin's "Dedication" to _A True Discourse of the Practices of Elizabeth Caldwell_, written, he says, by his "kinsman" Gilbert Dugdale and printed in 1604: "To the right honorable, and his singular good lady, the Lady Mary Chandois R. A. wisheth health and everlasting happiness."[13] In the remainder of the preface Armin writes, "Your good Honor knowes Pincks[14] poore hart, who in all my services to your late deceased kind Lord, never savoured of flatterie, or fixion: and therefore am now the bolder to present your vertues, the view of this late truth."[15] Unfortunately, no further clues as to the precise time and duration of the relationship with Lord Chandos exist; such information might be of help in determining the date of composition of _Two Maids_. In any case, a position with such a traveling company would have been

[12]Felver, _Robert Armin, Shakespeare's Fool_, p. 13, cites J. T. Murray, _English Dramatic Companies 1558-1642_ (London, 1910), pp. 28-30. See also R. B. Sharpe, _The Real War of the Theaters_ (Boston, 1935), p. 139.

[13]Grosart, p. xi.

[14]Hotson, pp. 112-114, convincingly demonstrates that Armin probably used an ermine, pronounced "armin," on his coat of arms; "a 'pink' was a small ornamental gash or cut; a modest diminutive for our Armin. Not even a pelt of the little ermine, but a tiny cut of it!" Thus the nickname.

[15]Grosart, pp. x-xi. Further evidence of Armin's connection with Lord Chandos' Company is provided in his _Foole Upon Foole, or Six Sortes of Sottes_, where he tells an incident which took place at Pershore in Worcestershire, during a tour of "the Lord Shandoyes players," at which he was himself present.

a natural springboard to his next employment: an actor-sharer in the Chamberlain's Men.

In 1599 or 1600 Armin joined "Shakespeare's" company. The precise time is difficult to ascertain for several reasons, but, since Felver's thesis is that Armin's clowning style and his character Tutch in Two Maids influenced Shakespeare's Touchstone and succeeding "witty fools," it should be important to determine whether Shakespeare knew either Armin or his play before writing As You Like It, the date of which is also the subject of controversy, though 1600 is generally thought to meet most requirements.[16] In 1600 Armin published both Quips Upon Questions (written in 1599)[17] and the first edition of Foole Upon Foole. In the prefaces to both of these he refers to himself as the "Clonnico de Curtanio Snuffe"[18] (Snuff, the clown of the Curtain). In the second edition of Foole Upon Foole (1605), he is "Clonnico del Mondo Snuffe," indicating that he has shifted from the Curtain to the Globe.[19] The Globe was being constructed in the winter of 1599, and the Chamberlain's Men

[16]Edmund K. Chambers, The Elizabethan Stage, III (Cambridge, 1923), 486. G. L. Kittredge, ed., As You Like It (New York, 1939), gives 1599 as the date.

[17]Chambers, II, 300.

[18]For an explanation of "Snuff" as another nickname for Armin, see Hotson, p. 114.

[19]Chambers, II, 300. Chambers also notes that there are other now non-existent editions of 1601 and 1602 "said to have been in the Harley Collection, and there is a reprint by F. Ouvry (1875)."

evidently moved into it from the Curtain between April and September of that year.[20] But it is not necessary to assume that Armin made the move at the same time, even though Kempe, his predecessor as clown in the company, probably left in February, 1599.[21] Baldwin has argued that since the Curtain and the Globe were both open during 1599, Armin could have been at the Curtain, after the Chamberlain's Men left, with Lord Chandos' Men until 1600, thus accounting for the preface of the 1600 Foole Upon Foole.[22] On the other hand, Armin may have joined the Chamberlain's Men early in 1599 before they left the Curtain, and his competition may have brought about the February departure of the decreasingly popular Kempe.[23]

Whatever the precise date of his joining the company, his name is definitely in the 1603 license for the

[20]Chambers, III, 403 and 415; also Sharpe, p. 139.

[21]Chambers, II, 326.

[22]Thomas Whitfield Baldwin, "Shakespeare's Jester: The Dates of Much Ado and As You Like It," MLN, XXXIX (1924), 451.

[23]Felver, Robert Armin, Shakespeare's Fool, p. 21. Frederick W. Sternfield (Music in Shakespearian Tragedy [New York, 1963], p. 108) and other scholars agree that the following lines from Hamlet, which is thought to have been performed shortly after Kempe's departure, are a criticism of his style and that Armin's adoption by the company was aimed at facilitating a shift to a more sophisticated kind of clown in the plays. "And let those that play your clowns speak no more than is set down for them. For there be of them that will themselves laugh, to set on some quantity of barren spectators to laugh too, though in the meantime some necessary question of the play be then considered. That's villainous and shows a most pitiful ambition in the fool that uses it." III.ii.42-51.

King's Men and on the Coronation list of 1604.[24] He played the roles of Touchstone, Feste, Lear's Fool, and others.[25] His publications from 1600 to 1605 have already been noted. Also in 1605 Augustine Phillips left him 20 shillings as his "fellow."[26] Until 1608 his books had been published anonymously, but in that year Foole Upon Foole, or Six Sortes of Sottes, a collection of anecdotes and reports on well-known mentally retarded figures of the period, was enlarged with some incoherent moralizing and retitled A Nest of Ninnies.[27]

In 1609 Armin published The History of the two Maids of More-clacke. After indicating in the prefatory epistle that the play had been performed "by the boyes of the Revels,"[28] he adds that "I would have againe inacted John my selfe, but Tempora mutantur in illis, & I cannot do as I would." Grosart infers from this (and Hotson does not object) that Armin "is too infirm to act the part."[29] Since he is also on the actor list of Jonson's The Alchemist (1610), Grosart, to validate his assumption of Armin's

[24]Chambers, II, 300.

[25]Felver, Robert Armin, Shakespeare's Fool, pp. 16 and 19. Also Thomas Whitfield Baldwin, The Organization and Personnel of the Shakespearean Company (Princeton, 1927), pp. 244-245.

[26]Chambers, II, 300. Also Grosart, p. viii.

[27]Available in John Payne Collier's edition, Fools and Jesters (London, 1842).

[28]See this edition, p. 104.

[29]Grosart, p. viii.

infirmity, assumes that the part "must have been acted much earlier than 1610." Yet the title page of the 1616 edition states, "Acted in the yeere 1610,"[30] and I can find no evidence in favor of an earlier date for this play. Surely there may have been other circumstances beside illness which could have prevented Armin from doing as he would, not the least of which is the possibility that he could persuade no one to produce Two Maids.[31] Furthermore, Armin was well enough early in 1609 to have some part in the publication of his verse translation of Straparola's Notte Piacevoli, The Italian Taylor and his Boy (Stationer's Register, 6 Feb., 1609). But there is no mention of him in the actor's list for Jonson's Catiline (1611).[32]

Thus five years elapse between his last known performance in The Alchemist and his death in November, 1615. During those years Armin would seem to have had the time, incentive, and developing skill necessary to write a play

[30]Chambers, III, 371.

[31]Felver (Robert Armin, Shakespeare's Fool, p. 73) assumes that Armin's phrase "I can not do as I would" refers to the time of the play's production by the Children of the King's Revels and that Armin means only that he couldn't take John's role at that time "because of his association with the King's Men, and because the other company was a boy's company."

[32]Chambers, II, 300. His deactivation is perhaps explained by the diminution of clownish roles in Shakespeare's later plays and his inability to fit the requirements of Jonson or Beaumont and Fletcher (see Felver, Robert Armin, Shakespeare's Fool, p. 69). His last spree of publishing, unless one accepts his authorship of The Valiant Welshman (1615), was done during a hiatus in theatrical activities caused by the plague which "kept the London theaters closed from July 1608 to December 1609" (Chambers, II, 214).

entered in the Stationer's Register on February 21, 1615. The Valiant Welshman was written between late 1610 and late 1614, years when Armin was between forty-two and forty-six years old. Since his authorship of the play is both a matter of scholarly dispute and highly relevant to my theories about the nature of the printer's copy and Armin's literary intentions in Two Maids, I provide old and new evidence of his authorship in an appendix.

Ultimately, however, the significance of Armin's life lies not in what he wrote but in what he did and was. He was the greatest comic actor of his time, a shaper, as Baldwin and Felver have shown, of Shakespeare's clowns and fools, and, apparently, a gentle and modest man.[33] John Davies of Hereford, in his Scourge of Folly (1610), wrote the following verses to him:

> To honest-gamesome Robert Armin,
> That tickles the spleen like an harmless vermin.
>
> Armine, what shall I say of thee, but this,
> Thou art a foole and a knave? Both? fie, I misse;
> And wrong thee much, sith thou in deede art neither,
> Although in shew, thou playest both together.
> Wee all (that's kings and all) but players are
> Upon this earthly stage; and should have care
> To play our parts so properly, that wee
> May at the end gaine an applauditee.
> But most men over-act, misse-act, or misse
> The action which to them peculier is;
> And the more high the part is which they play,
> The more they misse in what they do or say.
> So that when off the stage, by death, they wend,
> Men rather hisse at them than them commend.

[33]Austin K. Gray, "Robert Armine, The Fool," PMLA, XLII (1927), 673-685. Gray's article is a review of the then known facts of Armin's life, focusing on Armin's honest, kind, sympathetic personality.

But (honest Robin) thou with harmlesse mirth
Dost please the world; and (so) amongst the earth
That others but possesse with care, that stings:
So makes thy life more happy farre than kings.
And so much more our love should thee imbrace,
Sith still thou liv'st with some that dye to grace.
And yet are honest (in despite of lets),
Which earnes more praise then forced goodnesse gets.
So, play thy part, be honest still with mirth;
Then when th'art in the tyring-house of earth,
Thou being his servant whom all kings do serve,
Maist for thy part well played like praise deserve;
For in that tyring-house when either bee,
Y'are one mans men and equall in degree.
So thou, in sport, the happiest men doth schoole--
To do as thou dost,--wisely play the fool.[34]

[34] The Complete Works of John Davies of Hereford, ed. Alexander B. Grosart, II (Edinburgh, 1878), 60-61.

2.

DATE

It is an axiom of the Broadway theater today that "plays are not written but rewritten,"[1] and the recurrence, in modern scholarship concerned with the Elizabethan and Jacobean drama,[2] of theories of "interpolated matter" is evidence that the axiom held as well during Armin's career. Grosart, who first attempted to date the composition of Two Maids, found that though the bulk of the evidence favored an Elizabethan date (at least before 1603 and probably before 1600), he could account for certain passages only by assuming that they were injected into it after 1606.[3] Today we know far more about historiography, bibliography, and Armin's biography, but we are forced into the same conclusions, though for somewhat different reasons. The most we can be certain of in regard to the play is that at least one portion (and probably all of it) could not have been

[1]A remark by the demonstrably successful producer, David Merrick, made to the critic Jack O'Brien, who enthusiastically agreed, on the latter's daily radio program (WOR), June 9, 1966, during their discussion of the value of out-of-town tryouts.

[2]See, for example, Kenneth Muir in his discussion of the date of Macbeth, "Introduction" (Cambridge, Mass., 1952).

[3]Grosart, p. xvii.

written before June 14, 1597, and that it must have been in some playable form (probably as we now have it) by 1608. It will be best to establish the evidence for these "certainties" before moving into more speculative areas.

June 14, 1597, is the date upon which the Acts of the Privy Council reports that "Alice Stoite, a young woman of Dorset, was abducted by one Dinington and others."[4] Hillebrand, who has done the most systematic, antiquarian research of plays performed at Whitefriars, is unable to trace any more likely reference for Sir William's allusion in these lines:

> Yet remember Donnington's man, Grimes,
> Who for an heir so stolne and married,
> Was hanged, and the sergeant-at-armes,
> For assisting them did lose his place.
> (XXII.296-299)

It is, of course, possible that this line was added to an already nearly finished manuscript in order to buttress the verisimilitude of a barely credible plot. Armin's literary career began, after all, at least as early as 1590,[5] and it is not impossible that he had started the play before 1597, but, as we shall see, other evidence pushes the date of composition closer to the turn of the century. By the same token, we need not assume that the allusion to the abduction by Dinington (or Donnington) limits the date of the

[4]Harold Newcombe Hillebrand, "The Children of the King's Revels at Whitefriars," JEGP, XXI (1922), p. 328.

[5]In 1590 he supplied a preface to A Brief Resolution of the Right Religion; see Grosart, p. x.

play to within a year or a few months of the event. There is no need to denigrate Elizabethan powers of memory by assuming that audiences could not recall anything but yesterday's news. In reading the play for the first time, I was, myself, reminded of an incident which had taken place ten years before: an American soldier, for a time prisoner of the North Koreans, returned home to find that his wife, having heard him reported dead, had remarried.[6]

The very latest possible date for the play is, of course, 1609, the year of its publication (since it is not entered in the Stationer's Register, we cannot determine the exact time of year), but Armin's preface, "To the friendly peruser," gives reason for pushing the date back at least a year. He says of the play, in his customarily ambiguous fashion, that it is "a Historical discourse [Does he mean to imply that the story was based on an actual event? Grosart thinks so,[7] but I do not.], acted by the boyes of the Reuels, which perchance in part was sometime ["heretofore" (Grosart)] acted more naturally in the Citty, if not in the [w]hole."[8] If we take Armin at his word (there is no external support for his assertion about the play's production), the play must have been performed between 1606 and 1608, since that is the period in which

[6]New York Times, August 29, 1953, Sec. 2, p. 7.

[7]Grosart, p. xvi.

[8]See this edition, p. 104.

The Children of the King's Majesty's Revels (as they are called on the title page and by most scholars) were active.[9] Furthermore, his statement may be interpreted to mean that there were two separate productions, one by the "boyes of the Reuels" and another, earlier, one of only part of it. Since Armin is described in the entries of St. Bodolphe's register as a "player of Enterludes,"[10] it is quite possible that he performed the scenes of John i' th' Hospital as part of one of those interlude routines.

With those outside dates of 1597-1608 established, we may now review further evidence. First, we must not confuse, as Grosart does, evidence which establishes the time in which the play is set with evidence for its date of composition. The play is unquestionably set in the Elizabethan period: the monarch is referred to as "queene" (VII. 201) and as "her" (VII.181). There is also an allusion to Dean Nowell, who died in 1602.[11] But if the chief impetus to write the play was Armin's desire to recreate John i' th' Hospital, as "To the friendly peruser" implies, it is quite possible that Armin could be mentally reliving the past. He tells us in A Nest of Ninnies (1608) that John has been dead for some time,[12] yet he writes of him with

[9]Chambers, II, 64-66.

[10]Denkinger, passim.

[11]VII.156. Facts on Nowell are given in the DNB.

[12]Armin, Nest, p. 51. Furthermore, Armin's phrase in "To the friendly peruser" about John, "whose remembrance

affectionate memory then. And Dean Nowell was ninety-five years old and retired for thirteen years when he died in 1602; therefore, John's references to his relationship with the dean of St. Paul's are probably not meant to be current. Armin's play may have some of the qualities of a period piece.

R. B. Sharpe would place the play near 1602 on the basis of another allusion. Sir William's brother, the Governor of the Scilly Islands in the play, says:

> Sir that is France, a faire beseeming friend,
> On yonder continent stands Ireland,
> On this side Brittaine, and on that side Garsie,
> Islands besides of much hostillitie.
> (XVIII.12-15)

Sharpe finds that Sir Francis Godolphin, then in charge of the defense of the islands, wrote to Sir Robert Cecil, "on October 8, 1601, speaking of the spaniards at Kindsdale, 'I needs must write of the present dangerous estate of the isles of Scilly under my charge, being the fairest inn in the direct way between Spain and Ireland.'"[13] Sharpe does not give further details about the extent and duration of the concern for the islands, which would seem to have been justified during the whole long span of years of animosity between England and Spain and England and Ireland. Furthermore, Sharpe is characteristically and unconvincingly seeking to explain the play in terms of a personal feud which

---

I presume by appearance likely," indicates that John is no longer present.

[13]Sharpe, p. 224.

he says is the "real war of the theaters": "our play then, seems to have been contrived to interest relatives of the Godolphins...or rather...it was to amuse neighbors of the Godolphins and Killigrews by showing them in undignified--though sometimes pathetic--situations."[14] On the basis of such specious reasoning, one feels under no obligation to accept Sharpe's contribution to the dating problem under discussion.

Before going on to a review of the more controversial evidence of the date of composition (the evidence I have in mind is controversial because it involves interpretation of the nature of the play and evaluation of Armin's influence upon Shakespeare), we must consider the two main claims for Armin's significance as a playwright. The first claim, put forward by Baldwin,[15] Hotson,[16] and Felver[17] is that Armin, by his peculiar skills as a sophisticated clown and by his creation of Tutch, provided the seed from which grew Shakespeare's creation of Touchstone in _As You Like It_, which was probably written by June 1,

[14]Sharpe, p. 225.

[15]Baldwin, "Shakespeare's Jester," p. 451. In a note he says, "Cappell, _Notes on Shakespeare_, III, 494, says some authorities mention a 1599 edition of _Two Maids_, but neither Grosart nor the Malone Society in its reprint mentions such an edition or even the tradition of it."

[16]Hotson, p. 101, only argues for Armin's influence as an actor; he seems to accept a post-1600 date for the play. Austin Gray (p. 683), however, asserts that Armin played in _Two Maids_ before joining the King's Men.

[17]_Robert Armin, Shakespeare's Fool_, ch. III, _passim_.

1599, and definitely finished by August, 1600.[18] This means, obviously, that Two Maids must have been written before August, 1600, a conclusion not seriously contradicted by the evidence already given. But the second claim is that Two Maids is a parody of Shakespeare's major tragedies, which are all widely presumed to have been written after As You Like It and after 1600. Murry,[19] McGinn,[20] and O'Connor[21] all find in it imitations of Hamlet. It is not completely impossible to reconcile their position to that of Baldwin, Hotson, and Felver, since the plot of Hamlet was known as early as 1589 and "at least an early version of it was on the stage no later than 1600."[22] But Grosart[23] and I[24] also believe that passages of the play also imitate Lear (1605-1606) and Macbeth (1606). Clearly this latter claim is incompatible with the first unless the play underwent constant revision, and that is the hypothesis

[18]Albert Gilman, "Introduction," As You Like It (New York, 1963), pp. xxxii-xxxiii.

[19]John Middleton Murry, "Notes on Shakespeare," The New Adelphi, n.s. (March, 1928), pp. 252-253.

[20]Donald J. McGinn, Shakespeare's Influence on the Drama of his Age (New Brunswick, N. J., 1938), pp. 157-158.

[21]Frank O'Connor, Shakespeare's Progress (New York, 1960), pp. 101-102.

[22]Albert Weiner, "Introduction," Hamlet: The First Quarto (Great Neck, N. Y., 1962), p. 6. Weiner has Hardin Craig's endorsement.

[23]Grosart, p. xvii.

[24]See below, pp. 75-76 and 79.

with which I began this discussion.

There are three main structural elements of the play: (1) the comic interludes with John and the watermen; (2) the story of the two maids and their lovers, Toures and Filbon, which provides the conventional elements of intrigue, disguise, romance motifs, songs, the "wise folly" of Tutch, and perhaps some oblique parody of Romeo and Juliet (1594-1596); and (3) the domestic melodramatic comedy arising from James's presumed death, the Lady's bigamous marriage to Sir William, Humil's disillusionment with his mother's "adultery," the attempted murder of the Lady, and the parodies or imitations of Shakespeare's later tragedies. This break-down of the play makes it much easier to see how it could have been written first as a conventional comedy containing only the first and second elements, perhaps more fully expanded than we now have them. One can well imagine a young comic actor writing a play of this kind as a starring vehicle for himself. It would provide him the opportunity to play at least two roles, John and Tutch (and possibly Toures, who, like Armin, sings), which he may already have invented for curtain-raising routines. It is not relevant to the argument, however, whether or not Armin had previously played these characters in some form on the stage. It is clear that he was sufficiently interested in the nature and classification of kinds of "fooles" to write Foole Upon Foole (1600). The theory that some early version of Two Maids existed, actually focussing on the two maids, as the title suggests, rather than relegating them to a sub-plot as our text does, makes it possible to concur with Felver's and Hotson's arguments that the _play_, as well as Armin's style of clowning, influenced the creation of Touchstone. The passages which parody the tragedies, treated in detail below, all appear in Scenes XIII, XV, and XX, the ones dealing with Humil's discovery, revelation, and initiation into the mystery of his mother's "adultery." Armin may have invented the main plot at any time after 1600, when _Hamlet_ appeared in its earliest version.[25] He could then have revised the specific scenes and passages which suggest parody any time after 1606, probably before the production by the "boyes of the Reuels" (1607-1608).[26] The theory of an evolving text, therefore, accounts not only for Hotson's and Felver's claims, but for Grosart's, Murry's, O'Connor's, and my own as well, besides offering a possible explanation for Armin's reference to the play's having been performed "in part...if not in the [w]hole."

It only remains, then, to consider arguments against this theory. The first and simplest is that if the play had been written between 1600 and 1606, even if only in

[25]Weiner, p. 6.

[26]On pp. 15-16 of this discussion I give the time span for the boys' company as 1606 to 1608 on the basis of Hillebrand's speculation (p. 319), but he and Chambers agree that the earliest we can be certain of their operation is August, 1607, and since we must allow time for the parodied lines from _Macbeth_ to sink into the popular imagination, the later date is more suitable to my purposes.

part, the play would have been performed by the King's Men, to whom Armin was contracted. This objection is most easily met by the rebuttal that although Armin may have been required to offer it to Shakespeare's company, the company was not obligated to accept it, and, indeed, if they had accepted it, it would have been the poorest in their repertoire. Even Armin speaks modestly of it: "you shall find verse, as well blancke, as crancke, yet in the prose let it passe for currant."[27] On the other hand, Hillebrand[28] has shown that the Children of the King's Majesty's Revels were not nearly so discriminating, its properties being consistently second-rate, rights to them being inexpensively attained; therefore, they may easily be assumed to have taken a play which the King's Men had rejected.

The second objection hinges to some extent on the first. Baldwin and Felver accept the hypothesis that Two Maids would have belonged to the King's Men had Armin written any part of it while associated with them; therefore, they undertake a biographical study to prove that Armin had the opportunity and economic motive for writing a play in 1598-1599. They make their point convincingly[29] and I have

[27]"To the friendly peruser," p. 104.

[28]Hillebrand, pp. 318-319.

[29]It was Edmund K. Chambers (III, 210) who first assumed that Armin must have written and performed in his play before coming to Shakespeare's company in order to avoid a conflict of interest in giving it to the boys' company. Following this lead, Baldwin (Organization and Personnel, p. 452) sets out to discover Armin's whereabouts

no doubt that the previously mentioned first two elements were drafted in that time, but they do not and cannot prove that Armin would not also have had the opportunity and incentive to revise what he had written after 1606, especially since his major comic roles had already been written and his importance as an actor in Shakespeare's plays was diminishing by that time. In fact, it is not even impossible that the spoofing of the tragedies was partly the result of some resentment against Shakespeare's having become too serious to write rich parts for the clown; as I shall argue later, the play does seem like an attempt to jolly someone out of a dark and pessimistic mood.

To sum up, I believe that a theory of an evolving text best explains the various and contradictory evidence bearing upon the date for the play's composition. It seems most likely to me that Armin began writing the play in 1598-1599 as a light-comedy farce about the maids and John i' th' Hospital, but that over the next seven years he responded to the power of Shakespeare's major tragedies,

---

and activities before signing on with the Lord Chamberlain's Men in March or April, 1600. But Felver (_Robert Armin, Shakespeare's Fool_, pp. 21-24), still accepting Chambers' and Baldwin's premise (as he no doubt thinks he must in order to maintain his claim for Armin's influence on Touchstone), devotes three closely argued pages to attacking Baldwin's scholarship, bringing much new information to light to conclude that Armin joined the Lord Chamberlain's Men in the spring of 1599. Since I am denying the premise, as indeed I must in order to maintain an evolutionary theory, I have not felt it necessary to rehash the conjectured details of Armin's activities for the period either here or in my biographical section above.

developing a parody of the _Hamlet_ situation and adding lines which echo _Macbeth_ and _Lear_.

3.

TEXT

The title page of the 1609 edition reads as follows: "THE/ History of the two Maids of More-clacke,/ VVith the life and simple maner of Iohn/ _in the Hospitall_./ Played by the Children of the Kings/ Maiesties Reuels./ VVritten by ROBERT ARMIN, seruant to the Kings/ _most excellent Maiestie_./ [woodcut]/ LONDON,/ Printed by N.O. for _Thomas Archer_, and is to be sold at his/ shop in Popes-head Pallace,-1609."

Selection of a copy-text raised no difficulties. My collation of the eleven copies known to be extant shows that there was but one quarto, one edition, and one printing. There are eight copies in the United States and three in England, the latter being ruled out as copy-texts due to unavailability except on microfilm. Five of the eight American-owned copies are at the Folger Library, and each of them proved to be incomplete or otherwise imperfect. Of the three remaining American-owned copies, only one, and that one, fortunately, easiest of access, was printed after demonstrably proper proof corrections were made in the outer forme of Sig. C (see Appendix B). Therefore my copy-text is the quarto in the J. P. Morgan Library in New York, and it will hereinafter be referred to as *Q*.

Q. collates ¶^{2} A-H^{4}I^2; leaves ¶1^v and ¶2^v are blank; leaf ¶1 is the title page and leaf ¶2 bears the prefatory "To the friendly peruser"; ¶A carries the head title and the beginning of the play itself.[1] The text is set in ordinary roman, with speech prefixes and stage directions in the usual italic. Thirty-six lines of type to the page prevail, but E4^v and F2 have only thirty-five lines because the compositor ran verse on as prose. The pages are correctly numbered and given appropriate catch-words. In general the typographical details seem to have been carefully looked after; the appearance of the book is quite clean.

An examination of the running titles (*The History [ie] of the two/ Maid[e]s of More-clacke*) shows that at least sheets C-H were machined in two skeleton formes, Skeleton I imposing the outer and Skeleton II imposing the inner. Each of the eight pages on any sheet carries a running title rendered distinctive either by its spelling or by a recognizably flawed type-face; thus there are four varieties of each segment of the running title. In the chart below I have assigned alphabetical symbols to each

[1]Philip Williams, "The Compositor of the 'Pied Bull' *Lear*," *SB*, I (1949), 66n., states that "printing began with text gathering A...[and] the title page and preliminary matter...were printed along with the final two-page gathering by full sheet imposition." Unfortunately, Williams does not provide a basis for this latter assertion, and neither Dr. Dunkin nor I have been able to verify it.

of the running titles: J(4^v), K(1^r), L(2^v), M(3^r), N(1^v), O(4^r), P(3^v), Q(2^r), R(final page of text, which carries a version of "L" plus an ampersand), and S(head-title).

(o) I (i) II	J - K - L - M N - O - P - Q	Sigs. C-H
(o) (i)	L - K - N - S J - O - P - Q	Sig. A
(o-i)	N - O - P - Q	Sig. B
1^r - M 2^r - Q	1^v - P 2^v - R(L)	Sig. I

Although it is sometimes possible, by analyzing the distribution of type, to determine the sequence in which pages, formes, and sheets were composed or wrought-off, the evidence in *Q.*'s case is too contradictory to validate any conclusions.[2] For the same reason it is also impossible to determine whether *Q.* was set up by formes or *seriatim*. Had we definitive answers to these problems, we might be enabled to offer some scientific bibliographical explanation for the frequent mislineation of prose and verse which will be discussed in a subsequent section.[3] On the other hand, even

[2]When one finds in a text that the printer has definitely shifted from the use of W's and w's to VV's and vv's, one assumes that he has run out of the former; one then knows that he has redistributed his type where the W's and w's reappear; thus one can determine the sequence in which pages were composed. In *Q.*, however, no orderly pattern appears.

[3]I have been unable to determine whether the compositors worked by the forme or, serially, by the page because the existing evidence is both scant and contradictory. For instance, the word "division" is divided between Sigs. C1 and C1^v; normally this would be taken as evidence that the pages were composed serially because it is thought unlikely that a compositor could estimate his spacing needs

though Philip Williams[4] has shown that the play was set up by two compositors[5] (compositor A working on A1^{v}-A2, A3^{v}-A4^{v}, B3-B4^{v}, C3-C4^{v}, D3^{v}-D4^{v}, E3-E4^{v}, F3-F4^{v}, G3-G4^{v}, H3^{v}-H4 and compositor B setting up A1, A2^{v}-A3, B1-B2^{v}, C1-C2^{v}, D1-D3, E1-E2^{v}, F1-F2^{v}, G1-G2^{v}, H1-H3, H4^{v}-I2^{v} and the title page) who both worked on both skeletons, the information has not proved useful in elucidating cruxes since there is no pattern in the cruxes corresponding to the patterns in the mechanics of the book's printing. This may be as good a place as any to confess the disappointing fruitlessness of much bibliographical study of *Q.*; the confession is made not to disparage such study but only to suggest that the bibliographical evidence is as confusing as most other aspects of the play.

For instance, even the men responsible for printing, publishing, and selling the book share in the dubiously ambiguous character of the whole unlikely enterprise. *Two*

---

so precisely and so far in advance from the outer to the inner forme. On the other hand, the previously mentioned existence of two pages (E4^{v} and F2) which are short a line of type because some verse was run on as prose, indicates that the quarto was set by forme because if it were not, the compositor could have concealed his mistake easily by adding an extra line to those pages, whereas if it had been set by forme, he would have already planned the subsequent pages and found it cumbersome to make the correction.

[4]Williams, p. 66.

[5]D. F. McKenzie, "A List of Printer's Apprentices, 1605-1640," *SB*, XIII (1960), 129-130, reports that Jo. Reynolds and Thomas Corneforth were printer's apprentices to N. Oakes from March, 1607, to April, 1615, and from April, 1607, to July, 1610, respectively.

Maids is not entered in the Stationer's Register, and Thomas Archer, its publisher-seller, is a somewhat mysterious and perhaps even shady dealer who entered none of the six plays he published between 1607 and 1613.[6] Nicholas O[a]kes, the book's printer, has also been characterized as "somewhat of a refractory character, a printer of popular books at the risk of imprisonment,"[7] and one of the four "chief offenders"[8] against a parliamentary decree limiting the number of printers. But if these gentlemen were unpopular with the officials, they must have had some good repute with literary and theatrical people for they published works by Jonson, Shakespeare, Dekker, Heywood, Marston, and Webster, among others. O[a]kes, especially, enjoys today a high reputation for craftsmanship. Fredson Bowers, speaking of the "Pied Bull" Lear, says, "Okes was doing his conscientious best to produce the best text he could from his miserable manuscript, a copy so difficult to decipher that even the proof-reader at his comparative leisure could not always determine the manuscript reading."[9] Such a remark

[6]W. W. Greg, The Shakespeare First Folio (Oxford, 1955), p. 35n. See also Leo Kirschbaum, Shakespeare and the Stationers (Athens, Ohio, 1955), pp. 282-283, who details Archer's ventures and notes that he was "in trouble" and commanded to prison in 1621.

[7]Henry Plomer, A Short History of English Printers: 1476-1900 (London, 1916), p. 137.

[8]Plomer, p. 149.

[9]"An Examination of the Method of Proof Correction in Lear," The Library, 5th series, II (1948), 40.

might apply equally to Okes's work on Two Maids. Bowers' evaluation of Okes was supported ten years later with further evidence by John Russell Brown[10] and is warmly agreed to today by Robert K. Turner.[11]

Such endorsements, coupled with Greg's general admonition to trace corruptions and abnormalities to "peculiarities in the copy rather than...[to] the assumed incompetence of the printer,"[12] direct our attention to the state of the printer's copy. Grosart argues very weakly that since Armin's was a "name to conjure with," he could not be responsible for the stylistic barbarities of the play as we have it, and, therefore, we are warranted "in ascribing to the copyist and Printer..., and not to the author, much of its unformed and unpracticed style."[13] He adds that "it is simply impossible to exaggerate the carelessness of the copyist, or the corruption of the text.... It is thus manifest that (1)A very bad Ms. must have been furnished to the printer; (2)That the author could not have so much as read the Ms.; (3)That he had never looked at the proof-sheets."[14]

[10]"A Proof-Sheet from Nicholas Okes' Printing Shop," SB, XI (1958), 230.

[11]In a letter to me, 10/9/66, Turner, who has been collecting material on Okes for some years, says "Okes' compositors of the period...could certainly do good work. ... They were never responsible for the wholesale degeneration of a text."

[12]SFF, pp. 96-97.

[13]Grosart, p. v.

[14]Grosart, p. xx.

Wilfred T. Jewkes, however, rejects Grosart's reasoning, and insists that "Armin was responsible for issuing the play.... The text does not appear to be abnormally corrupt.... It is fairly clear that the copy for this play was a set of author's papers which had not been prepared for the stage."[15] Neither Grosart nor Jewkes presents the detailed evidence upon which their conclusions are based, and the opinions of both must be examined further.

Grosart's theory is built on the hope and faith that Armin could not have written so badly. He says "words are misused" (and so they are, see the discussion of "challenge" on p. 44) and that there are "ungrammatical interconstructions and imitations of sense, rather than sense proper" (for examples, see pp. 46-49 and many of the entries in Explanatory Notes), but he offers no proof for his assertion that these difficulties "belong to the corrupt text, not to the author."[16] He merely announces that "_Foole Upon Foole_ and _A Nest of Ninnies_ and _The Italian Tailor and His Boy_...make it manifest that Armin had a formed and individual style,"[17] but he gives no examples of this putative lucidity. _The Italian Tailor_, if it were thoroughly literate, which it is not, would not be very cogent proof for Grosart's assertion since it is a

[15] _Act Division in Elizabethan and Jacobean Plays_ (Hamden, Conn., 1958), pp. 284-285.

[16] Grosart, p. xxi.

[17] Grosart, p. xxi.

translation. The second book he mentions is an enlargement of the first, so that if it fails the test of literacy and lucidity, Grosart is utterly without evidence that Armin could write clearly. We ought, therefore, to examine a passage from _A Nest of Ninnies_.

Before doing so, we should remember that Grosart admits that in _Two Maids_ "the higher the language soars, the lower does it degenerate into rant, fustian, and unintelligibility."[18] I think this is equally true of _A Nest of Ninnies_. Armin is a lucid story-teller; in anecdote and exposition his style presents no marked irregularities or difficulties. But when he attempts to strike an attitude or generalize in any way, he becomes incoherent. A passage from _A Nest of Ninnies_ will demonstrate this stylistic inconsistency. I choose it more because it pertains to John i'th Hospitall, who appears in both the _Nest_ and _Two Maids_, than because it demonstrates my point; it is _relatively_ clear.

One of the incidents related about John hinges on his habit of replying to inquiries about the cost of an object, "A groat." To John, coats cost a groat, caps cost a groat, beards cost a groat. One day he was asked by a cobbler to deliver a pair of restored boots to a man who was scheduled to make a trip in order to pay a debt or forfeit a bond. The man could not make the trip without

[18]Grosart, p. xxi.

his boots, but John was interrupted on his errand when a stranger, seeing the boots, asked him what he would sell them for. "A groat," he replied, and the deal was quickly made. Thus the cobbler and the businessman were financially injured by John's simplicity. Armin tells the story simply but adds the following moral.

> The third jest of John shews morally many things; amongst which, things, I meane workes, are so cobbled that, to rid it with quicknesse, John may beare it up and down to the owner, while workmanship and time is merely abused--but it boots not 5 to meddle in this, least some say, ne sutra &c. But let me tel ye this, by the way, World: there are knaves in thy seames, that must be ript out. I, sayes the World; and such, I feare, was your father. O! no, sayes the crittick, he was that 10 silly gentleman that staid while the fools brought home his boots, and so forfeited his bond, that his good conditions lay at gage for it. Marry, yes, saies the World; and was after canseld at the gallows: for such as her lies in wait to cosin 15 simplycitie, and for a groat buy that which, well got, deserves a portgue. At this the cinnick fretted: and here they begin to challenge the combat.[19]

There is nothing here as difficult as many passages of the play, but the paragraph does prefigure some of those difficulties: ellipses by omission of a subject ("and...canseld," line 14); ambiguous pronoun reference ("it," line 3); vague or abstract diction ("conditions," line 13); and unconventional diction ("challenge," line 18, here used more idiomatically than at any point in Two Maids).

Grosart's characterization of such a style, then, as "individual" seems unjustifiably benign. I see no basis

[19] Nest, p. 55.

in Armin's other signed works for Grosart's certainty that the unintelligibility of Q. is due to the copyist's failures rather than Armin's, but in rejecting Grosart's reasoning, I am not necessarily rejecting his conclusion. I merely wish to make the point that only if one accepts Armin as the author of The Valiant Welshman (and the arguments for doing so, given in Appendix A, are, I think, sound but not compelling), can one be certain that he could write intelligibly at length. If we accept Armin as the author of Welshman and if we also assume, as I think we must, that O[a]kes' shop was responsible only for some expectable mechanical errors and not for the overall stylistic obscurity of the play, then we are left with two alternative explanations of that obscurity: (1) Armin provided a very rough set of foul papers to the printer or (2) a copyist badly botched the author's literate manuscript. If, like Grosart, we prefer to grasp at the second alternative, we must be prepared to demonstrate that the obfuscations are of a kind that a copyist, if he existed, was likely to make and we must be able to explain how and why he made them. I do not believe that either of these conditions for accepting the second alternative can be met, and, therefore, I favor the first hypothesis.

At the same time, Jewkes's assertions that Armin was responsible for issuing the play, that it is not "abnormally corrupt," and that the printer's copy was a set of author's papers not prepared for the stage seem to be in need of refinement. And even if we accept Jewkes's assertions, a fundamental question remains: if Armin bears the onus for *Q.*'s unintelligibility, must he be convicted of ignorance or negligence? That is, did he fail to recognize that, indeed, it does contain stylistic barbarities, or did he, at the close of his career, decide knowingly to publish a manuscript that was badly in need of revision? Again, favoring as I do the argument for Armin's authorship of *Welshman*, I prefer the latter of these possibilities though I can offer no explanation for it.

The best evidence that Armin was responsible for issuing the play is the existence of the prefatory epistle, which indicates at least that Armin instigated and sponsored the edition but does not tell us how carefully he prepared the printer's copy. The primary evidence that the play is not "abnormally corrupt" is that there are no glaring omissions from it, no loose ends of plot, no characters abruptly dropped or given unexplained appearances. The play has twenty-two scenes and 2111 lines, which seems normal enough in view of *Othello's* fifteen scenes and 3293 lines or *Macbeth's* twenty-nine scenes and 1994 lines. A few scenes, such as XXI, seem to begin *in medias res*, and occasionally the audience must infer that certain conversations have taken place which would account for the characters having knowledge that is not otherwise accounted for, but there is nothing in the play that clearly requires the assumption that something has been omitted.

Jewkes is probably also correct in asserting that the copy had not been prepared for the stage; although Q. does not have all the characteristics of unprepared copies, it has none of the characteristics of prepared ones. For instance, Q. does not markedly exhibit, as unprepared copies frequently do, an "inconsistency in the designations of characters in directions and prefixes."[20] In Q. character identifications are regular and uniform, though their names may be spelled or abbreviated variously (e.g., Mary-Marie, Humil-Humill, S. Will-Sir Will),[21] but these variations are more probably due to the preferences of the two compositors and their spacing needs. McKerrow argues that plays in which characters' names are consistent are "more likely to have been printed from some sort of fair copy, perhaps made by a professional scribe."[22] I do not believe that McKerrow's hypothesis runs counter to my claim that there is an absence of evidence of scribal mediation between Armin and the printer because in his context McKerrow is arguing that scribal copies tend to be superior to authorial ones, and surely it is not odd that an author would have his character's names firmly in mind while writing.

In any case, the absence of fourteen required speech

[20]Greg, SSF, p. 142.

[21]At X.23 the ferryman, normally identified as "Fer.," is identified as "Ferris."

[22]"A Suggestion Regarding Shakespeare's Manuscripts," RES, XI (1935), 464.

prefixes (at II.14, IV.2, VI.7, VII.160, X.30, XI.6, XI.107, XV.146, XV.151, XVI.7, XVI.34, XVI.37, XVI.134, and XVII.96) and the incorrect placement of three others (at VII.70, VII.77, and VIII.54) indicate that the copy had not been prepared for the stage. The unprepared state of the copy is further attested to by the probable omission of a brief line at XX.79 and the further omission of fourteen exits and entrances (at II.52, III.0.1, VIII.40, X.14, X.41, XI.92, XIV.85, XVI.190, XVII.0.1, XVIII.89, XIX.22, XX.54, XX.104, and XXII.185).

Further evidence that the copy was not used in connection with a performance lies in the style and content of the stage directions, which are abrupt and give no more detail than is required for an understanding of the text. Q. contains one hundred twenty-eight stage directions, of which eighty-five are simple exits and entrances. Two of the remaining forty-three are "permissive" ("Enter women for shewe" and "Enter...so many as may be"), being nearly definitive evidence that the copy was not a prompt book, and two others direct the actor subjectively, as an author might (Enter Humil "amazed" or "sadly"). Forty-one of the forty-three give details indicating disguise, costume, or required action (e.g., enter "reading" or exit "reeling"). I have added nineteen more, some of which, particularly those at V.18, 34, 36, 43, and 50, the reader may want to challenge. I have also, of course, restored the fourteen omitted entrances and exits.

Despite these clear indications that the printer's copy had not been prepared for the stage, staging from it would not be difficult for an experienced director because it is not obscure about _what_ is said and done but about the _meaning_ of and _motivation_ for what is said and done. The text is not seriously corrupt in the sense of being damaged by an outsider. Printer's errors are not relatively extensive or unusual in kind. Admittedly, some errors in lineation, such as those in the very last speech of the play and those already mentioned on p. 25, can, no doubt, be traced to the printer's negligence, but others may just as reasonably be traced to the writer's failure to distinguish verse from prose in his manuscript, a malpractice which Hardin Craig[23] says is not uncommon (see p. 99 for further treatment of this matter).

The significant source of suspicion of the text is not that relevant material is missing or that irrelevant material is present but that the existing material is stylistically opaque. All evidence is against the gross unlikelihood that someone would have bothered to "pirate" or mis-memorize the play. Nor is there any reason for believing that the obscurity, ellipticity, and involuteness of the following speech stems from a copyist's misreading of marginal or inter-linear revisions in the manuscript. The most persistent problem in explicating such passages

[23] _A New Look At Shakespeare's Quartos_ (Stanford, 1961), p. 25.

as the one to be cited arises in the attempt to interpret the logical and grammatical relationships between the phrases and clauses in the series:

> Mot as I am of Louers vnion,
> Contracted to a sollitarie life,
> By thus retayning singlenes of heart:
> Changing all doubts that the world affords
> But one, so to thy sweetest selfe,
> Which onely art idea of my thoughts:
> I vowe a reconciled amitie,
> Which violated, doos command my life
> To yeeld his intrest to the shade of death,
> May be, your father alienates our choice,
> And showes as sunne-shine threatning raine,
> To the all-hoping haruest present,
> Which to make cleare, the honourable word
> And fatherly regard in present office
> Haue past their speede in our attention.
> I know your father will receiue their on-set
> Soldier-like, ioying the siege begunne,
> Which tho resisted, bids them gladly come.
> (VII.29-46)

For this passage and others dealt with in the discussion of "Style" and in the Explanatory Notes it seems to me most logical to blame the author and his copy.

Nevertheless, since I tend to believe that Armin could and did write lucidly in _The Valiant Welshman_, I am obliged to believe further that for _Q_. Armin provided Okes with a set of completed but quite inadequately revised foul papers, whereas he provided the printer of _Welshman_ with a fair manuscript tentatively prepared for the stage. We find in _Q_., as I shall show elsewhere, the same sketchy characterization, the same broken and irregular lines, the same patchwork effect of many speeches that Una Ellis-Fermor[24] saw as

[24] "_Timon of Athens_: An Unfinished Play," _RES_, XVIII (1942), 270-283.

evidence of the unfinished state of _Timon of Athens_.

If I am right in the above conjecture, it is impossible to present now a "critical" text in the sense of one that represents "the form in which we may suppose that it would have stood in a fair copy, made by the author himself, of the work as he finally intended it."[25] It is probable that a fair copy never existed, no less one that fulfilled in any sense Armin's ideal intentions for it. The best we can do in such a case is present a text which would resemble the printer's copy of it if he had done his job faultlessly.

[25]W. W. Greg, _The Editorial Problem in Shakespeare_ (Oxford, 1954), p. x.

4.

STYLE

Unremarkably few critics have chosen to comment on Two Maids, but those few have frequently registered their dismay at Armin's style. The earliest evaluation is that of Alexander B. Grosart, who cannot believe that Armin is responsible for the play's "unformed and unpracticed style,"[1] blaming instead the copyist, the printer, or a corrupt text. He says,

> Words are occasionally misused, as by a foreigner.... But the ungrammatical interconstructions and imitations of sense, rather than sense proper, belong to the corrupt text, not the author. I am the more convinced of this by the easily noted fact that the higher the language soars, the lower does it degenerate into rant, fustian, and unintelligibility.[2]

Grosart is followed by John Middleton Murry, who confesses that he

> cannot imagine anyone (except Dr. Grosart,...) reading the "works" of...Robert Armin for their own sake. What plainly does emerge from a reading of his rather stupid works is that an actor of ordinary intelligence in Shakespeare's company remembered very little of any other plays save Shakespeare's...and where there is no Shakespearian reminiscence, of phrase, or cadence, Armin's verses are almost invariably doggerel, and his prose, if not fustian, thoroughly commonplace.[3]

[1] Grosart, p. vi.

[2] Grosart, p. xx.

[3] "Notes on Shakespeare," pp. 251-252.

Murry is seconded by H. N. Hillebrand, who finds "the style...fantastic in the extreme, being characterized by a kind of grammatical shorthand and preciosity of diction that drives the reader to despair. It is the style of a man determined to be 'literary,' and proud of his fund of Latin quotations."[4] And the most recent commentator on the play, Millicent C. Bradbrook, goes farthest in her derogation. Speaking of the lesser Elizabethan dramatists, she says, "easiness and facility marked most of the hack writers; lesser playwrights could degenerate into almost senseless mouthing--even allowing for the state of the text, Armin's Two Maids of More-clacke probably represents a low water mark."[5]

It is clear that the progression of critical estimate is toward increasing condemnation of Armin's style, even allowing for textual corruption. I have no wish to quarrel with that estimate as it applies to the style in Q., but I have argued elsewhere that Armin could and did write intelligibly in The Valiant Welshman. At this juncture the editor's function would seem to be to prepare the reader for the stylistic morass to be encountered by classifying and outlining sources of difficulty.

Perhaps the most obvious, if not the highest barrier in the way of comprehension of the play is Armin's

[4]"The Children...," p. 329.

[5]The Growth and Structure of Elizabethan Comedy (Berkeley, 1956), p. 56.

choice of words. First, one can point to his neologisms, some of which, like "vnder daunt" (XXII.135), are listed in no dictionaries and cannot reasonably have their meanings inferred from their context. Others are "splendious" (XVIII.16) for "splendid" and "transive" (XV.128) for "in a trance-like state" (both attributed only to Armin in _OED_), and "indored" (XXII.74 and XXII.241) for "endeared." Then there are words which, from their context, appear to be unintentional malapropisms: "retaines" (VI.66) for "sustains"; "consumption" (XX.41) for "consummation"; "obedient" (XVI.181) for "compliant (?)"; and "retrograde" (XIV.12) for "submissive (?)."

Some of the most baffling words in the play may very well arise from textual corruption: "false" (I.14); "moneth" (VI.49); "Mot" (VII.29); "Labits" (VII.89); "friending" (VII.122); "morning ries" (VII.177); and "looze" (XV.196). The fact that four of these all occur between signatures B2^{v} and B4, where there is at least one other misprint, "season" (VII.133) for "reason," may indicate that the text is especially corrupt in this section.

Armin also employs many words unconventionally if not idiosyncratically: "_Pagan_" (XXII.273), where the meaning is not at all clear though it is perhaps a metonomy for "lie"; "pull" (II.53) for "turn" or "chance"; "attempt" (III.22) for "undertaking (?)" or "act (?)"; "kick at" (XV.117) for "overcome" or "protest against"; and, finally, "challenge." Armin uses the word "challenge" in the most baffling, eccentric, inconceivable, and inconsistent contexts; it appears twenty-one times in the play, all but once in a predicate, and never incontestably in its most customary meanings of (1) to demand a contest with, (2) to dispute, or (3) to claim as due. In most cases (VII.4, VII.116, IX.20, XII.81, XII.94, XIV.32, XV.186, XVI.27, XXII.122, XXII.128, XXII.364) it could mean something like "demand," "request," "seek," or "claim." In others (I.48, XV.140) the context seems to require "defy." At VII.134 it seems to mean "threaten"; at VIII.86 "refuse"; at IX.14 "dispute"; at XIV.14 "bind" or "make responsible"; at XXII.260 "fulfill the requirements of" or "meet the demands of"; and at XXII.315 "desire."

This irresponsible use of words, plus a penchant for very abstract words and probably for ink-horn expressions, is reflected in the following speech:

> James. Tis true your mother challeng'd it: but he as angry as the raging morne, whose choller breathing shakes high battlements, puts her off with a pause of contrarie. I know it sir, her ioynter is subscrib'd too, which else to doe, sooner should earth to heaven presume a progresse, then the grant make firme what the antecedent challenges, your mother vpon this abandons from his bed, vowing bold absence. He inrag'd, giues way to all maligne and stubborne fashion of contempt. Such a cloze to day neuer had practise, such a wedding night, till this sad first neuer had purchase: you shall well agree them sir, to attone this iarre, vse means I pray you, twill become ye, well, when wrangling wrestles with such vilent iniurie, tis the sonnes office (IX.14-29).

This passage illustrates many of the stylistic hazards of the play; a full explication of it appears in the Explanatory Notes. We may here only enumerate its peculiarities: two appearances of "challenge"; an anti-climactic simile (unless "morne" is a misprint for "maine," i.e., open sea); a noun ("choller") used as an adjective; an unidiomatic phrase, "pause of contrarie"; a clause containing three conspicuous words of very uncertain and abstract meaning ("grant," "antecedent," "challenges"); another unidiomatic and pompous expression ("abandons from"); a fustian adjective ("bold"): an obfuscating redundancy ("all maligne and stubborne fashion of contempt"); unclear circumlocutions ("had practise" and "had purchase"); and a telegraphic clause of "grammatical shorthand" ("you shall [do] well [to make them] agree them").

Elsewhere in the play other singular, baffling, or inexplicable phrases occur, such as: "a point prevailing practice" (VI.32); "sit thee all to state" (XX.29) for "all sit in state"; "how and a woman" (XXII.32), presumably for "how _like_ a woman"; "How Goddess-like...[she]/ Stations the measure" (VII.125), the verb perhaps being a jargon word from dancing terminology, though I can find no evidence for it; "wits-charter" (VI.35); "plannet-stroke" (VIII.17); and "citty-proud" (XVI.168); not to mention quaint expressions like "report a flye a flye" (XV.53) for "call a spade a spade" and mild oaths like "grace a god, grace a queen" (VII.201) and "by my slipper" (XI.59).

Armin's grammar and usage is no less curious than his diction. In the passage already quoted, Grosart objected to "ungrammatical interconstructions," itself a term of somewhat uncertain meaning and for which Grosart gives no examples. One expects, of course, in a work of the Elizabethan-Jacobean period, a certain disregard for formal conventions which were not yet established, and, therefore, one is not discomfitted by irregularities in the agreement in number of predicate and subject, as at III.4-6 ("I am the round O/ Which...grieue"), IX.44 ("hels black motions tickles me on"), and XV.17-18 ("sandy minutes runs out"). Nor is one bothered by attempts to make one word do double duty, as in XXII.359-360 ("I will be generally laught at, once insooth I will"). Such unorthodox verb forms as "shals" (XI.7 and XI.84) for "shall we" cause little difficulty once one has become accustomed to them. But careless and ambiguous handling of direct objects is more distracting: at XXII.356 there is no direct object for "apprehends"; at XV.180-181 "respects" has two objects, "mother" and "womb," the first of which appears two lines before the verb and the second immediately after it. The grammar and syntax at VII.2-4 are even more baffling: "we, loues deitie/ Doos proclaime pardon to presume, and speake,/ Challenge libertie..."; here, either "we" or "deitie" may be the subject of "doos proclaime" (for further discussion, see Explanatory Notes).

The most consistently troublesome aspect of Armin's grammar is his use and abuse of personal pronouns. His first immediately noticeable departure from convention is to allow his "gentle" or "noble" characters to refer to themselves, at times, in the first person plural, whether in the nominative, accusative, or possessive case, apparently in affected imitation of the royal "we." From time to time, he also substitutes the personal pronoun for a more normal impersonal one (VII.37) and vice versa (X.20). More common is his failure to provide clear pronoun references and antecedents (XI.37-38 and XIII.4-6) or any at all (VII.112). Sometimes, as in V.53 ("By seeking you that lost not what we find"), he garbles his syntax and does not say what he means: "By finding you that lost not what we seek." If the previous example is evidence of a careless _auctorial_ transposition, it would, perhaps, be more fair to blame a corrupt text for such unintelligibility as "ly with him tonight, as I will with my Filbon, & by the morning _thinke but what is past, and you will reckon rightly you_, hele hold you three to one my medecine's true [my italics]" (XXII.345-347).

Rather than pursue Armin's technique of punctuation and proclivity for ellipses as isolated from his grammatical and syntactical practices, it is probably more instructive to observe these elements all combining to render a passage massively incomprehensible. For instance:

> Sir William. Right noble and my hearts indored
> friends,
> To preach your welcome, were to drowne the sea 75
> With floods of water. Be it knowne vnto ye,
> That your comming solemnely inuited,
> Hath that attendance appertaining as the Gods
> In their selected Bacchinals command,

Mary, the Nectar wants, and the Ambrotia, 80
Smiles in the presence of such earthly wines,
As the worlds compound furnishes with all,
Though it come short of lushius surfetting:
Yet willing furtherance makes the value meete,
In her best suite of entertaine, sit then, 85
And let our musicke rellish to the eare:
Such care and cost as love and welcome giues,
Not to prophane the best except the least,
As prologue to begin this worthless feast.
(XXII.74-89)

Here Armin, through Sir William, is indulging his most ornate style. The opening sentence, though anastrophic, is clear, the metaphor being a conventional twist on the proverbial idea of supererogation as "carrying coals to Newcastle." The next sentence, however, is thirteen and a half lines long, broken into three sections by two colons. In the first section, "attendance," "appertaining," and "selected" are sheer fustian, serving by their mere bulk to impose upon the reader a sense of ceremonial magnitude while they defy precise or meaningful definition. The punctuation of lines 80-81 forbids, or at least inhibits, adequate paraphrase, though presumably, despite the comma separating them, "Ambrotia" is the subject of "Smiles." "Mary," in the same lines, is an interjection, an oath, not a proper name, but the reader is virtually invited to confuse it for: (1) the subject of "wants," which is in the active voice when the passive "is wanted" (i.e., lacking) is required; or (2) a noun in direct address; or (3) the object of "wants." In line 83 "it" may have either "compound," "wines," or even "Ambrotia" as its antecedent. Not a single word in line 84 carries precise denotation, and the concluding comma gives inadequate warning to the reader that a pause at least as long as the one at the colon-stopped previous line is appropriate. Line 85, employing a periodic structure or word order, also seeks elegance in the mandarin phrase "suite of entertaine." The verb in line 86, "rellish," is somewhat baroque, if not just plain unidiomatic, and line 87 contains a compound subject with a singular verb. Finally, even allowing for the old spelling of "accept," Armin (or the printer) misleads the reader in the penultimate line by failing to provide him with a comma after an introductory infinitive phrase.

I have frequently referred to Armin's ellipticity, which Hillebrand calls "grammatical shorthand." It would be both cumbersome and repetitious to give further examples --cumbersome because the demonstration of ellipticity generally requires the reader's knowledge of a larger context, and repetitious because the Explanatory Notes are made up predominantly of expansions of cryptic passages. The most striking case may be the Earle's speech at XIV.1-10; other examples occur at XII.82-84, XIV.45, and XXII.101-102. Any of these might be used to document my repeated assertion that in much of _Q_. Armin has provided us only with notes and jottings to be polished later.

As a dramatic poet, Armin is at his best when he is prosaic and therefore understandable. Critical support for this judgment comes from Murry[6] who singles out the lines (XV.1-4), which he, and, later, McGinn,[7] believe to be in imitation of Hamlet, as "a favorable specimen of Armin's style": "The bird that greets the dawning of the daie,/ Signes with his wings, the midnight's parture." The lines are among the few wholly acceptable ones in the play, and they are thoroughly conventional (see Explanatory Notes). But one is less inclined to agree with Murry when he refers to the following mechanically incremental analogies as having "startling quality" (in the approbative sense): "as bare as January, when the trees/ Look like a girle, whose colour comes and goes as frost doos in the milke" (I.9-12). Murry also selects another passage for commendation; like the second it is a simile, and, like both previous ones, it is at least comprehensible: "yet honour makes them swell,/ Like clusterd grapes, till mature sweetness brings,/ Lussious conclusion" (XVI.158-160). Armin is less fortunate in three other figures involving the image of ripening nature. What does Tabitha mean, for instance, when she says that Filbon's "actions are like apricocks, they dangle and [I?] loue them" (XI.140-141)? Or why does the Earl, when he wants to reassure Sir William that his daughters will improve with age, say that "things at worst,/ Season in their decay [my italics]" (XIV.48-49)?

[6]"Notes on Shakespeare," p. 253.

[7]Shakespeare's Influence, p. 158.

Most baffling is James's lament:

> To make myself knowne but represents
> Mellow fruit falling into danger. O I am that
> Rotten ruin'd, and vnrellisht substance,
> Which on my owne vpgrowing tree falles off.
> By the times negligence undone I am.
> (III.8-12)

He compares himself to fruit, tree, and pruner, but actually has little in common with any of them. James makes no more sense in VI.2-4 when, presumably addressing the stars, he apostrophizes: "O you all wondring eies, Gaze till your fire flame, your eie-balles drop/ In moist imagination of this act." Why are the stars "wondring" rather than "knowing"? If eyes do indeed become hot and dry with gazing, in what sense do they drop their eye-balls? Or are eye-balls tears? And what is a "moist imagination"? It may be that we have here another example of unintentional ellipsis and catachresis; he may mean that the "eie-balles drop [tears] in moist recognition of this act." In attempting to soar, Armin stands on tip-toes and strains for what exceeds his grasp as the reader grows dizzy.

Armin might be considered more successful in his imitations of more Donnean, metaphysical conceits such as those at VIII.24-27 and XII.48-51 (for explication, see Explanatory Notes), but even in these cases syntactical problems arise. By and large Armin relies less upon figurative language than upon twisted rhetoric and high-flown diction for "literary" effects, and he avoids the Scylla of banality only by drifting into the Charybdis of nonsense. There are no underlying thematic images in the play, and only a few dramatic ironies, such as those at XXII.186-187 and XVIII.55, though Armin is probably most effective in the use of sarcasm or verbal irony, especially that directed by Sir William at Lady Vergir in the concluding scenes of the play. As one would expect, in the low comedy scenes there is a superfluity of quibbles, some bawdy, which excite only a modicum of mirth and less envy. Whatever stylistic talents Armin possessed, they are not to be understood in linguistic terms but in dramatic ones; his real style can be appreciated only in an examination of his handling of large theatrical modes and conventions, wherein he may be considered worthy of some respect for ingenuity and inventiveness. These matters are taken up in the ensuing pages.

5.

PLOT AND CHARACTERIZATION

Critical reaction to the plot of Armin's play has been nearly as consistent as the reaction to his style. Grosart calls it "involute, not to say absurd";[1] Murry calls it "stupid";[2] O'Connor calls it "preposterous";[3] and Hillebrand says it "degenerates into episodes which defy credulity."[4] Such epithets indicate the complexity of the affair and justify a detailed summary of the play's action at this point.[5]

A rich widower, Sir William Vergir, Knight of More-clacke, has two daughters, Mary and Tabitha, respectively beloved by and loving Sir Robert Toures and Filbon. The play opens immediately after the marriage of the knight to Mrs. Humil, a supposed widow who marries him chiefly for her jointure and that her son may be married, as has been promised, to Mary. On their return from the wedding James

[1]Grosart, p. xviii.

[2]"Notes on Shakespeare," p. 252.

[3]_Shakespeare's Progress_, p. 102.

[4]"The Children..., " p. 329.

[5]For the ensuing summary I am heavily indebted to Dr. Brinsley Nicholson, who performed this same task so well for Grosart in _Works_, pp. xviii-xix.

Humil, the bride's first husband, who had at some unstated time in the past caused her to be informed of his death in order to test her loyalty to him, makes himself known to her. On recognizing him, she drops her glove at his feet and announces that its finder shall be governor of the wedding feast. James assumes this task gladly, though he, together with the audience, is disturbed by the failure of his own son, Humil, to recognize him.

The second scene (by my division of the play) is an inconsequential comic interlude serving to introduce Tutch, an "artificial fool" in the knight's retinue, by means of a "low" dialogue with two watermen. Scenes III-VII serve largely to introduce the lovers, their suspicions of Sir William's ill-will toward the young men, and Humil's rivalry with Toures for Mary. These same scenes also provide some scant exposition of the relationship between James and the now Lady Vergir, and at the feast John i' the Hospital, a "natural fool" (and a mentally retarded inmate at Christ's Hospital), makes his entry to be introduced to the Earl of Tumult. Complications arise in Scene VIII when Sir William, after first promising the Lady her jointure, tells her that he will not consent to Humil's marriage to Mary. She retaliates by forswearing his bed. Then, aiming at higher marriages for his daughters, Sir William refuses Toures and Filbon, saying that Toures shall marry Mary, his eldest daughter, only "when shees dead and liues againe," and that Filbon shall have Tabitha "when you are from your selfe/ A woman." In response, the suitors resolve to disguise themselves and steal the girls away. In Scene IX James informs Humil of Sir William's retracted promise; Humil vows "mischiefe."

Scene X is another comic interlude with John and his attendants. In Scene XI Toures, disguised as a drunken tinker, gains entry by amusing Sir William, then whips Mary away on horseback from the back door. Meanwhile the knight intercepts a letter from Filbon to Tabitha, which Tutch has been bribed to deliver. Thereupon Tutch is dismissed, seeks Filbon, and is retained by him (in Scene XII). After the dismissal of Tutch, Humil captures Toures' page, who, under fear of whipping, divulges that the couple is to be married at Putney; so learning, Sir William orders Tabitha to be cooped up and departs for Whitehall, where the Earle now is, in order to obtain a warrant for a general search and a _ne exeat_. During his absence, in Scene XIII, young Humil discovers his father, whom he still does not recognize, in bed with his mother, and resolves partly from horror and partly to induce Sir William to fulfill his promise as to Mary, to make the fact known to the knight, who receives the news discreetly in Scene XIV. In XV Sir William returns, and to save his reputation conceals James in an inner room and then bids Humil go in to his mother's room and convince himself of the mistake he has made. The young man, having been convinced, exiles himself and is exiled from Sir William and the Lady. On his departure, Sir William calls forth the supposed guilty couple; at his wife's instigation James keeps his secret and appears penitent and humble; the wife is told to behave as though nothing had happened and is dismissed, while James is told to be ready to depart at the instant his absence is commanded.

In Scene XVI Tutch appears as a Welsh knight and Filbon as his servant; the Welsh knight is a suitor for Tabitha's hand, and so is co-conspirator Auditor, father of Toures, who now appears disguised as a wealthy merchant. Sir Rafe, Filbon's father, succeeds with surprising ease in convincing Sir William that the knight will make an appropriate husband for Tabitha. Fortunately for the conspirators, a priest, Sir Henry, is on hand and willing to perform the services. The suddenness of Sir William's and Sir Henry's acquiescence in the plan is not so surprising as Tabitha's, who, according to _Q._, agrees to it before knowing the identities of the Welshman and his servant. With the departure of the dupes, however, Filbon and Tutch discover themselves, and, exchanging clothes, the former proceeds with Tabitha to Putney, where they will be married.

Scene XVII shifts to the Scilly Isles, where Toures and some seamen are burying Mary, who has presumably drowned in a storm at sea. Our sorrow is abated, however, when, in the following scene, the governor of the islands, none other than Sir William's brother, Charles, thinking he had discovered a buried treasure, orders the coffin exhumed. As the trunk is opened, Mary "sits vp" and delivers herself of a remarkably self-composed speech. Scene XIX briefly discloses the conspirators' further preparations for marriage.

In Scene XX we learn that Humil has returned to More-clacke disguised as an apothecary and that in exchange for the promise of Sir William's daughter in marriage this "apothecary" has allowed himself to be induced to poison his mother under the pretense of cosmetizing her. Humil's true motives for agreeing to this plan are never made clear, but he speaks accusingly to her even after doffing his disguise until she reveals that James is his father; then they, with James, plot to dupe Sir William. As Scene XXI opens, Filbon and Tabitha have been married, and Henry is protesting against his unwitting part in the conspiracy; Auditor is still disguised as a merchant, and Filbon is resolved to return in some disguise to the still-continuing feast at More-clacke.

All the plots and counter-plots are now ripe for the denouement. In the final scene the guests are gathered, Sir William obliquely and sardonically taunts his wife, and Humil, as the apothecary, seems bent on the purpose of poisoning his mother. Tutch enters, disguised now as John, followed by Filbon disguised as a nurse. Tutch's witticisms are interrupted when Sir Rafe enters feigning irritation with his son for having married without his and with Sir William's consent. In his assumed rage he unmasks Filbon, who then claims that he has fulfilled the knight's condition that he should have Tabitha when he had become a woman. Then James, having just accused Sir William of murdering his wife (for she, according to their complot had left the room pretending sudden illness), brings her in after explaining that he is her husband and that she had recognized him. Next, Toures gives himself up to the vengeance of the father-in-law he has wronged, only to be saved by the timely entrance of Mary. Since she was to be married to Toures after she had died and lived again, their case is settled. Finally Sir William agrees to be "generally laughed at," and all ends satisfactorily.

The length of the summary is an index of the plot's complexity, but three main strands should emerge: (1) a main plot involving the Humil family's machinations against Sir William for the purposes of wresting some wealth, securing a dowried bride for the son, and preventing a bigamous consummation of an over-hasty marriage; (2) a sub-plot involving the conspiracy of the lovers and their aides for the purpose of overcoming the obstacles to their marriage erected unwisely by Sir William; and (3) comic interludes with John and his "retinue." Each of the two plots (the word is used in both aesthetic and conspiratorial senses) can be further analyzed into two sub-elements. The main plot uses the "Enoch Arden" situation of a husband returned to find his wife remarried and the Hamlet situation of a son who discovers his mother being unfaithful to his "father." The sub-plot features the two distinct adventures of pairs of lovers who are separated, on one side at least, by Romeo and Juliet-like parental interference and reunited by their paradoxical fulfillment of an amphibological "rash boon." The central figure in the play is Sir William, since the three groups of characters are related to one another by their relationship to him and react largely to expressions of his will, though James's pre-curtain gesture is the catalyst for the chain of events in the main plot.

Armin's almost absurd and often unnecessary reliance upon the disguise-device should not go unmentioned. Nine different disguises are used in the play as well as one concealed identity: Toures as tinker; Filbon as servant; Tutch as Robert Morgan; Humil as apothecary; Auditor as merchant; Filbon as Robert Morgan; Tutch as servant; Tutch as John; Filbon as Nurse; and James as governor. By this device Armin managed, among other things, to write a play in which there were four different parts for himself, quite a showcase for his versatility; he could and probably did play: John, Tutch, Tutch as John (and the two "Johns" are different, the first being a fool, the second a wit), and Tutch as Morgan. The "unnecessary" disguises are Auditor's (he accomplishes nothing in his disguise that he could not without it) and the shifting ones between Filbon and Tutch; if Filbon could imitate a Welsh knight as well as Tutch, there is no reason why he should not take that role in the first place since it was invented for him to marry Tabitha in.

The summary of the plot also reveals some other defects in the construction and character-motivation. Apart from the patently absurd implication at I.53 and VI.7 that James himself wrote letters announcing his own death, there being no attempt to explain how such letters came to be written or who wrote them, the only explanation of James's motive for sending them is at VI.13, the Lady's assertion that he put "to teast our weaknesse by [his] letters." (Note the Lady's pretentious affectation of the first person plural.) More important is the failure to explain Humil's motive for returning to More-clacke disguised as an apothecary (the possibilities and the evidence for them are discussed in the notes to XX.69-70 and XX.86 and 87-88). No more is it explained why Auditor should appear attired in "a Marchant's habite" (XVI.15.1) as a suitor to Tabitha; if he believed that this disguise would enable him to aid Filbon's pursuit of the girl (and why should he want to help Sir Rafe's son?), we ought at least to be told what his plan is. Other less significant but not less puzzling matters include Sir William's rejection of Toures and Filbon as sons-in-law in light of the Earl's assurances that he would provide them with the sum of money or property required by Sir William. Also unexplained is Tabitha's acceptance of the proposal made by the "Welch knight," since she nowhere clearly indicates that she has penetrated Filbon's disguise (but see my notes at XVI.141,

151, and 202-203). Armin's treatment of the effectiveness of disguises is also obscure at XI.13-14 and XI.28-29, where Madge and Humil, very conveniently, think they recognize the tinker Toures is impersonating. An unexplained contradiction occurs when at the end of Scene XI Sir William orders Humil to come with him to Putney but Scene XIV opens with Sir William at Putney and Humil still back at Moreclacke. And finally there are James's frequent and ambiguous expressions of fear of "torture" at XV.197 and 201, which make an assessment of his character difficult. In fact, the whole procedure of withholding the truth of James's relationship to Lady Vergir is very poorly explained by her hope of winning Tabitha for Humil. Nevertheless, these incongruities and inconsistencies are not evidence for thinking that the text is incomplete in its broad outlines; Armin, after all, wrote only two plays at the most (there is no evidence that others have vanished) and need not be expected to have mastered the craft of exposition.

Probably the only positive things we can say about Armin's characterizations are that the "homely milk-bole" maids speak on occasion with earthy gusto if not wit and that Sir William displays some complexity of personality in his treatment of the Lady. After he discovers her infidelity, his remarks to her are sardonic and psychologically convincing. He virtually tortures himself by insisting that she dress and behave as seductively as possible and uses irony toward her and James that can only hurt himself more than it does them (see XX.24-28 and XXII.28-56 and the appropriate notes). Aside from these two distinctions the blandness of the characters' personalities is revealed in the sameness of their speech, invariably a clumsy fustian. It would probably not be safe to concede that some of the more garbled, pompous, or affected speeches, such as Sir William's at XI.69-74 and XXII.74-89, are intended as such in order to demonstrate these traits in the character. Nevertheless, neither the main characters nor Armin's attitude toward them is simple; they are morally if not psychologically complex, and so, as I will demonstrate in the "Parodic Intent," is Armin's use of them.

No discussion of the characters in _Two Maids_ would be complete without a few words on John i' th' Hospitall, for if he had not existed, we should probably not have had the play.[6] The woodcut on the title page (also reproduced in _Shakespeare's England_, II, 236) shows either John or Armin's mimetic representation of him as a bearded figure "unmistakably in the uniform of a Christ's Hospital boy of Tudor times."[7] He wears a flat cap, a broad falling collar, a blue coat, and a petticoat showing behind the front

[6]There is good reason to believe that Armin's success in imitating John for his early "interlude" routines led him to undertake the writing of a play which would enable him to play the part again. See p. 16.

[7]O. H. T. Dudley, "John In the Hospital," a letter in _TLS_, June 17, 1949, p. 317.

or opening of the skirt. At his girdle are a pencase, an inkhorn, and a wallet or muckinder.[8] Felver adds that his stance is that of a man with a "wry neck, a lame foot, and a distorted hand."[9] Nearly all of the dialogue and antics given him in Two Maids are also given in A Nest of Ninnies.[10] Armin's attitude toward him seems to be less callous than affectionate, as is consistent with the broadly humane and unsentimental morality implicit in the rest of the play.

[8]Dudley says "wallet"; Felver, Robert Armin, Shakespeare's Fool, p. 18, says "muckender."

[9]Felver, p. 18.

[10]Nest, pp. 51-53.

6.

SOURCES AND ANALOGUES

There are no published suggestions of a source for Two Maids, and I do not believe that there is any. A story in Painter's The Palace of Pleasure, which provided Shakespeare with the sources of at least All's Well That Ends Well and Romeo and Juliet, comes closest (but still not very close) to Armin's plot. "Of Maister Thorello and Saladine"[1] tells the story of Master Thorello of Pavie, the generous host to Saladine, a visiting Sultan. Later Thorello goes on a holy voyage to Arabia with the Christians, telling his wife that if he does not return by a set time she should remarry. He is captured by Mohammedans and assigned to be the falconer to a Sultan who, happily enough, is Saladine. Saladine returns his former host's hospitality richly, so Thorello is reluctant to admit his eagerness to return home before his wife's term is up. Saladine discovers him in a dejected state on the eve of the term's end and provides him with a magical bed which will transport him momentarily from Africa to Pavie.

[1]The earliest known appearance of the story is in Busone da Gubbio's L'aventuroso Siciliano (ca. 1349). Painter's probable source was Boccacio's Decamerone, Giorn. X, November 9.

Thorello arrives just as his wife's wedding banquet is beginning. He disguises himself to observe her attitude toward her second marriage and is delighted to see that she seems mournful. He sends word to her that it is the custom of his country for a new bride to share a cup of wine with a stranger. She offers the cup and as she drinks, he drops from his mouth a ring she had given him before his departure. When she raises the cup to finish the wine, she recognizes the ring and rushes to embrace him.

> Then the company beinge intreated to sit and not to remove, Maister Thorello rehearsed in open audience what had chanced unto him from the day of his departure untill that time, concludinge with a petition to the bridegrome, that had newly espoused his Wyfe, that he woulde not be displeased if he tooke hir agayne. The new maried Gentleman, albeit it greeved hym very sore, and thought himselfe to be mocked, aunswered liberally and like a Frende, that it was in hys power to do wyth hys owne what hee thought best.[2]

The common elements are obviously the presumed widow's remarriage, the appearance of the presumed dead husband at the wedding, and the embarrassed resignation of the new husband. But it is equally obvious that the story provides no character equivalent to Humil, whose role is so important in Armin's work; furthermore, the tone and atmosphere of the two pieces are utterly different, though it must be admitted that Heywood, for instance, transformed another Italian romance from Painter's anthology into the realistic

[2]William Painter, The Palace of Pleasure (London, 1890), II, Tome II, 381.

domestic tragedy of A Woman Killed With Kindness and therefore we cannot be sure that Armin could not have brought about a similar metamorphosis.

Hillebrand remarks that the Toures-Mary sub-plot "savor[s] of the carefree invention of Heywood's Fair Maid of the West, which was written about the same time."[3] I am not quite certain whether Hillebrand is here intimating some influence of one playwright upon the other or whether his phrase "carefree invention" implies only a corresponding originality in the two writers. Karl Holzknecht, for instance, says that "for The Fair Maid of the West no more satisfactory source has been found than Heywood's own inventive imagination."[4] If Hillebrand does mean to imply an influence, it must, by his own dating, be one of Armin's influence upon Heywood, since Hillebrand is one of those who favors a late sixteenth century date of composition for Two Maids while Heywood's two parts of The Fair Maid of the West have 1607 as their earliest possible date.[5]

The common elements in Armin's and Heywood's plays are: (1) a blend of realism (middle and upper-middle class

[3]Hillebrand, p. 329.

[4]Outlines of Tudor and Stuart Plays (New York, 1947), p. 217.

[5]The second part of the play is widely believed to have a much later date, but John D. Lewis, in an unpublished doctoral dissertation (University of Kansas), entitled "Thomas Heywood's The Fair Maid of the West and Its Audience," argues that it followed the first part almost immediately, probably in 1607.

English settings and characters) and romance motifs (disguises, separated lovers, shipwrecks, and enigmatic riddles or oracles); (2) a husband, or in Heywood's case a fiancé, who writes prematurely to the heroine of his impending death; and (3) a heroine (*A Fair Maid*, II) who is shipwrecked and presumed dead by her lover. But the two plays are significantly different as well in that Heywood's misinformed heroine does *not* marry another, nor is there in Heywood's play any character similar to Humil or Sir William. Furthermore, Mary's case is more closely (though still not very closely) paralleled by the premature burial of Thaisa in *Pericles, Prince of Tyre*, tentatively dated 1606, though in that case we are much better prepared for the girl's recovery, and the problems raised by it are more complicated (see my note for XVIII.66.1 for further remarks on this parallelism).

Such a minor parallel as Quomodo's feigned death (as a test of the devotion of his wife and son) in Middleton's *Michaelmas Term* (1604-1606), which is merely a device to resolve a happy ending and not central to the whole plot, cannot be taken seriously as a source for Armin's play. And although a supposedly dead husband returns in time to interrupt the wedding of his wife in Marston's *What You Will* (1601), that play is satirical and farcical rather than comically melodramatic; more important, the wedding episode is only incidental to Marston's plot and, again, there is no character equivalent to Humil. But even

Middleton's and Marston's "analogues" are probably more relevant than the episode from _The Winter's Tale_ (1610) in which Florizel, like Toures, disguises himself as an itinerant tradesman in order to elope with Perdita.

Apparently the "Enoch Arden" situation, so popular in our twentieth-century soap operas (and occasionally in real life; see the story of the re-wed air force pilot's wife referred to on p. 15), was very rare in pre-nineteenth-century stories. Gellert Spencer Alleman,[6] in a survey of two hundred forty-one plays from 1663 to 1714, finds ninety-one successful clandestine marriages, like Toures' to Mary, and seventy tricked marriages (involving impersonation, disguise, duped parents and priests), like Filbon's to Tabitha, and twenty-six mock marriages, but not one of the latter involves bigamy or presumed-dead husbands, like that of Sir William and Lady Vergir. Indeed, Stith Thompson's _Motif-Index of Folk Literature_[7] lists not a single case of a son discovering his mother in bed adulterously, though there are single entries for a husband arriving home just as his wife is to marry another (N.681) and for a husband overlooking adultery for his reputation's sake (J221.1.1) and for an adulteress being betrayed by her child (J125.2). Similarly, Georges Polti[8] lists, besides _Hamlet_, only one

[6] _Matrimonial Law and the Materials of Restoration Comedy_ (Philadelphia, 1942), _passim_.

[7] (Bloomington, Indiana, 1955).

[8] _The Thirty-Six Dramatic Situations_ (Boston, 1944), entry 27D6.

case of a plot hinging on a son's duty to punish his mother to avenge his father: Brieux's *Simone* (1908).

In this section, then, I have outlined the plot and isolated the elements of *Two Maids*. I have also exposed the absence and/or insubstantiality of sources and analogues for the play, thereby suggesting the extent of Armin's originality. I hope to show in the next section that the real "source," if it can be called that, of Armin's play is the whole, imagination-reeling body of Shakespeare's major tragedies. I will attempt to show that our inept but humble little play found its inspiration in a serious and thoughtful but good-natured and admiring response to the great dramatist's "dark vision," which had eclipsed the earlier light one and thereby deprived "gamesome Robin" of the new clowning roles he would have liked.

7.

PARODIC INTENT

The most provocative critical comments on _Two Maids_ have been made by Frank O'Connor in his _Shakespeare's Progress_:

> When Armin wrote a play...., it was about a young man whose sensibilities were outraged by his mother's adultery (only apparent this time, one is glad to say). His name is Humil! That preposterous play of his, _The Two Maids of Mort-lake_ [_sic_], is to me the most moving of all Shakespearean documents, for it reveals all that the historical documents conceal; the tremendous impact on the imaginations of simple men that was produced by Shakespeare's daily presence: it is like the splashing waves on the shore after the great ship of literature has sailed silently by.[1]

This _aperçu_ is not the most provocative thing O'Connor has to say, however; in fact, John Middleton Murry had already observed that "the play has for [its] basis a sort of parody of the Hamlet situation" and had referred to Humil as a "caricature of Hamlet."[2] O'Connor, though, goes beyond Murry in two other respects when he says:

> [Armin] had an absolute passion for the work of Shakespeare...[especially] for the great tragic roles. Again it is the old story of the clown with the painted face who watches with jealous rage while Hamlet comes off, still lost in the cloud of his passion.[3]

[1]O'Connor, p. 102.

[2]"Notes on Shakespeare," p. 252.

[3]O'Connor, pp. 101-102.

I believe that O'Connor is right in broadening the influence upon Two Maids beyond Hamlet to include the major tragedies, but I believe his interpretation of Armin's psychology in doing so stems from a failure to appreciate the tone of Armin's play. I imagine Armin to have been an optimistic but tough-minded rationalist who had little sympathy for the tragic vision or the sense of "the pity of it all!" The line between parody and imitation is a hard one to draw, and in many of the parallel passages which follow one may be inclined to see, as O'Connor apparently does, bungled imitation rather than deliberately humorous distortion. But if we regard Two Maids as Armin's comic imitation of Shakespeare's tragic action rather than as a failed attempt to mimic Shakespeare's language, we may see a distinction between parody and imitation as clear as the one revealed by Shakespeare's parody of Lyly's language in I Henry IV, II.iv.438-461, and his imitation of any of several predecessors' plot in Romeo and Juliet.

In Hamlet four months have elapsed since the death of the hero's father and two since the marriage of his mother; yet the grieving son recognizes and vows fealty to the ghost of his father while the dishonored mother does not even see the ghost. In Two Maids an undefined but presumably brief time has elapsed since the announced death of the hero's father and no time at all since the widow's marriage; yet the unmourning son fails to recognize his living father and later betrays him while the widow-bride acknowledges and remains faithful to him. Had Armin merely been trying enviously to imitate Shakespeare, he would not have drawn the differences so sharply. Both Humil and Hamlet believe that their mothers have adulterously betrayed their husbands, and both are shocked, outraged, and intent upon revenge. The distinctions between the two situations are also relevant, for Hamlet is outraged because his noble and true father has been murdered and betrayed for the sake of an ignoble uncle, and therefore his outrage demands a corresponding indignation in the audience. Humil, on the other hand, is not incensed in behalf of his real rather, whose earlier departure and presumed death he resents (IX.33-39) but in behalf of his stepfather, a vain man capable (like Claudius) of conspiracy to murder. Humil's motive for revenge is not the restitution of a loved one's honor but a combination of resentment against the injury done his own honor by his mother's loss of reputation and an impious hope that he can ingratiate himself with his stepfather (XIII.27-29), thus winning the well-endowed hand of his stepsister by exposing the mother's treachery. Thus, even if Humil's interpretation of the apparently scandalous event were valid, his dignity, in comparison with Hamlet's, is travestied and demeaned. I do not believe that this deflation of the hero is due to Armin's artlessness, for, as we shall see, the morality and dignity of virtually every character in the play is torpedoed by the author's skillful irony and cynicism.

Nearly all of the passages identifiable as probably intentional parody occur in Scenes XIII and XV, the ones occurring shortly after Humil's discovery of his mother and James in bed together on the very night[4] she has wed Sir William. Humil utters three lengthy soliloquies: the first of thirty lines, composing the entirety of what I call Scene XIII; the second, of twenty-two lines, opening Scene XV; and the third, of twenty lines, early in Scene XV at 61-81.

Here is the first: "Enter Humil Sadly," immediately after discovering his mother and James in bed together.

O I am slaine with wonder.
Hath this life left in it a little breath,
To blow out treason, reeke yee cloudes of shame.
Putrifie all imagination, hold her at stearne,
There let her sinke, neuer to win againe, 5
Honours recouery, shall I say and thinke it?
O--
Haue I not beene in bed to night, and so
Talke idly wanting sleepe, or rose from rest,
As many troubled doe, acting like life, 10
Awaking dead, for in that flattering feare,
Perchance her reputation may be saued.
No I am certaine in my feare, tis true,
In yond black closset lies a wicked woman,
(I will not say my mother, that names lost) 15
In the twind brazings of the slaue her man.
In Iames his armes, and shall I suffer it?
O--
To blab, it were to harould out my shame,
In quarter'd scutchin of black obloquie, 20
To murder one were most imparciall;

[4]As is common in Elizabethan and other drama, the time scheme of the play is vague, but most evidence indicates that the events take place within approximately thirty-six hours, though it is probably impossible for Mary to have been shipwrecked, buried on the Scilly Isles, exhumed, and returned to More-clacke in a little more than twenty-four hours, as the play demands.

Againe to turne hilles on this sinne,
Would write me baude, but to be nobly satisfide
Is a content licens'd from equity.
The knight shall know it, I will write to him, 25
Startle his bold imagination with pale feare,
Rouse his reuengefull spirit on them both,
And make me hopefull of his loue neglected,
Forgiue me world, heauens iustice puts me on,
And though a sonne, Ile punish both or none. 30

The only verbal echoes of Hamlet here are at lines 8-12 in the cadences and concerns of the famous:

...to die, to sleepe,
To sleepe, perchance to dream, I there's the rub,
For in that sleepe of death what dreams may come
When we have shuffled off this mortall coyle
Must giue us pause.

But the disillusionment, the sense of universal decay, the lurid image of "twind brazings," and the conviction that "heauens iustice puts me on" are also found in Hamlet.

The second soliloquy begins on a more definite Shakespearean note. McGinn[5] cites its first four lines as echoes of Hamlet, I.i.150-167, which I reproduce here, abstracting the significant matter:

The Cock that is the trumpet to the morne
Doth with his lofty and shrill sounding throat
Awake the god of day. . . .
This bird of dawning singeth all night long
. . . .
But look the morne in russet mantle clad
Walkes ore the dewe of yon high Eastward hill.

The passages in question are similar in imagery, rhythm, syntax, and diction but are also descriptive commonplaces; the first lines are especially instructive of Armin's poetic style: of the significant words in the two

[5] Shakespeare's Influence, p. 158.

passages ("bird-cock," "greets-is," "dawning-trumpet," "daie-morne") only Armin's verb is more precise or specific than Shakespeare's, otherwise Shakespeare is more concrete and connotative in his imagery. Here is Humil's second soliloquy, which, like Murry, I give in full as an example of Armin's imitation of Shakespeare:

> The bird that greets the dawning of the daie,
> Signes with his wings, the midnights parture,
> And the sleetie deaw moistning the cheekes
> Of morrowes welcome: giues earnest of the morne:
> Yet all secure, adultrate lust dos sleepe, 5
> And I the hatcht yong of this troden henne,
> Stands Centinell to her idolatrie.
> Blow you sweld windes and crack the battlements,
> Rouse their incestious luxurie with feare
> Of whats to come, yet that were my mishap, 10
> No silent aire fan on them baudie breath,
> That as they reeke in their licentious loue,
> Diuell may seale sure, and Morpheus so pleas'd,
> May to their pastime adde affliction
> Deliuer'd by the hand of him thats wrongd, 15
> And stands indebted to his desteny:
> Yet are they as the hower, whose sandy minutes
> Runs out at pleasure till the period comes,
> Fast sleeping, and enioy their quiet,
> Rouse the black mischiefe from thy ebben cell, 20
> Land in the bosomes of this twin in lust,
> Him whose heapt-wrong calles vengeance to be iust.

Aside from the first four lines, already discussed, one cannot fail to notice at line 8 the striking similarity to Lear's memorable "Blow, winds, and crack your cheeks!" (III.ii.1). Armin may be characterizing Humil as one of those self-conscious young men bent on dramatizing themselves in an effort to make their lives imitate the art they admire. I will return to comment on Armin's possible reasons for reminding his audience of _King Lear_ later. More like Hamlet (or even Othello) is Humil's morbidly affecting focus upon the physical image of the lovers, "this twin in lust."

The third soliloquy combines the language of _Macbeth_ with the psychology of _Hamlet_:

> Scarlet is scarlet, and her sin blood red,
> Wil not be washt hence with a sea of water,
> Is this my hand, or is the fire fire?
> Whose scorching heate dissolues relenting mettall,
> When as it tries the substance; yes, and I 65
> Make knowne my mother is an alien,
> From my blood, so to fall off, and perish
> Euen in her pride of blisse, damn'd be the slaue
> That so attempts her spotlesse chastitie
> To ruine, I know that yet smooth looke, 70
> Plotted, contriu'd, and woon her with deuise,
> She neuer knew a double character till now,
> But single singler she euer rulde,
> Euen modesty her selfe, _Vesta_ resignd to her,
> And vertue hand in hand at barly-breake, 75
> Ran the swift course, none but a hound of hell,
> Hunted this fawne of fortune to his kennell,
> But my mother, forgetting her degree,
> Dos captiuate loue, life and liberty,
> By one deedes practise, wicked, nay farre worse,
> Fatall disgrace, honours created course. 81

The first two lines of this third soliloquy inevitably remind the reader of Macbeth's question:

> Will all great Neptune's ocean wash this blood
> Clean from my hand? No, this my hand will rather
> The multitudinous seas incarnadine,
> Making the green one red.

Humil's question in the third line was probably detonated by Macbeth's: "Is this a dagger, which I see before me,/ The handle toward my hand?" (II.i.33-34). At the same time Humil, like Hamlet, dwells on his mother's "double character," her hypocrisy. And McGinn[6] points out that the phrase "fall off," in line 67 of Humil's speech, may have

[6] _Shakespeare's Influence_, p. 158.

been picked up from the Ghost's lament to Hamlet: "O Hamlet, what a falling-off was there" (Hamlet, I.v.47).

Armin's Shakespearean echoes are not confined to Humil's three soliloquys. Just before the Ghost lamented his "falling off," he accused Claudius of his murder. "O, my prophetic soul! My uncle!" Hamlet exclaimed (I.v.40). When Humil learns that James is his father, he exclaims: "O you prophetique Fairies" (XX.84). Armin also lifts at least one and probably two phrases from the speech in which Hamlet tells Horatio of his plan to trap the King by means of a play: "Vulcans stythye" appears at XV.154 and in Hamlet at III.ii.89, and "cutted guilt" (XV.103) is probably Hamlet's "occulted guilt" (III.ii.82). Furthermore, Humil's question, "was I bewitcht,/ That thus at hudman's blind I dallied/ With her I honored?" (XV.169-171) recalls, "What devil was it/ That thus cozen'd you at hoodman blind?" (Hamlet, III.iv.76-77). Finally, and perhaps not very significantly, Sir William considers but rejects the possibility of feigning madness as a solution to his embarrassment (XV.217).

For the sake of completeness, this account of parodic passages must include notice of two other works treated irreverently by Armin. Like Jonson in Every Man in His Humour (I.v.57-58), he burlesques the notorious hyperbole and bombast of Kyd's The Spanish Tragedy (III.ii.1-5):

O eyes! no eyes, but fountains frought with tears;
O life! no life, but lively form of death;
O world! no world, but mass of public wrongs,
Confused and filled with murder and misdeeds!

Tutch, when discovered by Sir William in the act of delivering Filbon's mash note to Tabitha, proclaims:

O life no life, but messe of publicke wrong,
Day turne to night, for I ha liu'd too long.
(XI.110-111)

In the next scene (XII.43-46) Tutch takes off on a popular ballad about "Mary Ambree," who in the original is portrayed as chaste and courageous:

Ile nere sell my honour for purple nor pall:
A mayden of England, sir, never will bee
The whore of a monarcke, quoth Mary Ambree.

But Tutch's version, which keeps the same refrain as most of the stanzas in the original, is less ceremonious:

Mortall downe, thistle soft,
She laid her selfe vnder to keep him aloft,
And euer she said, come turne thee to me,
And was not this bonny lasse Mary Ambre?

(See Explanatory Notes for XI.110-111 and XII.43-46 for further discussion of these two passages.)

I have previously indicated that I do not share O'Connor's view that these allusions to or parodies and imitations of Shakespeare's tragedies are manifestations of the clown's envy of the tragedian. On the contrary I believe that in the context of the comedy they are ironic rejoinders to Shakespeare's tragic vision. The effect of the play is to reassure us of the likelihood of social or communal success in avoiding potential tragic traps. Armin's characters are neither so noble nor so damned as

Shakespeare's tragic figures. It is as if Armin were shaking his head in wryly amused tolerance at the humanity and fate of those figures, telling them all that, as Oscar Wilde would say, "life is too important to be taken seriously." No, Humil-Hamlet, your mother has not betrayed your father, it only looks that way. No, Humil-Edmund, your father has not rejected and disowned you, it only looks that way. No, Sir William-Lear, your daughters have not vilely repudiated you, they have merely behaved like unsophisticated but sensible young women who will take the necessary steps to win their mates. No, Sir William-Othello, your wife has not villainously betrayed you but only remained loyal to her true husband. No, Toures-Romeo, your virginal beloved has not been cruelly snatched from your wedding bed, it only looks that way. Not even the Macbeth-like ambition of Sir William and Lady Vergir for socially improving marriages for their children will be allowed to come to fruition in Armin's comically deflated world of the middle classes. And these painless conclusions to potentially devastating situations are not contrived to satisfy some naively Panglossian complacence on Armin's part.

If Armin's characters suffer no abiding pain, they nevertheless denude themselves of dignity, for they are a most conniving and politic lot. Sir William not only falsely promises his daughter to Humil in order to secure Lady Vergir's consent in marriage (and he does this twice, the second time unknowingly, when Humil is disguised as the would-be murderer of his mother, an apothecary), but he also responds to the discovery of his wife's "adultery" with a mere petty and hypocritical regard for his "reputation," the appearance of his honor. One may criticize Othello for gullibility or for self-indulgence and romantic self-deception, but he is unquestionably a grander personage in his passion and his revulsion from Desdemona's putative sin than Sir William is in his circumspect avoidance of scandal and his subsequent conspiracy to murder. But Sir William is not knave only, he is also fool, for he has himself been gulled into marriage by a fortune-hunting widow who is primarily interested in procuring a wife for her son, and as the play concludes he must resign himself to being a "iesting-stock." He has been cuckolded by his wife's husband, defied by his daughters, betrayed by his servant, and outwitted by his sons-in-law.

If Lady Vergir is tricked and victimized by false promises into the marriage, she too does not hesitate to use "policie" (VI.26 and VI.58), attempting to extort fulfillment of those false promises by refusing to consummate the marriage. Thus the ambitious and materialistic Lady is deceived by both her husbands (the first pretends to be dead, apparently to test her fidelity), betrayed, denounced, and perhaps nearly killed by her son,[7] and is unsuccessful

[7]It is not clear in the play whether Humil actually intends to murder his mother or merely pretends to be

in her plot.

The son for whom the Lady so degrades herself is one who is unmanly enough to encourage her to secure him a wife in such a fashion, who fails to recognize his own father, and who callously betrays his own mother largely out of a selfish desire to ingratiate himself with a step-father who has already scorned him. The family's failures in securing their objectives only illustrate the extent to which they are dominated by what Conrad, in _The Heart of Darkness_, calls "the flabby devil."

The young Romeos of the story, Toures and Filbon, are hardly more heroic. If we cannot fault them (as an audience imbued with stricter ideals of authority might have) for defying their vulgar and willful superior, a man who seeks to "b[u]y honor" (VIII.61-66) for his daughters, Toures falls short of the romantic ideal when, while playing Pyramus to Mary's Thisbe, he resorts to rhetoric rather than self-slaughter and when he lightly assumes the disguise which his friend Filbon had perfected and had been planning to use himself (XII.35-37). Filbon, in turn, has no scruples about deceiving Henry (a foolish, vain, simpering version of Friar Laurence) into performing an illicit marriage, also invoking "policie" (XII.63) as a justification. We should not be surprised by his duplicity however,

---

willing to do so in order to win Sir William's confidence. I think he actually intends to do so, but see my notes at XX.69-70, 86, and 87-88.

since his father, Sir Rafe, invokes the same concept (XVI. 142) and does not scruple to aid the young men in defrauding his former friend and superior of the one thing he holds dear, at the same time doing whatever he can to avoid responsibility. Not even Tutch, who is first compromised by Filbon, emerges unscathed in Armin's portrait gallery of calculating parents, whining and weak-kneed lovers, faithless sons, disobedient daughters, doubting husbands, pompous aristocrats, and petty traitors. When we compare Tutch to Lear's Fool, we must think not only of his desertion of Sir William but of his whining self-pity at the prospect of having to face Sir William without Tabitha's or Filbon's protection (XXII.234-237).

The morality of the remaining characters is more difficult to assess. Surely even an Elizabethan conservative must have allowed for the perversity of Sir William in judging the girls' filial disobedience, and one feels certain that Armin intended them to be regarded as "homely milk-bole things," coarse, perhaps, but not mean-spirited and probably charming in their simplicity and single-minded search for mates. Aside from his lapse of sense in testing his wife, James is decently if weakly concerned for the embarrassment he must cause Sir William and is no more exasperated by Sir William's attempt on his wife's life than Sir William was by James's instantaneous seduction of _his_ wife. Throughout the play the Earl is a figure of good-will but almost seems, again, like a parody, by virtue of his ineffectuality, of Shakespeare's omniscient Dukes in Measure for Measure, A Midsummer Night's Dream, and The Winter's Tale.

Armin's own morality is best understood by comparing it with the one suggested by Louis B. Wright in his account of the popular themes of the drama of the time. Wright describes a period of growing class consciousness in which commercial theaters catered either to the middle or upper class, satirizing one or the other. Of the many money-making themes for Elizabethan plays, which Wright lists, the only element which Armin capitalized on was the interest in domestic triangles and actual or threatened murder. But Wright adds that "the tragic relations of husband, wife, and illicit lover provided a vehicle for theatrical sensation capable of running the gamut of sentimentality or pandering to the grosser appetites of the multitude, while at the same time it preached a sermon against the crying sins of murder and adultery."[8] He goes on to cite many passages of overt moralizing by repentant sinners, which have no parallels in Two Maids. There is clearly nothing sentimental about Armin's handling of his theme, nor do I think that such an item as James's entrance "garterles" deserves to be regarded as "pandering to the grosser appetites." The only moralizing in the play is that directed by Sir William against drunkenness (XI.69-74)

[8]Middle Class Culture in Elizabethan England (New York, 1935), p. 607.

and by his brother Charles (XVIII.58-60) against the use of tobacco and by the preacher Henry (XVI.125-127) against the abuse of selling church benefices. It is unlikely that Armin meant any of these seriously since in the first two instances the Vergir brothers are castigating characters who are not actually guilty of the vices (Toures is not really drunk, and the buried chest does not contain tobacco) and in the third instance the speaker is made to appear ridiculous and is squelched by Sir William himself (XVI.128 and 132). Early in his career Armin did write a preface to a "pious" religious tract,[9] but being a playwright he was naturally anti-puritan, and his only "religious" figure in the play is portrayed as inept and alternately self-congratulating (XVI.129-132) and cringing (XXI.72-74). This is not to say that Armin would necessarily have endorsed the advice of his mentor Tarleton "to pull downe the Churche and set up the Ale-house,"[10] but that he, unlike the self-righteous Henry, recognized the artistic value of the indirect literary attack by means of parody, satire, and comic ridicule.

A further clue to his intentions in resorting to the indirect attack is provided by an examination of his curious nomenclatural practice. Why has he set the play in

[9]Grosart, p. x.

[10]Richard Tarleton, in a preface to Barnabe Rich's _Faultes, Faults, and nothing else but Faults_ (1606), cited by Wright, p. 605.

More-clacke? Although he may have liked the alliteration in the title, when compared to the more exotic-sounding title of _The Two Gentlemen of Verona_ one can only conclude that he deliberately chose the clattering name for purposes of parody, as if one were to write of _Pericles, Prince of Poughkeepsie_ or _Hamlet His Highness of Hoboken_. The political leader of the world of the play is given the title of Earl of Tumult; surely not a gratuitous absurdity but a kind of allegorical clue to Armin's mocking attitude toward his creations; as we have already seen, the relationships between all of the characters are almost incredibly disordered and tumultuous when measured by the criteria of "right reason" or "natural order," which are the relevant criteria of the Elizabethan-Jacobean world. The Earl of Tumult seems unaware that he is the Momus of More-clacke, where men become women, women die and live again, and artificial fools (Tutch) become "natural" ones (John). If Felver is right in calling the play "a strong candidate for [the] prize [for] the most complex and baffling intrigue comedy in all English drama,"[11] it may be that Armin intends to reduce to absurdity the extent of intrigue and conspiracy and deception among those aspiring to greater social "honor" in the petty aristocracy. There may be nothing extraordinary about the name Sir William Vergir, but Tutch (XVI.99), in the role of Welsh Sir Robert Morgan, refers to him as

[11] _Robert Armin, Shakespeare's Fool_, p. 16.

William Perger, or Berger (Burgher), and the name aptly describes him as a virgin burgher. His wife, also oddly, has no Christian name or given name in the play. Humil is certainly an appropriate name for the debased and humiliated Hamlet. The plain names of Mary and Tabitha also seem to be designed to de-romanticize the common and domestic objects of worship. The least explicable appellation is that of Auditor, which sounds like the title of a man's office, but he is twice referred to (XIV.30 and XVI.108) as "Master Auditor" or "Auditor," not as "the Auditor," as one would expect if this were his title. He, too, is given no family name, but, more oddly, his son is called Sir Robert Toures, and no tower of strength is he. Sir Rafe has no family name either, and his son is Filbon or *bon fils* (good son). I see no significance in the name of James Humil. But the low comic characters have suitable names: Wat is not only an abbreviation for "waterman" but seems also to be the common nickname for Walter, since he is referred to in direct address as "Wat" rather than as "the waterman," and Fer is not only an abbreviation of "ferryman" but also a nickname for Ferris, by which he is designated in the speech tag at X.23. Furthermore, the wise folly of Tutch-John (XXII.171-177 and 181-184), who reminds Sir William "That honest men want,/ And knaues get money," while "all the world" are "beggars" serves as a *touchstone* for the foolish "policie" of the ambitious pharisaism of the rest of More-clacke's inhabitants.

I trust I shall not be accused of humorlessness for treating the characters of a light comedy in such moralistic terms. In the first place, the lightness of the comedy is problematical; much of Sir William's fustian attitudinizing could be played either broadly and farcically or dourly and menacingly. When seen for the first time, the play may very well keep the audience in some suspense as to whether it will end in the violence of melodrama or the embrace of comedy. There can be no doubt about which genre it ultimately belongs to, but Armin's comedy emerges essentially from his technique of ironically measuring the mundane life of the petty nobility against the grander experience projected in Shakespeare's tragedies. The virtue of the technique is that it becomes a double-edged instrument, providing at once a rationalist, common-sense critique of high tragedy as a departure from "nature" and a moral index by which to measure the ignobility of the smaller, deflated reality.

To sum up, _Two Maids_ is comparable in its effect to Barbara Garson's _Macbird_: both plays are sprinkled with Shakespearean phrases and measure vulgar characters by Shakespeare's noble heros, but Armin implies that real life is not only not so noble but also not so tragic as life portrayed in Shakespeare's tragedies. Armin parodies rather than imitates the plot or action of his model and imitates rather than parodies the language. Garson burlesques Shakespeare's language and imitates his plot.

8.

EDITORIAL PRINCIPLES AND PRACTICES

For reasons stated in "The Text," my copy-text is the J. Pierpont Morgan Library quarto. Adhering to the principles enunciated by modern textual scholars, I have attempted to present a critical, old-spelling text that would, as closely as possible, satisfy the ideal intentions of its author.

No substantive or semi-substantive deviations from the copy-text have been made silently. In order to retain the general texture of the copy-text I have reproduced its old-spelling accidentals, making no attempt to render spelling uniform throughout; thus "reach" (I.38) becomes "reatch" (XII.76), "widdow" (I.8) becomes "widow" (I.40), and the _doe_-_do_, _Ile_-_I'le_ disparities and the like are allowed to stand in order that students may pursue Williams' studies of the two compositors.[1] I have not "corrected" Armin's usage when he fails to use an apostrophe in the possessive case or to make verbs agree in number with their subjects or when he uses apostrophes in contractions inconsistently.

[1]"The Compositor of the 'Pied Bull' _Lear_," _SB_, I (1949), 59-68.

On the other hand, I have corrected misspellings which Armin and the print setters would have recognized as such; thus "lighly" (XXII.130) and "sithes" (XV.214) are corrected to "lightly" and "sighes" and footnoted. When misspellings could be emended in more than one way (e.g., "detie" [VII.2] equals "ditty"? "dutie"? "deitie"?), I have made the emendation, provided a footnote, and discussed the possibilities in the "Explanatory Notes" at the end. The same procedure obtains when the copy-text is not legible (e.g., "prolong" or "proloug" [XXII.89]). I have not changed "too" to "to" or "two," or "I" to "aye," but when there is doubt as to which of these or other modern words is meant, I have discussed the problem in the "Explanatory Notes" (e.g., "plaste" equals "placed" and "past" equals "paced").

Punctuation, too, has been altered as little as possible, though perhaps more than one would wish necessary. Elizabethan conventions in punctuation often seem arbitrary to those unaccustomed to them, but one soon adjusts to the "comma-splices" and the penchant for end-stopping lines for oratorical rather than rhetorical or grammatical reasons. My primary purpose in repunctuating has been to restore Armin's apparent intentions rather than impose modern practices upon the text. Thus when the copy-text prints a comma or no mark at all at the end of a speech, a period has been supplied and footnoted. The same holds when marks are clearly misplaced as in "Regard her not, for she talkes,

Id'ly Filbon" (VII.20). This line is altered to "Regard her not, for she talkes idly, Filbon." Such compositorial errors in pointing or capitalization, when clearly due to anticipation, reversal, or oversight are corrected and footnoted. On the other hand, there are a number of passages in the play which are to us ambiguous or meaningless as punctuated in the copy text, and must also have been so to its early readers; in such cases I have assumed the editorial responsibility to punctuate the passage as I deemed fit, to footnote all changes, and to direct the reader to an Explanatory Note discussing the problem and possibilities. Armin, or his printer, sometimes concludes a question with a comma or period rather than a question mark; in such cases I have not altered the punctuation if the interrogative word order is used, but when the declarative word order is used, as in VIII.18, I have made the change as an aid to the reader. The reader should also be aware of the printer's practice of sometimes substituting question marks for exclamation points.

In the text proper only a very few minor alterations are done silently. (1) Arabic numerals are written out; (2) the long "f" is modernized, and "W's" are used for "VV's," but "I" and "i" are kept for "J" and "j," and "V(v)" and "U(u)" are presented as in the text; (3) fount cases are corrected as required by altered end-punctuation or relineation; (4) display capitals and ornamental initials are replaced with regular capitals of the appropriate fount;

(5) the spacing of words, elisions, lines, and sections is normalized; (6) nasals are expanded; (7) the exclamatory ô is changed to O; (8) the initial letter of an italicized word, which is often not italicized in Q., has been italicized; (9) catch-words and running titles have been dropped, but ampersands, even at the beginning of verse lines, have been maintained. In speech prefixes, however, abbreviations have been silently expanded and the spelling made consistent, while the stage directions have been silently normalized, especially in regard to capitalization, though inconsistencies in spelling of names are allowed to stand. Omitted speech prefixes have been supplied in brackets, and reassignments of speeches have been footnoted and further discussed in the "Explanatory Notes." Lengthy stage directions are centered on the page, but brief ones, especially those requiring gestures to accompany specific lines, are maintained in the right-hand margin. I have also shunned the original printer's practice of economizing by running two or three brief speeches on one line; these have been expanded. Furthermore, I have followed Clifford Leech's practice, in his editions of The Revels Plays, of assigning to stage directions which occur on separate lines from the text the number of the immediately preceding line followed by a decimal point and 1, 2, 3, *etc*. Thus the line 105.3 indicates the third line of stage direction following line 105. At the beginning of a scene the lines of a stage direction are numbered 0.1, 0.2, *etc*. Stage directions

have been added, in brackets, when the copy-text does not provide necessary exits and entrances and when I have felt it useful to indicate the person to whom a speech seems to be directed or when stage business is suggested by a speech. All abbreviations of proper names and titles in the stage directions have been silently expanded.

Aside from occasional stage directions the only significant addition is that of scene divisions, which are bracketed. I have divided the play into scenes on the principle that a cleared stage indicates a new scene. Jewkes[2] has shown that for production purposes these divisions are natural, and they also make it possible to avoid cumbersome four-digit numbers in lineation and to facilitate discussion of the play's structure.

Limitations of marginal space have prevented me from indicating the pagination of the copy-text in my text. To compensate for this omission, I have provided virgules to indicate that a new page was begun at that point in the quarto and listed the catchwords for each signature in Appendix C.

Grosart's edition has been collated point for point, but since he reproduces his copy-text almost point for point, except for occasional and inconsistent substitutions of colons or semi-colons for commas or the equally occasional addition of a hyphen or apostrophe or grammatical correction,

[2] _Act Division in Elizabethan and Jacobean Plays_, pp. 7-9.

I have not seen fit to record his alterations unless they influenced me in repunctuating a difficult passage. Many of his notes have been incorporated and acknowledged in my "Explanatory Notes."

Press variants, all of which occur in the outer forme of signature C, are listed in Appendix B.

The "Explanatory Notes" explain not only obscurities in the text but my handling of all editorial problems, such as emendations and relineations. They also contain suggested readings, as opposed to incorporated variants, critical and interpretive comment, biographical and historical background relevant to specific passages, literal expansion of allusions and figurative language, and whatever other kinds of help or speculation seem appropriate. In them I have frequently felt it necessary to confess ignorance, perplexity, and uncertainty in the hope that future readers will add to our understanding of this largely neglected play.

Finally, the problems of lineation are so complex as to deserve extended treatment. Aside from the explication of obscure passages, perhaps the severest trial of editorial patience has been prompted by problems in lineation. The copy-text prints much verse as prose and, probably, some prose as verse. As Armin warns us, we shall find "verse as well blanke, as cranke."[3] I have felt obliged to alter eighty-seven passages, amounting to

[3]"To the friendly peruser," see below, p. 104.

eighteen per cent of the text (383 out of 2111 lines). Only a third of those alterations was undertaken with any measure of confidence. There are several considerations precluding more positive assessment of the remaining two thirds.

The most general reasons for uncertainty in this matter stem from more basic uncertainties (discussed in "Text") about the relationship between Armin's intended ideal text and our actual copy-text: it is usually impossible to determine whether the lineation of the copy-text reflects errors by the printer and/or copyist, or is the product of Armin's carelessness or ignorance, or some combination of these. Whatever the cause, Armin's prose and verse, as they appear in _Q_., are often indistinguishable, though not as often as _Q_. would indicate.

Some notion of the extent of the indistinguishability may best be grasped by an analysis of three pages of "verse" chosen at random from _Q_. The first of the three pages, sig. A3 (III.3-35), is the most regular: of the thirty-three lines printed as verse only one is a short, one-line speech and only two others, one from the beginning and one from the end of a speech, are abnormally short; twenty-one (or better than two-thirds) of the full-length lines contain ten syllables, four contain eleven, three contain nine, one has thirteen, and one eight. The page is also quite typical in that only eight of the thirty-three lines lack end-punctuation. The second exemplary page, sig. E3^{v} (XV.161-196), is the least regular: of its thirty-three "verse" lines only five are short, single-line speeches and only two others are short, speech-ending lines; but only ten (or one-third), including two couplets, contain ten syllables, two contain nine, four have eleven, seven have twelve, one has thirteen, one fourteen, and one fifteen. Furthermore, only thirteen, or less than half of the full-length lines, are end-stopped. Needless to say, I have relined much of this "verse." The third exemplary page, sig. E4 (XV.196-232), is the one following the second page and shows a quite different pattern: of its thirty-six "verse" lines only three are short, single-line speeches and only three more are short, speech-end lines; twelve of its thirty full-length lines contain ten syllables, four contain nine, two have eight, six have eleven, five twelve, and one thirteen; only three of the lines are not end-stopped. To sum up, two-thirds of the lines on the first page are decasyllabic and three-quarters are end-stopped; less than a third of the lines on the second page are decasyllabic and only half are end-stopped; about forty percent of the lines on the third page are decasyllabic and ninety percent are end-stopped. With such variety and irregularity it is difficult to establish a norm by which to measure dubious passages.

Passages which I have relined may be placed in one, and sometimes more than one, of six categories. The first type of passage is that which, though printed as prose, contains two or more lines of rhymed iambic pentameter. Such rhymed exit lines as

> _Filbon_ farewell, my husband thinke on me,
> I am thy treasure but thou bear'st the keie
> (XXI.66-67)

should obviously not be printed, as _Q_. does, as prose. The second type of mislined passage is that containing irregular but rhymed verse (e.g., II.50-52, VII.85-86, XI.129-134, XVI.94-97, XVII.85-88, XIX.16-17, XX.82-83, XXII.171-176, XXII.340-341, and XXII.348-349). Again, the presence of rhyme seems adequate justification for relining the passages as verse. And alterations in the lineation of the third type of passage can still, like those in the first two types, be undertaken with confidence; these are passages which despite their appearance in _Q_. as prose can be scanned as regular blank verse (I.9-12, VII.101; VIII.1-6, 10-12; XI.162-164; XV.127-129, 249-252; XVI.61-65; and XXI.6-8, 18-19).

Whereas alterations of the first three categories can be made with some confidence in the interest of maximizing the amount of clearly recognizable verse in the play, some readers may be less inclined to accept editorial meddling with lines which are already cast as verse in _Q_. (as at I.5-6; XV.143-150, 190-193; XVI.171-182; and XXII.374-383). The first instance will be discussed presently; in the second case mislineation arose from running-on sequential speeches by different characters. In the last and most egregious example a series of couplets has been buried in line-middles by mislineation; this passage is the clearest case of textual corruption in the play as it is most obvious that Armin could not have intended the lines to appear as they do in Q. In the remaining three examples of this fourth type, as in all of those of the fifth type, the editor, no matter what his decision, exposes himself to charges of incompetence; these are cases in which I have recast already irregular lines into different but often still irregular lines with the intention of isolating rhyming lines or of increasing the number of end-stopped lines or, at least, of creating some regularity where little or none existed before.

The fifth category is the largest, containing fifty-six separate passages, and the least justifiable, being composed of passages of Q.'s prose which I have recast as admittedly irregular verse. Most of these changes can be justified by one of three possible situations: (1) when a single speech is printed as a mixture of verse and prose (e.g., VII.181-188, XV.236-245); (2) when the same character's surrounding speeches are in verse (e.g., VI.17-18, 28-29; VII.6-15); and (3) when surrounding speeches by other characters in the scene are in verse (I.5-6, 41-42; V.83-86; and a great many in Scenes XV and XVI, which provide an inexplicably disproportionate number of lineation problems). At times, too, I have made alterations when I suspected that the compositor had simply been unable to fit a long hexameter on a single line and then practiced a false economy by running lines together. There are also two cases of clearly compositorial responsibility for mislineation: E4^{v} and F2 have only thirty-five lines instead of the usual thirty-six; this is no doubt due to the erroneous treatment of the speeches at XV.244-252 and XVI.87-97 as prose.

As Grosart has rightly said, "the apparent prose will be found to scan as well (i.e., sometimes as ill) as that printed in verse,"[4] so that my aim has been to maximize the number of end-stopped, alternating stress, decasyllabic lines, taking into account Armin's free use of: (1) short lines at beginnings and endings of speeches; (2) extra-metrical unaccented syllables; (3) iambic tetrameters; (4) headless lines; (5) initial trochees; and (6) hexameters, especially those made up of a trochee plus iambic pentameter. All too often one is put to the task of separating not gold from dross but flour from talcum powder; I have performed the operation as delicately as my blunted instruments of perception would permit, footnoted the passage in question, and often discussed my reasoning in the "Explanatory Notes." In only two cases (VII.94-97 and XI.20-22) have I recast from verse to prose.

I have already mentioned that the metrical irregularity of _Q._'s verse deprives the editor of a norm. There is another convention which might have helped to reduce

[4]Grosart, p. xx.

editorial anxiety, however, had Q. obeyed it with consistency. In Elizabethan drama we expect "low" characters to speak in prose and noble characters to speak in verse, as a general rule. And Armin's lowest characters (Tutch, Wat, Fer, John, Boy, and Nurse) do generally abide by this convention. But the lovers (Mary, Toures, Tabitha, and Filbon) serve both comic and romantic functions which are not always clearly separable; at such times, neither is the metrical quality of their speech. But most troublesome are Sir William, Lady, James, and Humil, who in Q. frequently alternate from verse to prose within given scenes (e.g., Scene IX) and sometimes, if the print-setter were to be trusted, even within single speeches. Hardin Craig has offered an explanation for a similar but not identical state of affairs in Pericles (1609):

> The text seems worse than it is, because no quarto, except possibly the 1608 version of King Lear [also printed by Okes], has so much verse printed as prose. Some of it appears to be the result of marginal revision, but the quantity is so great that one is obliged to believe that the reviser wrote a great deal of his verse in the form of prose, a practice not without parallel in Shakespeare and other Elizabethan writers.[5]

By this remark Craig indicates that despite the writer's calligraphic practices, his intentions were to write verse; this would seem to be an especially justifiable assumption in dramatic or ceremonial scenes in which the majority of speeches are in verse.

Nevertheless, such an assumption can be only

[5]A New Look at Shakespeare's Quartos, p. 25.

tentative at best in such scenes as the first one in *Two Maids*. Here only fifty-six lines comprise twenty-seven speeches. Of the twenty-seven speeches seventeen are of one line, often a very short one, and therefore not objectively identifiable as verse, though two (I.34 and 40) might be called regularly iambic with one extra-metrical syllable. Of the ten multi-linear speeches, *Q.* prints five as verse and five as prose, which I have recast as verse. Obviously such a balance provides no norm, especially since prose and verse are about equally divided between "high" and "low" characters. The first speech in verse (lines 2-4) contains two regular iambic pentameter lines and a half line of iambic trimeter; thus it is conventional and certainly identifiable as verse. The second verse speech (lines 5-6), however, can be so designated only by virtue of its typography, not its rhythms: *Q.* prints line five with twelve syllables having no regular metric pattern and line six with three (or four, depending on elision of "flowers") patternless syllables. I have regrouped the words and printed them as a headless iambic pentameter line followed by a regular iambic half-line. The third speech printed as verse (lines 24-32) contains only four clearly regular lines (26, 27, 28, 32), allowing for a final unaccented syllable in line 27. Three of the remaining five lines (24, 29, 31) contain only eight syllables, line 24 having only one sure iamb, line 29 none, and line 31 two. The remaining two lines (25 and 30) are quite irregular, line 25 having only one sure iamb and line 30 only two. In the fourth verse speech (lines 43-45) only the first and third lines can be called regular, line 44 containing an extra unaccented syllable somewhere in mid-line unless "they are" is contracted. Of the five speeches printed as verse, then, only the fifth (lines 46-57) is a secure example of blank verse, all but two of its lines (49 and 53) being regular.

This analysis of the five putative verse passages offers little aid in evaluating or redefining the five "prose" passages, since the "verse" provides no norm against which to measure the "prose." The first of the "prose" passages (lines 9-11) is surely in the _language_ of poetry but a good deal of manipulating is required to transform it into blank verse. _Q._ prints:

> I will not say as poore as Iob, but as bare as Ianuary,/ when the trees looke like a girle, whose colour comes and/ goes as frost doos in the milke.

This can be recast and scanned as follows:

> I will not say as poore as Iob but as bare
> As Ianuary when the trees looke like
> A girle whose coulour comes and goes as frost
> Doos in the milke.

Even if we assume a contraction of "but as" in line 9, the "verse" is barely satisfactory. On the other hand, merely by capitalizing the initial letter of the second line of the second "prose" speech in _Q._, we can transform the passage into verse no more irregular than much that appears throughout the play:

> Twas wont to be a rich widdow and a poore knight
> But now false a knight rich and the widdow poore.

The hexameter in line 13 is by no means unusual, but, unfortunately, the editor finds no justification in the more regular verse passages of the play for eliding by apocape the extra-metrical syllable in the fourth foot of line 14. In fact, there is no evidence in the play that Armin practiced any elision or contraction; had he done so, the editor's burden of rationalizing the apparent metrical chaos would have been much lightened. The two remaining passages requiring relineation as verse in Scene I present no major obstacles. Lines 18-19 can be regrouped to form two regular iambic pentameter lines, and lines 41-42 illustrate Armin's common practice of compensating for syllabically or accentually short lines by following them by long ones. Since he wrote for a theater audience rather than a reading audience, he did not scruple to follow a line containing extra-unaccented syllables with a headless one, so that the aural, if not the visual, effect was one of metrical regularity.

To sum up, I have relined some of _Q._'s verse and much of its "prose," on the grounds that _Q._ does not reflect Armin's intentions because (1) the compositor has sometimes not duplicated his copy; (2) that copy sometimes probably reflected Armin's calligraphic practices rather than his prosodic intentions; and (3) the copy was in a rough, unpolished state.

THE

History of the two Maids of More-clacke,

VVith the life and simple maner of IOHN
in the Hospitall.

Played by the Children of the Kings
Maiesties Reuels.

VVritten by ROBERT ARMIN, seruant to the Kings
most excellent Maiestie.

[Woodprint]

LONDON,

Printed by N.O. for *Thomas Archer*, and is to be sold at his

shop in Popes-head Pallace, 1609.

To the friendly peruser

GENTLEMEN, Cittizens, Rustickes, or quis non, I haue
boldly put into your hands, a Historical discourse,
acted by the boyes of the Reuels, which perchaunce in
part was sometime acted more naturally in the Citty,
if not in the hole. Howsoeuer I commit it into your 5
hands to be scan'd, and you shall find verse, as well
blancke, as crancke, yet in the prose let it passe for
currant, I would haue againe inacted Iohn my selfe, but
Tempora mutantur in illis, & I cannot do as I would, I
haue therefore thought good to diuulge him thus being 10
my old acquaintance, Iack, whose life I knew, and whose
remembrance I presume by appearance likely. Wherein I
whilome pleased: and being requested both of Court and
Citty, to shew him in priuate, I haue therefore printed
him in publike, wishing thus much to euery one, so 15
delighting, I might put life into this picture, and
naturally act him to your better contents; but since it
may not be, my entreaty is, that you would accept this
dumbe show, and be well wishing to the substance.

Yours euer as he is merry and frolicke, 20

ROBERT ARMIN.

The Historie of the two

Maides of More-clacke.

With the life and simple manner of Iohn

i'the Hospitall.

[Dramatis Personae

Sir William Vergir: a well-to-do knight of More-clacke and father of Mary and Tabitha, the two maids of More-clacke.

Mary Vergir: Sir William's eldest daughter, one of the titular maids, romantically pursued by and in love with Sir Robert Toures.

Tabitha Vergir: Sir William's second daughter, romantically pursued by and in love with Filbon.

Lady Vergir: bride of Sir William, formerly married to James Humil, whom she presumes dead.

James Humil: first husband to Lady Vergir, presumed dead, father of Humil.

Humil [Junior]: son of James and Lady Vergir; would-be suitor to Mary, who has been promised to him by Sir William; in Scene XX he appears disguised as an apothecary.

Sir Rafe Filbon: father of Filbon [Junior] and acquaintance of Sir William.

Filbon [Junior]: son of Sir Rafe and suitor to Tabitha; to court her, he appears in Scene XVI disguised as the servant to a Welch knight, then as the knight himself; in Scene XXII he appears disguised as the nurse to John.

Auditor Toures: father of Sir Robert, acquaintance of Sir William, and friend to Sir Rafe; apparently auditor of one of the Queen's offices; to help Filbon in the latter's attempt to secure Tabitha as a bride, he appears in Scene XVI disguised as a merchant and suitor to Tabitha.

Sir Robert Toures: son of Auditor Toures and suitor to Tabitha; to abduct her, he appears in Scene XI disguised as a tinker.

Earle of Tumult: friend and occasional guest of Sir William; also benefactor to Robert Toures and Filbon Junior.

Governor: Sir Charles Vergir, brother of Sir William and governor of the Scilly Islands.

Henry: rector or vicar of Putney, a parish in the gift of Sir William.

Tutch: a quick-witted clown, first a servant to Sir William and then to Filbon, whose marital goals he aids by disguising himself first as a Welch knight, then as the knight's servant (he and Filbon exchange disguises in Scene XVI), and finally as John (in Scene XXII).

John i' th Hospital: a mentally retarded "natural" kept by the City at Christ's Hospital, affectionately regarded by Sir William.

Madge: a kitchen maid to Sir William.

Waterman and Ferryman: two clownish servants.

Nurse: a woman appointed to look after John.

Boy: an attendant to John.

Lords, Gentlemen, attendants, Master of a vessel, and sailors.

Ladies "for shew" and servants.]

[Scene I]

Enter a maide strowing flowers, and a

seruing man perfuming the doore.

Maid. Strow, strow.

Man. The Muskadine stayes for the bride at Church,

The Priest and himens cerimonies tend

1. strow] Strow Q.

To make them man and wife.

Maid. By my maiden-head a ioyfull time, 5

Ile paue their way with flowers.

Man. While I perfume.

Maid. Some say this widdow's rich.

Man. I will not say as poore as Iob, but as bare

As Ianuary, when the trees looke like 10

A girle, whose coulour comes and goes as frost

Doos in the milke.

Maid. Twas wont to be a rich widdow and a poore knight,

But now false, a knight rich and the widdow poore.

Man. How euer honour is most rich, no matter who is

poore./ 15

Maid. I would my fortune were no worse.

Man. Thine may be better.

Maid. So much if't be thy wil, if euer knight

Were gul'd, be it in me, in me I pray. _Enter Humil._

Humil. What are the waits of London come? 20

Man. Yes sir.

Humil. Play in their highest key then.

Man. Sound Hoboyes. _Hoboyes play._

5-6. _Q. prints_: "By...their/ way...flowers." 9-12. _Q. prints as prose_: "I...Ianuary,/ when...and/ goes...milke." 14. But] but _Q._ 15. _Q. prints as prose_: "How...who/ is poore." 18-19. _Q. prints as prose_: "So...were/ gul'd...pray." 23. Sound] sound _Q._ _Hoboyes play._] _Q. prints at line_ 22.

Humil. Make the Gods daunce, cause Iouiall mirth.
Musike in heauen for this earthes marriage 25
Is a triumphant concord to vs all,
To me tis seal'd by promise for his daughter,
Who in our blood shall simpathize, sayes I,
She shall be ours, bedded, although some
Mennace a riualship, yet the sure card 30
Giues the trick ours, and we shall winne,
Since in my mother it doth first beginne.

Enter the solemne shewe of the marriage, Sir William Vergir, Earle, Lords, Auditor, Sir Rafe, Sir Robert Toures, Filbon, others.

Enter Lady, Mistres Mary, Mistres Tabitha, and some other women for shewe.

After all.

Enter Iames a cittizen, father to Humil.

Iames. Good morrow sir.
Humil. A good one to thy selfe, to vs tis seasond.
Iames. A marriage sir? 35
Humil. I and a good one friend.
Iames. Because tis rich.
Humil. Good reach at starres, y'faith tis true.
Iames. In whom sir, if I may be bold.

24. mirth.] mirth _Q_. 34. seasond.] seasond, _Q_.

Humil. A knight of _More-clack_ to a London widow. 40

Iames. My burdned soule saies I, a Knight of More-
clack

To the widow _Humil_, iust, tis she./

Humil. By this the blessing of the holy rights,

Rellish is in them, they are married, at least

Faire for it, I must witnesse to't, fare-well. _Exit_. 45

Iames. How ignorance pleades nonage, in his eie

He knowes me not, tis not the Lyons kinde,

Whose nature challenges right property

Of perfect being, if it were,

Humil would _Humill_ know, that him begot, 50

To be what now he is. Married againe,

And her first husband liuing, blame her not,

Tis my owne proiect, thanke my letters,

That falsifide our deaths black funerall,

Into her mornefull hearing, follow it, 55

Thinke on thy soule, diuide that bitter band,

Knit by the closure of a mutuall hand. _Exit_.

[Scene II]

Enter two watermen with luggedge.

Waterman. I rest ye sir.

41-42. _Q. prints as prose_: "My...More-/ clack...she"; she.] she, _Q_. 44. Rellish is] Rellishes _Q_. 48. property] property. _Q_. 51. is. Married] is married _Q_.

Ferryman. At whose suit Wat?

Waterman. At the bridegroomes, ile not a foot further till I haue eaz'd my shoulders.

Ferryman. No nor I, we are asses right, we carry prouender, but are not the better for't. 5

Waterman. As how?

Ferryman. Thou't not beleeue breads bread, till it be tasted, I say to thee, in this trunk is prouender.

Waterman. Be an asse till thou proue it. 10

Ferryman. Heres money which will buy it.

Waterman. O by a figure, I say to thee thou art an asse.

[Ferryman.] How?

Waterman. By thy burthen. 15

Ferryman. No otherwise, thats not so good.

Waterman. Because thou hast eares.

Ferryman. Are all asses that haue eares?

Waterman. Are all truncks laden with money that are heauy? 20

Ferryman. Indeede I confesse in that I am an asse, but I thinke so.

Waterman. By such surmise thou makest it prouender./ We are water-men, and thinke because wee see a man comming, and that I am his first man, heele be my 25 first fare, when another gets him.

10. Be] be Q. 21. Indeede] indeede Q.

<u>Enter Tutch the Clowne, writing.</u>

Ferryman. Come, you are bookish.

Waterman. And thou blockish, say rights right, and no more.

Ferryman. Se sirha Mr. <u>Tutch</u>, what an officer? 30

Waterman. Yes, hees booking in, Mr. <u>Tutch</u>, <u>salue</u>, <u>sis salue</u>.

Ferryman. <u>Iubio te saluere</u>, <u>aue</u>.

Waterman. He heares vs not.

Tutch. Let me see. Capons, Turkeis, Small-birds, 35
Beefes, Muttons, Partridge, Plouer, Wood-cocks.

Waterman. Meaning vs, good morning, and many sir.

Ferryman. And many Mr. <u>Tutch</u>.

Tutch. Are ye come water-squirts, are ye come?

Waterman. And why sir, water-squirts? 40

Tutch. Because you shoote water, and so do they, but ha ye that will doo't, my dainty element dashers.

Ferryman. Do't and stand to't Mr. <u>Tutch</u>, if wee might spend it sir. <u>Enter Humil</u>.

Humil. Well said honest knaues, beare in, but say 45
wheres <u>Iohn</u> i'th hospitall, and's nurse?

Waterman. At hand sir.

Humil. Tis well, away, and <u>Tutch</u> tutch the tippes of their tongues, with our seller suckets.

Tutch. Ile tutch the tippes of their tongues, & their

35. see.] see <u>Q</u>.

tongues tippes, 50

Ile baste their bellies and their lippes

Til we haue ierk't the cat with our three whippes.

[*Exeunt*.]

Humil. Married? tis ended, and the next pull mine.

At a faire fleece, a golden one,

The eldest daughter is my hope, 55

What then rests in it, O you winged lap-wings,

Farthest cry, when we come neerest to't.

Quando pecus omnia sub vmbra ruminat antiquos

paulilum vocitamus amores. *Exit*.

[Scene III]

[*Enter Iames*.]

Iames. Tis done too late to aske why so.

Tardie intrusion as a Cipher plaste,/

Fils but vp roome, while substance in the other

Makes number pretious, I am that round O,

Which with a sigh, as sad as is my soule, 5

Grieue all too late, what now befits my mone,

But black despaire, and die in't do,

To make thy selfe knowne, but represents

Mellow fruit falling into danger, O I am that

50-52. *Q. prints as prose*: "Ile...tongues/ tippes...ierk't/ the...whippes." 54-57. *Q. prints as prose*: "At...hope,/ what...cry,/ when...*umbra ru*-"

Rotten ruin'd, and vnrellisht substance, 10
Which on my owne vpgrowing tree falles off,
By the times negligence, vndone I am,
Would that I had dide indeede, and not in word.
These il tun'd words like discords sounded harsh
And yet were thought true musick, well, well, 15
Ile take my stand, and as she passes by
Note if her glories dash not all my hopes
With base forgetfulnesse of what she was,
My picture can she not forget, may be,
Old loue may yet liue in this new-born Lady. 20

Enter the solemne order of the Bride-groomes return from Church, and as the bride goes by, she beholds Iames *the cittizen with earnest eye, & speakes aside.*

Lady. I am woonder strocken in my selfe,
O you all-seeing, pardon my attempt,
My second choice hath laid siege to my soule,
And my disloyalty hath in that witnesse
Slaine the concurrances of after ioy, 25
Euen so he look't that had my maiden heart,
Euen such was he, whose farre estranged death
Gaue me this licence of ill libertie,
To do, and vndo, O forgiue me then,
Weake in my sect, my fault to the best of men. 30

Lets fal her gloue,

Iames *takes it vp*.

Sir William. New wedded Lady, & our mornings bride,

What is't that troubles ye?

Lady. A losse but being small.

Earle. No matter for the losse,

You find a purchase, equals any crosse./ 35

Lady. Let it go then. *Exeunt*.

Iames. She knowes me and this constant accident

Subscribes to't, how can she excuse,

This double deede, this false neglect of loue?

O women how you dally in your trust, 40

How quickly you forget late liuing life,

And bury the remembrance in your smiles.

And ye this morning for the dead do sigh,

And shed your teares in bosome of new choice.

How haue I sifted your loose difference, 45

For euer being president against all.

Glad am I at this oportunity.

Who landed me euen in the iawes of feare

Swallowing my destiue happinesse

To vtter ruine of herselfe and me. 50

If the vnconstant aire whistle abroad,

That *Humil* liues, then *Humils* widow dies

30.1-30.2. *Q. prints at line* 32. 35. find] fiud *Q*. 37. She] she *Q*. 42. smiles.] smiles *Q*. 43. do] to *Q*. 44. choice.] choice *Q*. 50. me.] me *Q*.

In desperat scandall, rackt and tormented,
In the remembrance of old wretchednesse,
Which to preuent, plots cunningly contriu'd 55
Must buckler my repute so weakly wiu'd. *Exit.*

[Scene IV]

Enter Sir Robert Toures, and yong Filbon.

Toures. Lost her gloue?
[Filbon.] So she makes knowne.
Toures. Ile find it to my euerliuing glory.
And the next triumph, weare it in my helme
Daring all gallants in defence to approue, 5
S. *William Vergirs* Lady owes this gloue. *Exit.*
Filbon. If my good fortune challenge such account,
To find it by my friend or industry,
Ile prick it on a pole, and with my launce,
Curuet with nimble speed, in course of armes, 10
And as I snatch it by a curious passe,
Cry in lowd eccho, here is for her loue,
Who on her wedding day did loose this gloue. *Exit.*

[Scene V]

Enter the two maiden sisters, Mary and Tabitha./

Mary. The Bride, our new made mother lost her gloue.
Tabitha. I sister, so she saies.
Mary. Ile seeke no further, for it is in vaine.

Tabitha. Especially when quicker eyes then ours,
Arch in the browes of loues two votaries, 5
Lord how they'le bragge to find it questionles,
Twill proue a ransome of a thousand kisses,
Amorous glaunces, modest curtesie,
O how these flaterers can insinuate,
And stretch an inch of length to an el of wide. 10
Heeres much in office for a little pay.
A gloue God wot.

Mary. I sister, so they say, go to ye wanton you
He that shall marry thee, is matcht y'faith,
To English rash, or to a Dutch snap haunce, 15
You will strike fire with words--

Tabitha. Who I? now as I liue sweet _Moll_.
If _Filbon_ marry me, as by this light.

[_Points to light held by Mary_.]

Mary. And wincke.

Tabitha. Tis hard to iuggle with the diuell, we maides 20
So simper in each others quantity
As we know fashion ere it be deuiz'd
Forsweare you one, and Ile forsweare--

Mary. The other, iust euen so,
Shall I be plaine with thee-- 25

Tabitha. Youle answere, no.

10. wide.] wide _Q_.

Mary. I.

Tabitha. No I.

Mary. I no.

Tabitha. I know you will not, therefore let him go, 30

I loue my _Filbon_ as men loue good clothes,

Put them on euery day.

Mary. And I loue _Toures_ as I loue my sleepe,

Embracing thus, folding most deerely.

[_Fondles candle_.]

Tabitha. Your louer nightly, as you wish him yearely. 35

Mary. In troth in such a sort: [_Gestures suggestively with candle_.]

Tabitha. As children play with stones, to make them sport.

Mary. You make me blush _Tabitha_./

Tabitha. At the thing ye wish,

Plague on the cat that loues nor milke nor fish. 40

We are all maidens pictures, faine we would,

Yet we cry away away, when away we should.

Mary. Yet againe. [_Gestures with candle again_.]

Tabitha. Neuer yet.

Euer so when so our matters fit. 45

Mary. They are returnd. A gloue or no?

Enter Toures and Filbon.

46. returnd.] returnd, _Q_.; no?] no. _Q_.

Toures. No, but the gloue I sought not, I ha found.

Mary. Where is't man?

Toures. You'r the gloue, which stil I seeke to weare

Make me happy, match it to a paire. 50

[*Takes her by the hands*.]

Mary. Be these for euer matches.

Tabitha. How can ye find the gloue was neuer lost?

Filbon. By seeking you that lost not what we find.

Tabitha. Indeed a willing losse, is losse of gaine,

Where louing finders pitty loosers paine, 55

I will not say, enioy so much the rather,

Because gift giuer cries out on the father.

But if I durst, I would, till when,

Vnmatch our gloues, each take his owne againe.

Enter Sir William, Iames, Earle of
Tumult, Auditor, Sir Rafe.

Sir William. It is inacted by the brides faire word, 60

Who findes her gloue, is this daies gouernour.

To manage all our pastimes in the house,

And thou art he, the onely conquerour,

Of prize and honour, then enioy it.

Iames. You giue and I receiue, is this my office? 65

Sir William. Sign'd and deliuer'd.

Iames. I take it on me, musicke triumphes come,

Since fortune cast her fauours in my fist,

Ile be most prodigall.

Yet with modesty I am a Cittizen. 70

Vnlook't for welcome, and vnthinking come,

To receaue honour in a statesmans roome./

Yet to this presence I will still addresse,

Loue, paines and duetie in this businesse. _Exit_.

Earle. In this is fortune blind, whose deeds are dangers, 75

Giuing her graces not to friends but strangers.

Toures. Prooue on my fortunes how so ere they stand,

I hold my fairest fortune in my hand.

Mary. The like doe I. _Enter yong Humil_.

Filbon. And all the fairest fortunes I would proue, 80

Is onely this, to enioy my dearest loue.

Tabitha. The like I wish.

Humil [_Speake aside_]. All happinesse liue in thy choice,

In hers, all mischiefs, horrour, lest our selfe

Participate in tender of our choise, 85

Freely deliuer'd in the sight of heauen.

Sir William. What newes?

Humil. The wedding dinner breaths his last.

Sir William. And wee will visit it; on forward there.

Exeunt.

83. _Speake aside_.] _Q_. _prints at end of line_ 82. 83-86. _Q_. _prints as prose_: "All...hers/ All...of/ our...heauen."

84. lest] les _Q_.

[Scene VI]

Enter _Iames_ _and_ _Ladie_.

Iames. So faire and fortunate to be thus false,
Wedded to two. O you all wondring eies,
Gaze till your fire flame, your eie-balles drop
In moist imagination of this act,
Before the first be dead to wed a second. O. 5
Lady. Why writ you dead in your last letters?
[Iames]. Sick was I, and no likelihood of life.
What then, was that a iust excuse
To varnish ouer this base counterfeiting? no,
I'le make it knowne. 10
Lady. I care not, I will thus excuse it,
All opposite of iniurie was yours,
Putting to teast our weakenesse by your letters,
Which carrying credit, woman in her will,
Guiltlesse is causer of this open ill. 15
Iames. Had I beene thus aduiz'd, but all too late
Acquainted with your speede, I had preuented
What now is past and done.
Lady. Why did you not? Baud to your owne misdeede,/
Three quarters guiltie of this accident, 20

5. O.] O _Q_. 7. _Q_. _assigns this line to the Lady, beginning James' speech at the next line_. 10. I'le] Il'e _Q_. 17-18. _Q_. _prints as prose_: "Acquainted...is/ past...done."

That might & would not stop the hazard,
Will ye now heape vp miracle,
And make it worse in note, by adding too't
A bauins blaze, 'tis not so soone extinct,
Being fierce of flame, quensht must it be, 25
By water-course of sounder pollicie.

Iames. I am from my selfe in this, what shall I doe?
O I am madde, and mischiefe mennassis
Vnwitting of all purpose.

Lady. Why did I cast my gloue, 30
Proclaim'd the finder stickler of our sports,
But to a point preuailing practise?

Iames. I know not how.

Lady. Leaue all to me, women that wade in sinne,
Haue their wits-charter to authorize it, 35
And they haue antidotes that to digest,
Which better iudgements lose themselues in,
Let me alone.

Iames. To ly with him the while.

Lady. Tis true to ly with him, but not in sheetes, 40
To vse the flourish of a womans skill,
In windes and turnings, other lying,
My new made husband iniures not the old,
As I am simply false, I will be found

24. 'tis] t'is _Q_. 28-29. _Q_. _prints as prose_: "O...all/ purpose." 38. Let] let _Q_.

Constant to death, knowing my businesse 45

Is to heale vp the fractures of the time,

And to salue vertue in her taint of ill.

Iames. I build on this.

Lady. Some moneth.

While I possesse the glory of my name, 50

Attendances according, marrie our sonne

Vnto his eldest daughter, that's the point

Of all: regaine my ioynter next,

'T is not amisse to satisfie your debts,

These two atchieu'd, the third is bedding,/ 55

And if this braine beguile him not of that,

Say I am single: no, since blame sits nie,

Behooues giue care to vse true policie.

Iames. Our sonne.

Lady. Aside. *Exit* [*Iames*]. *Enter Humil*. 60

Humil. Mother the noble guest expects ye,

The present meeting doos neglect it selfe

Where our faire bride is wanting,

Pray come in, you doe them wrong.

Lady. I am not well, and this commanding aire 65

Retaines my health, I came to fetch it,

Wherefore inricht with what was ours before,

We yeeld fresh duetie and attend them.

Humil. Will you be mindfull of our marriage, mother?

54. 'T is] T' is *Q*. 60. *Exit*.] *Q*. *prints at line* 59.

Begin so happily in yours. 70

Lady. I shall indeauour in it, come. *Exeunt*.

[Scene VII]

Enter Mary, *Tabitha*, *Toures and Filbon*.

Tabitha. Close and husht, not a fly stirring,
While they feede hungerly, we, that loues deitie
Doos proclaime pardon to presume, and speake,
Challendge libertie, now by my maiden-head.
Filbon. Sweare not loue. 5
Tabitha. Can you forbid my oath? Sir I will sweare,
& till I lacke it, say, nought shall confine me,
I had rather feast in fancies pittance,
Then to feede gag'd with attention,
Soothing euery bit with curiositie: 10
No, I can fill my bellie in a minute,
Satisfie my stomacke in a breath:
Louers digest their sighes, and chow their spleene,
While other appetites fall hungry to't,
And let them greedily graze on. 15
Mary. What's all this?
Toures. Louers talke anything.
Filbon. I vnderstand ye not.

2. deitie] detie *Q*. 6-15. *Q*. *prints as prose*: "Can...&/ till...feast/ in...soo-/ thing...in/ a...digest/ their... appetites/ fall...on." 14. to't] toot *Q*.

Tabitha. I would not that you should, for I speake
Greeke.

Mary. Regard her not, for she talkes idly, _Filbon_. 20

Tabitha. Be you aduiz'd then sister, I'me a foole./
Yet not so simple but I talke by rule,
I say, dine they that list, I will not, for my dish
Drest to my hand is here, here let me feede,
[_Gestures to her parts_.]
'T is the maids modicum, God send vs speede. 25

Mary. In that I claime a part,
Who euer feedes this dish hath _Maries_ hart.

Tabitha. So then said I well, ye wicked thing.

Toures. Mot as I am of Louers vnion,
Contracted to a sollitarie life, 30
By thus retayning singlenes of heart:
Changing all doubts that the world affords
But one, so to thy sweetest selfe,
Which onely art idea of my thoughts:
I vowe a reconciled amitie, 35
Which violated, doos command my life
To yeeld his intrest to the shade of death,
May be, your father alienates our choice,
And showes as sunne-shine threatning raine,
To the all-hoping haruest present, 40
Which to make cleare, the honourable word

20. talkes idly,] talkes, Id'ly _Q_. 25. 'T is] Ti's _Q_.

And fatherly regard in present office
Haue past their speede in our attention.
I know your father will receiue their on-set
Soldier-like, ioying the siege begunne, 45
Which tho resisted, bids them gladly come.

Mary. Pause in that trust, giue eare.

Enter Iames with the musitions.

Iames. Sound proclamation,
It is inacted by the bride and bride-groome,
And by our selfe chiefe in authoritie, 50
That all receiue their pleasures
From the most high in this assembly
To the lowest, all pastimes are made free,
Dauncing, carding, dicing reuelling,
And other dues of times fit merriments, 55

[Takes up glass.]

--Vnto the bride and bride-groomes health./

Tabitha. The daies short, and the night's

Filbon. Stop there.

Tabitha. I will, to pleasure thee.

Iames. There take your places. 60
And in your sweetest key of musique strokes
Sound pleasant melody, eccho those sounds
Which true-loue-hearts, in concords chiefest grounds

54. reuelling,] reuelling. Q. 55. of times] oftimes Q.
59. thee.] thee, Q.

Haue their blest being, vse art in times,

Which may giue welcome to our noblest guests. 65

Enter Humil.

Toures. We are betraid, yong Humill is at hand,

Daunce, and excuse it so. [They dance.]

Filbon. Sound musique there.

Toures. Content, a dance, and in againe.

[Humil.] Content, no daunce, yet in againe. 70

Toures. It is vngently don to snatch her so.

Humil. I snatch but that which promise saies is mine,

Haue I offended?

Toures. I.

Humil. Right what is wrong. 75

Toures. Here?

[Humil.] Or where you dare, go seeke in Brainford, go.

Toures. Brainford?

Iames. Put vp, or I shall be offending vnto one,

[To Toures] Against the brides sonne, dare ye? 80

Humil. I repent not what is done, come you with me.

Toures. So slaues by violence do hurry hence,

The rights of--

Iames. Peace, we on you do impose command.

Yeeld duty in it: hall, a hall there. Musique sound, 85

And to the bride do consecrate this round.

70. Humil] Toures Q. 76. Here?] Here, Q. 85-86. Q. prints: "Yeeld...there./ Musique...round."

<u>Enter all the traine to daunce</u>.

Sir William. Squire of the day, cul out your gadding bucks.

Select your light-heel'd does,

Open your Labits, turne them to the toiles;

We that are <u>Venus</u> Huntsmen may partake the sports. 90

Earle. You'r a gallant woodman sir.

Auditor. My sonne for one.

Sir Rafe. And mine the other./

Sir William. Good my daughters for them both, a course or so, go too, lead on, the bucks that haue imployment for these does, are not these giddy gamsters, i'le be the forester and looke too't.

Toures. Heare you that?

Mary. A lightning before heat.

Filbon. Your fathers aire is harrald to his tongue. 100

Tabitha. A knowes the coate, but thinkes not who shall weare it.

Sir William. Ther's two and two.

Iames. A coople more, too makes no show,

Our measure is for three.

88-90. <u>Q</u>. <u>prints</u>: "Select...Labits,/ Turne...may/ partake ...sports." 94-97. <u>Q</u>. <u>prints</u>: "Good...both,/ A...imploy-/ ment...the/ Forester...too't." 101. <u>Q</u>. <u>prints as prose</u>: "A...shall/ weare it." 103-104. <u>Q</u>. <u>prints as prose</u>: "A... is/ for three."

Auditor. Why then the bride. 105

Sir Rafe. And bridegroome.

Sir William. O sir, pardon me.

My ioints were oild to pleasure, but now, not.

Iames. Then I with her.

Sir William. You! O, your authority commands her. 110

[_Music sounds_.]

Iames. Harke. [_They dance_.]

Lady. It giues his luster light.

Iames. My warrant wins, where his dos loose the right.

Humil snatches Mary from Toures and dances.

Sir William. My sonne in law growes bold.

Good againe, heres much to do in loue, 115

One simply stands, not challenging his owne:

And reason, _Mary_, chance is yet vnknowne.

No, nor in you sir, though my son,

Words past contriue, but after deedes cry done.

Auditor. Brook'st thou this disgrace. 120

Toures. O sir, no remedy, what Iustice liues so free.

And to her owne is friending.

Auditor. I am mad to thinke on't boy, but--

They daunce a measure.

Toures. How Goddes-like the elder of the two,

Stations the measure, it is a Iouiall sight, 125

117. vnknowne.] vnknowne _Q_. 122. friending.] friending, _Q_.

Where beauty gilds the pauement with her light.
How sullen _Saturne_ tooke her by the hand/
With frosty feeling, in whose icy touch,
She shrunke her hold, but with a iealous eie,
She glanst on me, fearefull that standers by 130
Should be inricht with't: now she smiles me faire,
Guilding my torture with an after hope.
Thus moroliz'd, I reason on my right,
Her loue thus challeng'd by inferior might.

The daunce ends.

Enter Iohn, Nurse, Boy, all in blew coates.

Sir William. After this dalliance here comes other sport. 135
Pray ye attend him gallants: How now _Iohn_?
Tardi venientis Iohn, you must be whip't.
Quaso preceptor, non est tibi quid.
This silly sot, my Lord, so please you heare him,
Vtters much hope of matter, but small gaine. 140
An old wife nurst him, which we call blind _Ales_.
She dying, left him to the citties keeping.
Which in their Hospitall they thus nurst vp
Amongst the bounties of their other deeds:
Many besides, now you shall heare his fellow 145

127. hand] hand. _Q_. 133. reason] season _Q_. 134.2. _Q_. _prints this stage direction below line_ 138.

Aske him such questions as his simplenes
Answeres to any: sirra let me heare ye.

Boy. Iohn, how many parts of speech be there?

Iohn. Eight, the vocatiue, and ablatiue, caret nominatiuo O. 150

Boy. What say you to reddish Iacke?

Iohn. That it does bite, Ha, ha, ha.

Boy. Where ha you been Iacke?

Iohn. At Powles friend.

Boy. Who saw you there? 155

Iohn. Mr. Deane Nowel, O hee's a good man truly.

Boy. What did a giue thee Iack?

Iohn. A groat, looke here else.

Boy. What wil't do with it?

[Iohn.] Carri't home to my Nurse. 160

Boy. I'le giue thee a point Iack, what wil't do with it?/

Iohn. Carri't home to my nurse.

Boy. I'le giue thee a fooles head Iack, what wilt do with it? 165

Iohn. Carri't home to my nurse.

Boy. Carry a fooles head, what a foole art thou?

Iohn. Should I goe home without it? whose foole now?

Boy. Who toles the bell for Iohn? *Iohn toles the bell, as if a pul'd the rope.*

163. Carri't] carri't *Q.* 169. *Q. prints the stage direction at* 170.

Iohn. I know not, 170

Boy. When dide a?

Iohn. Ene now.

Boy. Hoo *Iacke* hoo?

Iohn. My Nurses chickin. Ha, ha, ha.

Earle. A silly ignorant, is a euer so? 175

Sir William. Neuer otherwise, a cleanly Idiot, what's
put on him in his morning ries, is as you see it.
This old woman is his Nurse. *Enter Messenger.*

Messenger. So please your honour you are sent for to
the Court,
The Court goes from Richmond to White-hall. 180

Earle. We will attend her, kind sir *William Vergir*,
Our times bride-groome, to your selfe and you.
We wish as we haue euer done, all loue,
And for our present entertainement rest
Indebted to your bounty, if a Courts amends 185
Haue in its power of satisfaction,
You command it, this acknowledg'd euer,
Your poore acquaintance but an honourable friend.

Auditor. We will attend your coach.

Earle. Sir, be mindfull of our seruant *Filbon*. 190
What wants in him to weie downe loue with gold,

172. now.] now, *Q*. 173. hoo?] hoo, *Q*. 184-188. *Q*. *prints as prose*: "And...your/ bounty...satisfacti/ on...poore/ acquaintance...friend."

Our fauours shall supply. *Exeunt*.

Sir William. Tis a light weight, their portions if they poize no better, will to the worlds beleefe, grow lesse not greater, but let them passe, I weie 195 them as they are. Come Nurse, follow vs *Iohn*.

Exit after.

Nurse. Wipe your nose, fie a slouen still, looke ye be mannerly, hold vp your chinne, let me see ye make your holiday legge, so my chucking, that's a good lambe, do not cry for/ any thing, *Iohn* if ye doe. 200

Iohn. No Nurse, grace a God, Grace a Queene. *Exeunt*.

[Scene VIII]

Enter Sir William and his Ladie.

Sir William. Shreeke no more in my eare, I pre-thee peace.

I graunt I made such promise: but what then,
Shall I for that so set her on the racke,
When her faire fortunes looke a better way,
With the small proffer of your giddie sonne? 5
No: you shall pardon me.

Lady. Youle let me haue my ioynter yet.

Sir William. Yes that, three hundred by the yeare t'is thine,

194. they] they, *Q*. 1-6. *Q*. *prints as prose*: "Shreeke...I/ graunt...that/ so...bet-/ ter...no:/ you...me." 8. t'is] ti's *Q*.

But for your sonne to wed my eldest daughter.

Lady. Why, he doth merit her in my accord, 10

And tis no wrong in you, to dip her blood

In the selfe dye that wee are in.

Sir William. I grant his merit, but her shining value,

Made golden glittering by my vantings,

Lookes to a higher promintoria, 15

From which tower, when your sonne gazes,

It affrights him, yeelds him plannet stroke.

Lady. He shall not haue her then?

Sir William. Beleeue it wife.

Lady. He shall. 20

Sir William. Ha.

Lady. I will not bed with you till then.

Sir William. What?

Lady. I ha said it, and when posture of our word

Takes his bace beeing, I will die the death, 25

Into our wedding sheetes shall mischiefe come,

Before my bodie breake your word with me,

Euen on your wedding day.

10-12. Q. prints as prose: "Why...tis/ no...wee/ are in." 13-17. Q. prints as prose: "I...made/ golden...pro-/ mintoria...af-/ frights...stroke." 13. value,] value Q. 14. glittering] glittering, Q.; vantings,] vantings Q. 16. tower] sower Q. 18. then?] then. Q. 24-28. Q. prints as prose: "I...his/ bace...sheetes/ shall...word/ with... day."

Sir William. Nay then vp with the lists, againe it
shall not be. 30

Lady. I care not, thinke you I doe, keepe your word
in that when I breake mine.

Sir William. No more, be stranger to my bed, doe doe.
Haue I of nothing made thee much and wilt thou--

Lady. Yes I will, haue you of protestations, othes, 35
and vowes made these loose fractures: lawfull bee
it then for me to shun the make-peace bed, since
strife sets such diui/sion betwixt man and wife, I
am most firme in't.

Sir William. Very well, tis not amisse. [*Exit Lady*.] 40

Enter Auditor, Sir Raph, and their sonnes
Toures & Filbon.

Auditor. The night drawes on, tis time to part.

Sir William. At your pleasures gentlemen.

Sir Rafe. Your gallant daughters will be next.

Sir William. Or not at all, for I am past it now.

Auditor. And we are praid vnto, our sonnes are
gentlemen, 45
What resteth then, but we saile nearer to the point?

Sir William. What point?

33-34. *Q. prints as prose*: "No...Haue/ I...thou--" 40.1. *Q. prints*: "Enter...Filbon, and their sonnes." 46. What] what *Q*.

Sir Rafe. Of mariage, past betwixt vs in our promises.

Sir William. Indeede to one I promis'd her waight in gold,

Vnto the other which I loue as deare, 50

Her waight in siluer, now gentlemen,

What goods haue you to equall these large promises?

Auditor. Why all we haue.

[Sir William.] But twill not serue,

The big auouchments of my promises 55

Controlles you all, and all mens else, ye all,

Vnder degrees of Earles, Lords, or as Potent.

To toule them on I eccho these large sommes.

Sir Rafe. Vnualued must your sommes be to such choice,

Honour lookes high aboue such pettie price. 60

Sir William. Looke honour high as heauen,

Our earthly reach doth leauell in that eie,

And with the imbellishment of richer worth

Ile by, and out-by the imprisond scope,

Of reaching blood, what will not value doe 65

Where strong abillitie dos reach his hand,

And they haue beautie too, which ioyned to riches

Will proffer faire: tho not so quaint

As courtly dames or earths bright treading starres,

48. mariage, past] mariage past, *Q*. 49-52. *Q*. *prints as prose*: "Indeede...vn-/ to...now/ gentlemen...pro-/ mises?" 54. Sir William] Sir Rafe *Q*. 57. Potent.] Potent *Q*.

They are maids of More-clacke, homely milke-bole
things, 70

Such as I loue and faine would marry well.

Sir Rafe. It was a promise in you to be kinde.

Sir William. Ile forward with that promise, you loue/
my eldest.--

Toures. With my soule. 75

Sir William. And pittie to deuide that loue, then
hearken me, when shees dead and liues againe, shees
yours, not till then.

Toures. Then neuer but in death.

Sir William. You loue my yongest daughter. 80

Filbon. And will euer.

Sir William. Pray ye doe: but when you are from your
selfe a woman, she is yours in marriage.

Filbon. Woman to woman ioyned twere wonderfull,
But in more maze of wonder I should be, 85
What I doe challenge to participate,
And from my selfe liue to deuide in other.

Sir William. Faith not till such a wonder.

Sir Rafe. Ist not enough to scandall thy true word?
But are we slighted thus with fantasies, 90
Impossibilities, dead and aliue againe,
Manhood infuzd in woman: tis not generous. Exit.

Auditor. Come sonne vpon my blessing

85-87. Q. prints as prose: "but...chal-/ lenge...in/ other."

Take from thy eies thy heart adoring shine,
Offer no more thy altar bearing thoughts 95
To one so gyant-like, whose reach sits hie,
Aboue the compasse of a gentill eie. *Exit*.

Sir William. You haue your answeres, gallants.

Toures. We like it not.

Filbon. Nor will we so except it. 100

Sir William. Fore-warnd come neare my house,
Rapes, fellonies, and what may else be thought on,
I will with heauie impositions
Surcharge ye with, if not with pistoll shot,
I will defend my selfe and these I keepe. *Exit*. 105

Toures. Liue I to heare this?

Filbon. Conuay them from him, let vs.

Toures. In disguise.

Filbon. Or not at all.

Toures. That way or none. *Exeunt*./ 110

[Scene IX]

Enter Iames and Humil.

Humil. *Iames*, when I put thee from my thought, let me
be hudwincht from all fortune, thy pertaking
gentlenes is such, as I doe loue thee, troth I doe.

Iames. God continue this good league.

Humil. Wot'st what newes? 5

98. You] you *Q*. 2. all] all, *Q*.

Iames. No.

Humil. The louers are expulst, and my faire hopes shine the clearer: what wilt say when I doe marrie this Knights eldest daughter?

Iames. That you are then possest. 10

Humil. She is mine contracted in her fathers word.

Iames. New broken sir.

Humil. Ha.

Iames. Tis true your mother challeng'd it: but he as angry as the raging maine, whose choller breathing 15
shakes high battlements, puts her off with a pause of contrarie, I know it sir, her ioynter is subscrib'd too, which else to doe, sooner should earth to heauen presume a progresse, then the grant make firme what the antecedent challenges, your 20
mother vpon this abandons from his bed, vowing bold absence, he inrag'd, giues way to all maligne and stubborne fashion of contempt, such a cloze to day neuer had practise, such a wedding night, till this sad first neuer had purchase: you shall well agree 25
them sir, to attone this iarre, vse meanes I pray you, 'twill become ye, well, when wrangling wrestles with such violent iniurie, tis the sonnes office.

Humil. Tis the diuels office and not mine, to hell 30

15. maine] morne Q. 27. 'twill] t'will Q.

obedience, if he breake his word.

Iames. You had a father loued ye better.

Humil. He loued me as a king in a play his seruant,
who nere seeing him giues kind applause, but small
vtilitie: my father in my child-hoode loued and left 35
me to the worlds eie, in bold necessitie, I thanke
him for it, since he di'de my mother hath her chance,
mine wants the proofe, stand by times minion and
inconstancie. oh./

Iames. Haue patience. 40

Humil. Yes, whereunto? sith all my hopes ly leuell
With despaire, such milk-sops in whose breasts,
Lingers a lagging hope, to them is patience
sufferable;
But to me, horror, and hels black motions tickles
Me on to mischiefe, and I will-- *Exit*. 45

Iames. So.
Now swims vpon the maine, such shipwrack-soules,
As the windes rage splits on the rocks of danger.
I, my wife, and sonne all three, now heaue, and
Feare of sinking, makes vs timorous. 50
Should we be sheluing on the shallow beach,
The seas rough gusts might scatter our intents,
So idle purchase might be gathered vp,
From our so sodaine shipwrack: No my state

54. From] from *Q*.

Stands yet secure: though maim'd yet is not foil'd: 55
But salu'd by wise occasion may make good
This sodaine ouerflow of tide and flood. *Exit*.

[Scene X]

Enter Iohn i'th hospitall, and a
blew-coat boy with him.

Boy. *Iohn*. Where had'st this bread and butter?
Iohn. The crow did giue it me.
Boy. But take heede the kite tak't not from thee.
Iohn. I'le choake first.
Boy. *Iohn* shal's play at counter-hole i'th cloister? 5
Iohn. I ha nere a counter.
Boy. Ile giue thee one for a point.
Iohn. Do, and i'le play hose go downe, O sir, *Willy* is
a good man truly, heer's good custard and capon, and
good bread and butter too. 10
Boy. Now *Iohn*, i'le cry first.
Iohn. And i'le cry lagge. I was in hoblies hole.
Boy. I ha won this *Iohn*, now for another.
Iohn. I'le ha't againe will I will O. [Enter Nurse.]
Nurse. What's the matter, making my sweet lambe cry?/ 15
Come *Iohn* we must to London, on with your cleane
muckender, and take leaue of sir *William* and his
Lady. Gods me your point, where is it *Iohn*?

14. ha't] hate *Q*.

Iohn. The crow has it, and did win it at counter hole.

Nurse. I'le whip ye for it, take him vp, loose your point lambe, fie, vp with him sirha. 20

Iohn. Good Nurse now, no more truly O, O.

Enter watermen.

Ferryman. Where's this suck-egge, wheres Iack a boy: come ye moueable matron, wheres this tugegge, away away. 25

Nurse. Ile take leaue of Sir William and go away.

Exit.

Ferryman. Now my Iohn iuggler, your nose is like Lothbery conduit, that alwaies runs waste.

Boy. Whats his name Iohn?

[Iohn.] Sternigogilus, ha, ha. 30

Ferryman. What?

Boy. A goggle eye, a wanton eye, a madcap, so a meanes.

Ferryman. Wat?

Waterman. Hollo.

Ferryman. Trim boat, turne head, we're at hand muschrumpe, we come boy, we come. Enter Nurse. 35

Nurse. Come Iohn, our leaue is taken.

Iohn. Haue ore the sea to florida, and was not good

22.1. watermen] waterman Q. 23. Ferryman] Ferris Q.
23-25. Q. prints as mixed verse and prose: "Where's...boy:/ Come...tugegge,/ away away." 36. we] We Q.

King *Salomon*, *Tom Tyler*. *Sing*[s].

Ferryman. O well sung Nightingale, a boord a boord there, ha rip there. [*Exeunt All*.] 40

[Scene XI]

Enter Toures in a tawny coate like a tinker, and his boy with budget and staffe, Toures tincks vpon his pan drinking.

Toures. Boy, you vnderstand me, though the liquor haue renst me, remember your businesse boy.

Boy. Yes master.

Toures. Tis rare to be a tinker boy, worke inough, wench inough, and drinke inough, is't not boy? 5

[Boy.] I maister./

Toures. Boy where shal's haue doings, Ile clout any womans cauldren, boy.

Boy. Master, tincke on tis time, for we ha nere a penny. 10

Toures. Pawne budget boy, Ile ring in boy, ha ye any worke for a tinker, a ti, ti, tinker. *Enter Madge*.

Madge. By my maiden-head tis hee, the merry tinker of Twitnam boy, is't not?

Boy. Yes flowre i' th frying pan, he stops holes well, tis he. 15

Madge. Has his old songs still, has he not?

15. i' th] it'h *Q*; well,] well. *Q*.

Boy. Yes, and new to boote.

Madge. And be not these tinkers knaues? vpon their backs they beare a long picke, with a staffe i' the end. He shall ha worke, Ile breake way for him, and call out the gentlewoman to heare him sing. 20

Boy. Let them all say what they can. [*Sings*] "Dainty come thou to me." We shall ha worke maister.

Toures. Draw boy, *homo armatus*, boy, Ile pepper your pans, where's my dogge boy? 25

Enter Sir William, Humil, Lady, Mary, Tabitha.

Boy. Your Dame has him, and will meete you at Putney.

Humil. Indeede whats a tinker with out's wench, staffe and dogge.

Lady. Is this the tinker you talke on? 30

Humil. I madame of Twitnam, I haue seene him licke out burning fire brands with's tongue, drinke two pense from the bottome of a full pottle of ale, fight with a Masty, & stroke his mustachoes with his bloody bitten fist, and sing as merrily as the sobrest Querester. 35

Madge. Come tinker, stop, mend.

Toures. Ile tickle your holes.

20. i' the] it'he *Q*. 20-22. *Q*. *prints as verse*: "they... end,/ He...and/ Call...sing." 23. can. ...me."] can...me. *Q*. 26. where's] Where's *Q*. 27. Your] your *Q*.

Sir William. Hee's out of tune for singing now.

Toures. Out of tune and temper too, thus can dainty liquor do. Sing boy. 40

Boy. Relish maister, relish, a note aboue *ela* maister, sol, fa, me, re./

Toures. *A maiden sitting all alone,* *Sings*.

Vnto her selfe she made great mone, 45

Sorrow set vpon her cheeke,

And she look't greene as any leeke:

Her friends did aske her cause of care,

But she cri'd out in her despaire.

O stone, stone ne ra, stone na ne ra, stone. 50

Tabitha. Cold comfort in a stone.

Toures. *Docters came her pulse to feele*,

And Surgions with their tooles of steele,

To dig, *to delue*, *to find her paine*,

But all they did it was in vaine, 55

Still on her back this maiden lies,

And with an open throat she cries.

O stone, stone na ne ra, stone ne na ne ra stone.

Tabitha. Better and better by my slipper.

Toures. *Old wiues they made answere thus*, 60

Greene sicknes was most dangerous.

And oate-meale eating is a food,

That neuer yet did maiden good,

42. *ela*] *eta* Q.

Tut, tut, tut, tis nothing so,
Still she cri'd out with paine and wo. 65
O stone, stone ne na ne ra, stone ne na ne ra, stone.
Till she was deliuered of a chopping boy, and all
was as I am, *Omne bene*.

Sir William. What a disfiguring diet drunkennes
Layes vpon man. A beastly appetite 70
Lingers the body where such glutnous meanes
Swelters in surfet of desire and ease.
I am an enemy to my selfe to thinke
That man is slaue so to continuall drinke.

Toures. Knight, feast, knight, a good celler keeper 75
knight. I'le cusse thy daughter knight.

Mary. Howes that?

Toures. Shals not busse knight, shals not neb?/

[*He puts his arms around her*.]

Sir William. Thou art in the straits *Moll*, and the
pirots shot will sincke thee, therefore yeeld. 80

Toures. I am thy *Toures*, being thus disguisd, am come
to steale thee, then be sodaine *Moll*.

Mary. Nay then y' faith. *Exit*.

Toures. Knight shals drinke at dore like beggers? no,
ile in knight, see thy seller, is thy seller in 85

66. stone.] stone *Q*. 69. diet] diet, *Q*. 70. man.] man, *Q*.; appetite] appetite? *Q*. 71. meanes] meanes, *Q*. 73. selfe] selfe, *Q*.; thinke] thinke, *Q*. 85. knight,] knight *Q*.

dept, knight dare he not show his face? your black
iacks are my elder brothers, knight, shals not shake
hands with our brothers knight? *Exit reeling*.

Sir William. Follow him, looke he steale nothing.

Madge. Tinckers steale nought but drinke & maidenheads, 90
Ile watch him for one, if you allow losse of the
other. [*Exit*.]

Sir William. Wheres *Tutch*? *Enter Tutch*.

Tutch. Sir.

Sir William. Who waite you on? 95

Tutch. On the world sir.

Sir William. And what saies the world to ye?

Tutch. To me sir? *Giues Tabitha the letter as he talkes*.

Sir William. To you sir, what a message? letters, ha,
daughter i'le be your secretary, nay hide not, 100
iuggle not with me, ile once be secret to your
thoughts, yfaith I will.

Tabitha. Tis a carde of lace sir, which he bought me.

Tutch. I bone-lace sir.

Sir William. Bone-lace subscrib'd too like a letter, 105
lace weau'd of ten bones, ist so? euen so.

[Tabitha.] O *Tutch*.

Tutch. O mistres now am I tri'd on my owne tutch,

98. sir?] sir. *Q*.; *Giues Tabitha*] *Giue her Q*. 98.1. *he*] *she Q*. 100. i'le] il'e *Q*.

I am true mettall one way, but counterfeit an other:
O life no life, but messe of publicke wrong, 110
Day turne to night, for I ha liu'd too long.

Tabitha. From _Filbon_.

Tutch. Yes from _Filbon_, woe to the day, time, and hower.

Tabitha. Wherefore./ 115

Tutch. That I brought this newes from your louer therefore.

Sir William. Pull off your coate.

Tutch. I neede not sir, tis ready to fall off, yet if I doe, tis the time of yeare, the fall of leafe sir, 120 and seruingmen do drop their coates, there sir.

He puls it off.

Sir William. Begone, come no more neare my house, if thou do thou art a fellone, are you the carrier, are ye indeede, must loue make you his mercurie, must _Filbon_ send by you? my owne betray my owne, to him, 125 your a knaue, they shuffle ye about, ile deale the cards and cut ye from the decke, you vnderstand me, go.

Tutch. Gang is the word, and hang is the worst,
Wee are euen, I owe you no seruice, 130
And you owe me no wages, short tale to make,

129-134. _Q_. _prints as prose_: "Gang...are/ euen...short/ tale...be/ short...fields/ report."

The sommers daie is long, the winter nights be short,
And brickill beds dos hide our heds,
As spittell fields report. _Exit_ _Clowne_.

Sir William. Wife coope vp our ginnie henne, that 135
wants this treading, you gossip, to your closset,
Filbon shall, if we want will, yes yes what else.

Lady. Come daughter.

Tabitha. I denie _Filbon_ to his face, bring me to him,
I will iustifie that all his actions are like 140
apricocks, they dangle & [I] loue them.

Sir William. You doe. _Enter_ _Madge_.

Madge. Alas sir, mistres _Marie_ is with the Tincker
gone, and at the backe dore horst, I see the
gelding, twas a dapple gray. 145

Humil. Hell and damnation. _Exit_ _Humil_.

Sir William. Death and torture.

Tabitha. Christmas gambuls, father, shooing the wilde
mare.

Sir William. Am I a iest to laugh at now, indeede, 150
indeede.

Enter _Humil_ _after_ _the_ _boy_.

Humil. O not so fast sir, I am for your race, and will
out strip ye, if ye run no faster, speake what was
this tincker?

Boy. Tincker sir./ 155

Humil. I, thy master.

Boy. My master is a knight, who _Ioue_-like in the shape of such a thing, came to see _Daunie_ in this shoure of gold.

Sir William. _Toures_ was it? 160

Boy. _Etiam_, _ita_, _ego_ I sir.

Tabitha. Now fortune at the fairest, go with thee,
Thou hast beene cunning in this stratagem,
And I doe giue thee ioy with all my heart.

Sir William. You doe huswife. 165

Tabitha. Wishing a whirle-winde in the like disguise,
Fetch me hence smoothly, I am lawfull price.

Sir William. Wheres _Iames_?

Lady. At London.

Sir William. I will thither too, since the diuell 170 driues I am the second, lock her vp, safe be it your charge. _Exeunt_ _Ambo_.

Humil. What for this counsellor, concealing rape and ruine of your childe?

Sir William. Whip him. 175

Boy. I shall neuer indure it.

Sir William. Vnlesse you doe betray this trust, and tell vs to what cabbinet he hath conducted her.

Boy. To Putney, O to Putney sir, where theile be

162-164. _Q_. _prints_ _as_ _prose_: "Now...thou/ hast...thee/ ioy ...heart." 163. cunning] comming _Q_. 166. disguise,] disguise. _Q_.

marryed. 180

Sir William. At my parsonage, God amen, no other hospitall to shadowe them but mine, am I the patron of so hard mischance, that my owne of my owne shall cosin me, ile thether, sonne your company?

Humil. No, ile to Richmond sir, preuent them there. 185

Sir William. No sir, you shall with me, thats the next office, for your selfe, delaying due, in other all things ready, you will then serue your selfe, nor he nor you shall carue so to your appetites.

Humil. Your pleasure sir. *Exeunt*. 190

[Scene XII]

Enter Filbon and Tutch.

Filbon. For my sake turn'd away?/

Tutch. Yes, my master turnes a new leafe, and so must I sir, twas for your letters sake.

Filbon. Is there no hope?

Tutch. What doe you call it when the ball sir hits the stoole? 5

Filbon. Why out.

Tutch. Euen so am I, out, out of all hope euer to come in to crum my porrage at his table sir.

Filbon. Welcome to mine, then honest *Tutch*, but speake thy minde, thinkest thou she will continue firme? 10

Tutch. Firme sir, yes, vnles you take her for a ioyne

stoole, sheele continue firme, she feedes on ye,
dreames on yee, hopes on ye, and relies on ye,
telling her father what a friend you are, protesting 15
and molesting to the hole house of your good parts,
vowing to God and man if she haue not you, she will
haue nothing: for any mans pleasure, sheele not liue
if not for yours.

Filbon. I stand resolu'd. 20

Tutch. She wishes that ye should, or sheele not trust
to ye.

Enter Sir Rafe.

Sir Rafe. Sonne seest thou yong Toures?

Filbon. Not since our last repulse in loue, since when
I stand affected vnto singlenes of life. 25

Sir Rafe. Then art thou stable in my thoughts, but let
me whisper to thee boy, young Toures in a Tinckers
habit hath her stolne, to whom his heartie adorations
were to this houre consecrate, shees gone, and her
old doting father got to complaine him at the court, 30
how twill worke I know not.

Tutch. Like wax, sheele take any impression, sir she.

Filbon. Like a tincker say ye?

Sir Rafe. Certainly euen so.

Filbon. Twas my owne proiect father, hee applauded it, 35

13. stoole,] stoole. Q. 22.1. Q. adds "and Filbon."

knowing my fashion of that counterfeit, to be so
sure, as no man could forgoe me.

Tutch. But himselfe sir, tis a point of law, arraigne
him vpon _ipse facto_./

Filbon. And art thou stept beyond me? where to night 40
thou slepst: soft be thy pillow: easie be thy rest,
& may thy bed be.

Song.

Tutch. _Mortall downe, thistle soft,_
She laid her selfe vnder to keep him aloft,
And euer she said, come turne thee to me, · 45
And was not this bonny lasse Mary Ambre?

Enter Auditor, and doth whisper with Sir Rafe.

Filbon. _Mary_ indeede she hath resign'd to me hard
choyce,
Neare am I but as arrowes a farre of,
Seemes to the shooter neighbor to the marke,
Till it proue otherwise, so I 50
Furthest from fauour am, though seeming nie.

Tutch. Change your marke, shoot at a white, wil say,
come sticke me in the clout sir, her white is
black, tis crept into her eye, and wenches with
black eyes the white's turned vp are but as custards, 55
though they seeme stone cold, yet greedily attempted,
burning hot, and such a wench is she sir.

Filbon. I know she loues me.

Tutch. Most affectionately burnes in desire for ye, but key cold through her father, she stands to 60 freeze while others are appointed to thaw the ice, not you.

Filbon. I must vse pollicie.

Tutch. The onely man, I will assist you sir.

Filbon. I thanke thee, and I will preuaile in't. 65

Auditor. I thinke sir, if I see my house to night, there will come warrants to make open way to their recouery, thinking they are with me, whom I protest I haue not seene, and vnacquainted with her subtill stealth, am now as cleare as is the babe new borne, 70 I neither knew of it, nor where they are, I do beshrow their hearts, right I haue in him for it.

Sir Rafe. Sleepe in my house then, so my word shall make your answere stronger, I haue a sonne, I wish him so possest, but not with violence, yet say he 75 doe climbe high, and reatch the top bough with a stricter course, I knowing not the manner nor the meanes, acquites me, and God giue/ them ioy, my oath is cleere, and that's my warrant.

Auditor. Sir, I will trouble you to night, by this 80 sad time his mone doth challenge comfort, and the

61. ice] Ice Q. 64. sir.] sir, Q. 73. Sleepe] sleepe Q.
78. giue] giue, Q. 80. night,] nigh, Q.

councell whose loues he hath so often visited,
heartned on by the Earle of Tumults meanes, they
will adde present purpose as he begges it.

Sir Rafe. But if the Earle know of my sons discharge, 85
sign'd by his carelesse answere, 't would allay his,
hot endeuours with a cold responsall; but cease
that, the time shall come--

Filbon. Tis mine, the cause and all, pine let mee in
them, if the sonne of hope shine as a troubled 90
meatuare in the sky; tis our fates fortune, and no
matter cause no remedy.

Auditor. True vantings of resolue, tis late, and
custome challenges no right in me to be so
hurtfull to my selfe, the euenings aire is rawe 95
and cold.

Sir Rafe. Filbon follow vs, be you more temperate.
You see what hurry threatens in this misdeede,
Wounds deepe are dangerous, though they hardly
bleed.

Filbon. Sir I am lessond. 100

Tutch. As the boyes at schoole
Practice their knowledge by contrary rule? Exeunt.

85. But] but Q. 86. 't would] t'would Q. 94. me] me, Q.
98. threatens in] threatnings Q.; misdeede,] misdeede Q.
99. bleed.] bleed Q. 100. lessond.] lessond, Q.
101. schoole] schoole? Q. 102. rule?] rule. Q.

[Scene XIII]

<u>Enter</u> <u>Humil</u> <u>sadly</u>.

Humil. O I am slaine with wonder.
Hath this life left in it a little breath,
To blow out treason, reeke yee cloudes of shame,
Putrifie all imagination, hold her at stearne,
There let her sinke, neuer to win againe, 5
<u>Honours</u> recouery, shall I say and thinke it?
O--
Haue I not beene in bed to night, and so
Talke idly wanting sleepe, or rose from rest,
As many troubled doe, acting like life, 10
Awaking dead, for in that flattering feare,
Perchaunce her reputation may be saued.
No I am certaine in my feare, tis true,
In yond black closset lies a wicked woman,
(I will not say my mother, that names lost)/ 15
In the twind brazings of the slaue her man.
In <u>Iames</u> his armes, and shall I suffer it?
O--
To blab, it were to harould out my shame,
In quarter'd scutchin of black obloquie, 20
To murder one were most imparciall;
Againe to turne hilles on this sinne,

6. <u>Honours</u>] <u>Homers</u> <u>Q</u>.

Would write me baude, but to be nobly satisfide
Is a content licenc'd from equity.
The knight shall know it, I will write to him, 25
Startle his bold imagination with pale feare,
Rouse his reuengefull spirit on them both,
And make me hopefull of his loue neglected,
Forgiue me world, heauens iustice puts me on,
And though a sonne, Ile punish both or none. *Exit*. 30

[Scene XIV]

Enter Earle, and Lord, and Sir William, the Lords, and Sir Williams two men bearing torches.

Earle. You that binde vp in secrets of the night,
Dayes benefites going to rest,
As peacefull birds, lodg'd in a sanctuary,
Smile at our Courtiers care, whose industry
Rules in the silent and all shadowing night, 5
Suites that are breathles in a troubled day,
Haue their abiding in our cares at night,
Hard censur'd, and atton'd by late aduice,
Saluing the worlds scares, as we would your care
Knew we the burthen of it. 10

27. Rouse] Rose *Q*. 2. rest,] rest; *Q*. 3. sanctuary,] sanctuary. *Q*. 4. industry] industry, *Q*. 6. day,] day. *Q*. 7. night,] night. *Q*.

Lord. With vs the morn is mated with the moone
And we are retrograde to what you doe.
Esteeming conscience, benefite and good.
Challeng'd in seruice of our country:
Sir though our blood affirme vs labour free, 15
It bindes thee more to busie industry,
Wonder not at our late vpsitting therefore.
Sir William. Your honours toile in our extremities,
But we vnthankfull merit contrary,/
Thinke it a want and weaknesse in our kind, 20
I poste and labour in a toile my selfe,
Seeking my owne: midnight to me is noone,
And all the houres of dull past night,
Sun-shine eclipses, that do much molest me,
Pardon me that am so tedious. 25
Earle. Seeking your owne?
Sir William. My eldest daughter is conuei'd from me,
Hurri'd away, as theeues by violence
Conuey their booties from the true mans store.
Toures, Auditors sonne hath done this deede. 30
A rescue noble Lords.
Earle. Rescue and right, challeng the benefite.
Sir William. A warrant for a generall search,
Restraints for Cinck-ports, and all passages,

18. honours] humors Q. 26. owne?] owne. Q. 30. Toures, Auditors] Auditor, Toures Q.

That theeuish water doth dispoile vs of. 35

Earle. It shall be sign'd i'th morning,

Draw the contents as you affect the meanes,

And let attendance vrge the early act.

Lord. Good night.

Earle. God morrow is it not? 40

Sir William. Betwixt them both.

The morall of my misery seeking too late,

That to recouer which I lost too soone.

Lord. And yet in each you stand indifferent.

Sir William. I must, till perfected by you, 45

Either late losse, or timely victory,

Recouering what I feare is past aduantage.

Earle. Hope the best sir, things at worst,

Season in their decay, as children mend,

Bent in their eye to ruine, yet they pause 50

Resting in grace, does reobtaine at will,

Opinion in rash iudgement, dooming ill.

Lord. Good rest, for we go too't.

Sir William. The peace of happinesse be with ye,

I will retire me to my Inne, and wish,/ 55

Howres as short as momentary breath,

For till the morning, minutes howres be,

And howres yeares, such is reuenge to me,

Might I enioy it?

58. reuenge] reuengd Q.

Man. Sir. 60

Sir William. My man, a midnight messenger, what is thy
haste in Leathe steept? speake is that all one, one
all, that we call daughter, gone too, is she?

Man. No sir.

Sir William. Wherefore starest thou so wildly, say, 65
weart thou asleepe and wakened? com'st to vs hers
without thy better part? and sent abroad, leauing
thy wits at home.

Man. Your sonne sir, in all haste sends you his
talles, wishes your wit and iudgement sodainely, 70
read and regard sir.

Sir William. Giue the torch. [Reads.] If you wil see
my mother & your wife, fellow'd in bed make haste,
Iames your man writes on your pillow &c. my eies are
witnesses to their adulterie. 75

Seruant. Whats the newes?

Man. Plague on these iauntings, once we shall be old,
& then this trotting life will linger in our bones,
all howres are our nights, we dally with our owne
destruction. 80

Sir William. It cannot be, or if, or if, what if? if
it be so I am vndone, poison'd am I with faire
promises, no maruell tho you doe forsweare my bed,

62. Leathe] leathe; steept?] steept, Q.; one,] one? Q.
72. torch.] torch, Q.; If] if Q.

if yet againe, if what make I here when treason is
at home, away. [_Exeunt_.]

[Scene XV]

Enter yong Humil.

Humil. The bird that greets the dawning of the daie,
Signes with his wings, the midnights parture,
And the sleetie deaw moistning the cheekes
Of morrowes welcome: giues earnest of the morne:
Yet all secure, adultrate lust dos sleepe, 5
And I the hatcht yong of this troden henne,
Stands Centinell to her idolatrie.
Blow you sweld windes and crack the battlements,
Rouse their incestious luxurie with feare
Of whats to come, yet that were my mishap,/ 10
No silent aire fan on them bawdie breath,
That as they reeke in their licentious loue,
Diuell may seale sure, and Morpheus so pleas'd,
May to their pastime adde affliction
Deliuer'd by the hand of him thats wrongd, 15
And stands indebted to his desteny:
Yet are they as the hower, whose sandy minutes
Runs out at pleasure till the period comes,
Fast sleeping, and enioy their quiet,
Rouse the blacke mischiefe from thy ebben cell, 20
Land in the bosomes of this twin in lust,

Him whose heapt-wrong calles vengeance to be iust.

Sir William. [*Off stage*.] Locke fast that dore and leaue me.

Giue me your light, Sonne *Humil*?

Humil. Father. *Enter Sir William and his men*. 25

Sir William. Thou seest I am obedient at thy call.

Exit seruants.

I come as messengers that bring their bale,

Sign'd in their lookes, be well aduis'd,

Thou makest a chalenge goes beyond all grace,

Should it be false. 30

Humil. It is my loue to you that makes me step

Heart-deepe in disobedience to my mother.

Wretch that I am to thinke her so,

It makes me desperat of prioritie,

Forethinking my beginning to be bace, 35

Conceau'd in such mistrust and frailty,

My front hath that impression still,

Adding a blush to my distemperature,

And I am crest-falne in sanguinitie,

Pray ye beleeue me, would it were not so. 40

Sir William. Enough watch & be secret, I will enter,

Sit as the night rauen or the skreeking owle,

Ouer my portall, menasing ill chance

To all within: for death is to my blood

A blessing, while this feuor killes, 45

Almost my intellect or better part,/

Yet shees thy mother, and no sonne but hates
His owne disgrace so highly merrited,
And I beleeue thee.

Humil. Sir, trueth is trueth, my conscience and
religion 50
Bindes vp in me, and since I doe proclaime
Detraction from my blood, by her misdeede,
Giue me leaue to report a flye a flye,
It if offend the vertue of mine eie.

Sir William. Tis true. 55
And yet me thinkes it should not be,
How hardlie will this scandall take impression,
Where resolu'd christianity dos dwell?
But I will trie the gold, perhaps tis base,
Who knowes the hearts affection by the face. Exit. 60

Humil. Scarlet is scarlet, and her sin blood red,
Wil not be washt hence with a sea of water,
Is this my hand, or is the fire fire?
Whose scorching heate dissolues relenting mettall,
When as it tries the substance; yes, and I 65
Make knowne my mother is an alien,
From my blood, so to fall off, and perish
Euen in her pride of blisse, damn'd be the slaue
That so attempts her spotlesse chastitie
To ruine, I know that yet smooth looke, 70

64. Whose] whose Q.

Plotted, contriu'd, and woon her with deuise,
She neuer knew a double character till now,
But single singler she euer rulde,
Euen modesty her selfe, _Vesta_ resignd to her,
And vertue hand in hand at barly-breake, 75
Ran the swift course, none but a hound of hell,
Hunted this fawne of fortune to his kennell,
But my mother, forgetting her degree,
Dos captiuate loue, life and liberty,
By one deedes practise, wicked, nay farre worse, 80
Fatall disgrace, honours created course.

Sir William. Foole, foole, foole. _Enter Sir William_.

Humil. Ha./

Sir William. Light bubble swell and breake, would'st thou beleeue
All this, and giue a glosse to slaunders crueltie: 85
Ripening reproch it selfe with thy fond eare,
O _Humil_, _Humil_.

Humil. Sir.

Sir William. Thou art a villaine, and hast cast vp hilles
Against heauen it selfe: when sonnes vnto 90
Their mothers are so false, O where is grace?

84-87. _Q. prints as prose_: "Light...thou/ beleeue...ripe-/ning..._Humil_." 89-92. _Q. prints as prose_: "Thou...against/ heauen...false,/ O...shew/ her face."

Hudwinckt from honour, sham'd to shew her face.

Humil. Is it not so?

Sir William. Trust thy owne eies, go, thou shalt see a sight

Will melt thy stubborne spleene in pittie, 95

Sweetely she sleepes, whose innocent respect

Smiles in her dreames, thy childlike gouerne,

Laughing lowd in their simplicitie,

While waking mischiefe seekes that to vndoe,

Which true requir'd, stands centinell vnto, 100

Goe and returne with shame.

Humil. With shame, diuell of mischance whats this?

Did I not see their culted guilt looke big?

Was I in traunce of my beleefe, ha, was I?

Can be no iugling in it: can there? *Exit*. 105

Sir William. No thou art constant as the northren starre,

And I as giddy as the vntam'd Leopard,

That sees no meanes but dire destruction,

Flinging his foame to poison in his waie

Mans mischiefe, plotted to his ouerthrow: 110

He told me true, O that I liue to thinke so,

Or they so wretched to deserue the thought,

Soundly they slept, whose slumbers kild me waking,

Yet to recouer halfe slaine reputation,

99. waking] waking, *Q*. 103. culted] cutted *Q*.

Done haue I, what to purpose practiseth. 115

If it preuaile, our honour so preseru'd

Will kicke at all malignant crueltie

That taints our name with euer liuing skorne,

Fortune be for me, I will that recouer,

Which diuell him selfe cries guilty too, my fame/ 120

The flight it wings, imps feathers of renowne,

That left al's lost, my birth-right tumbles downe.

Enter Humil amazed.

Humil. Sir I am sorry.

Sir William. How can they excuse such wanton loosenesse,

Know they I stand here to thunder vengeance 125

On their luxury.

Humil. My mother's fast asleepe, and I awake,

Am in a transiue maze, vnwitting how

To make my peace with God, herself and you.

Sir William. Why, are they not together? 130

Humil. Not in bed.

Sir William. Thou should'st with Argos hundred eyes,

115. practiseth.] practiseth Q. 116. preseru'd] reseru'd Q. 122. downe.] downe, Q. 124-126. Q. prints as prose: "How ...loosenesse,/ know...luxury." 127-129. Q. prints as prose: "My...tran-/ siue...her/ selfe...you." 130. Why,] Why Q.

Search in the chinkes and corners round about,
It cannot be but she is extant there,
Ha, is she not? 135

Humil. I am confounded in the search,
Please your iustice be my torture,
I haue murdered innocence,
Sorrow is not the way, death is the least,
I challenge cruelty and vrge the exactest 140
Point of perill, slaue that I am to liue.

Sir William. A sonne, a sonne, to do so to a mother.

Humil. Fare ye well, rather then be a witnes
Of my wrong, I will not see my selfe in't,
Go thou worse then. 145

[Sir William.] Ile sacrifice to the diuill, that tempted thee,
All thy distempered thoughts, cry mercy to her sectes.
To spotlesse innocence be free,
Say all thy treasons, build on slippery ice,
And thou art frozen cruelty. 150

135. Q. prints at end of 134. 136-141. Q. prints as prose: "I...iustice/ be...the/ way...ex-/ actest...liue." 143-145. Q. prints: "Fare...wrong,/ I...then," 146-150. Q. prints: "Ile...thy/ Distempered...sectes./ To... treasons,/ Build...cruelty,"

[Humil.] Sir, for your wrongs, if you remit black
torture,
Tis my hell, and I appeale to sterne rigor,
O you sonnes, whose true obedience shines in maiesty,
While mine more vgly is then Vulcans stithye,
Smels ranker then despised Hemlocke, 155
Curse and ban him, I am your subiect to't.
And euery mother, whose snow innocence,
Feeles soft and tender, as the downe on palme,
Rate my rebellion with a blisseles name,
And for my sake giue misaduenture aime./ 160
Guide 'hem to me, say I am such a sonne,
Through whom a mother is so soone vndoone.

Sir William. Let me not see the while thou liu'st away,
Let thy repentance shew it selfe in this,
Not to be seene where thou hast done amisse. 165
Catiue depart.

Humil. I will, this tongue that slandered--

Sir William. Be her slaunder still.

Humil. It is too much already, was I bewitcht,
That thus at hud-man blind I dallied 170

151-153. Q. prints: "Sir...tis/ My...sonnes,/ Whose... maiesty." 154. is then Vulcans stithye] then is vulcans tithye. Q. 155. Hemlocke,] Hemlocke Q. 156. to't.] to't Q. 157. innocence,] innocence; Q. 162. vndoone.] vndoone, Q. 167. slandered--] slandered, Q.

With her I honor'd? O you times how haue you
Nurst me, but no more, _Humil_ hath branded on his
Mothers name, an AEthyops blacknesse, and
A spotted staine, forgiue me that and all. _Exit_.

Sir William. What need I to afflict reuenge on him 175
That on himselfe exasperates, farewell
Thou pride of sonnes, who to a father
In supposition onely, and by law,
Art all so louing, that thy mother dalling
With wantones as girles with gauds, thou not 180
Respectes the womb that brought thee forth,
But ill attempting so, and so thou rumorst,
As the fault ripe in act, is blowne to aire,
And though her sonne thou vtter'st what they were.
Thou shalt not loose by't. Now it fits, 185
I challenge from the offence some right,
And adde confine to this adultery.
Wife, wife, rise and come forth.

Enter Lady, in her night gowne,
and night attire.

Lady. Call ye sir?

176-186. _Q. prints_: "That...pride/ Of...and/ by...dalling/ With...respectes/ The...attempting/ So...act,/ Is...thou/ Vtter'st...by't/ Now...right," 184. were.] were, _Q_. 185. by't.] by't _Q_. 187. adultery.] adultery _Q_.

Sir William. Yes, take my closset key, let forth your louer, 190

Giue me some ease by way of reason yet,

And 't will allay our discontent,

O God so new to marriage, and so stale,

Couldst thou so soone reuolt, so soone, ha?

Enter Iames unready, in his night-cap, garterles with the Lady.

Iames. I must acknowledge all. 195

Lady. O No, some better looze,/

This will but adde to mischiefe torture.

Vse patience now, be reconcil'd to feare,

Be doue-like humble, and leaue that to me.

Iames. How can I, when the brand is on my brow, 200

But by exclaime, giue ease to torture?

My braine is scar'd, and I am liueles in't.

Sir William. Kneele not.

Ambo. A sentence, let vs dy.

Sir William. No maruel though you vow this abstinence 205

When deputed by him, you shunne my bed,

You do deserue your iointer well,

190-193. _Q_. _prints_: "Yes...louer,/ Give...t'will/ Allay... and/ So...ha?" 191. 't will] t'will _Q_. 197. torture.] torture _Q_. 198. now,] now _Q_. 201. torture?] torture, _Q_. 202. in't.] in't? _Q_.

To admit a fellow in a true mans place,
I thanke ye for it, yes.

Lady. Sir. 210

Sir William. No, no words I know you can alleadge,
The diuell has scripture for his damned ill,
And this dos neighbor it, go and attire ye,
Be smilefull, and expresse no griefe in sighes,
Rather be tickling sportfull, topt in pleasure, 215
Then daunted any way, that me concernes.
To vse the mad-mans guise, but I am past it,
Since what is done, no reference hath to wish,
I am for credit sake, supportable, al's well,
Content am I to be senseable, and feele my 220
Fortunes as I may, ranking my selfe with such,
As sometime liu'd in my repute most base,
Faith all is well beleeue it, I am satisfied:
I know you do repent, and that's my remedy,
Other amends I looke not for, In, and attire ye, 225
But [to *Iames*] stay you with me.

Lady. I am obedient. *Exit* *Lady*.

Sir William. Go thou shame, neuer till now possest,
And in a breath confounded, sir, you see your wrongs
Shine through the horne, as candles in the eue, 230
To light out others, thinke you this misdeede,
Merits saluation?

214. sighes] sithes *Q*. 215. pleasure,] pleasure. *Q*.

Iames. I must acknowledge contrary./

Sir William. Wilt thou for all this spight,

Yet vse me kindly in the next? 235

Iames. Command me sir.

Sir William. Not for the second, this mistake me not,

Rather to binde thee from it, if hereafter,

Fashion of frailty summon vs to feare--

I must be plaine, and therfore thus: 240

Looke when soeuer I hold vp this finger,

Signing my lippes with it, and cry begone,

Euen then be speedy to depart the land.

If not, all power of mischiefe that I can,

I will and so resolue. 245

Iames. Sir, I am ready to the minute.

Sir William. It may be, other reasons wil restraine me

As causelesse motiues, not seeing guiltinesse.

In needy sequences perhaps our heart

Will in itselfe take truce with this mischance, 250

Or if it doe not, yet attend our spleene,

It wil be better for ye.

234. Q. prints: "Wilt...in/ the next." 239. feare--] fear Q. 244-245. Q. prints: "If...will/ and...resolue." 249-252. Q. prints as prose: "In...take/ truce...our/ spleene ...ye." 250. mischance,] mischannce Q.

Iames. In humble duty.

Sir William. Goe, giue coppies of good countenance
to

Our friends, thinke all is well, for so it is, 255
I that am all in griefe, am all in suffering,
I forgiue the reason, fare ye well. Exit [Iames.]
What I will do, is bar'd vp in this closet,
The key that opens it, is my reuenge.
Turn'd by a hand whose palme dos itch with fire 260
Til al consume, a cuckold, cuckold Sir William is.
Its euen so, would I were yet the last or least,
But not by thousands. Go too then, am I
All alone in this? Who is't that tongue calles
man
That is assured of his wiues condition? 265
None, or if any, there the Phoenix liues
Vnfellow'd, be his fate renown'd while mine
Is mockery, and a Iestiue stock, to
All that knowes me. O you starres blaze fire,
Till this abuse be quench'd by my desire. Exit./ 270

254-257. Q. prints as prose: "Goe...our/ friends...griefe,/ am...well." 261. Sir William is.] William sir is Q. 263-264. Q. prints: "But... this/ Who...man." 263. thousands. Go] thousands go Q. 264. alone] alone, Q.; this?] this Q. 268-269. Q. prints: "Is...me./ O...quench'd/ By...desire."

[Scene XVI]

Enter Tutch like a welch knight, and
Filbon as a seruant waiting.

Tutch. Harke ye Morris.

Filbon. I Sir.

Tutch. Where is Tailer? dudge me, will knog his pad,
What is chirken with cold button done, say you.

Filbon. Excellent, this is welch indeede, O my honest 5
Tutch.

[Tutch.] Sausebox, rowly powly, am I not your master?

Filbon. You are sir, pray ye pardon me.

Tutch. You must haue your left eie Diamiter wise,
Fixt on my right heele, and all the offices 10
A seruant owes in dutie to his Master, performe
As naturally as if the fortie shilling time
Were come, lest I leaue talking welch,
And crack your pate in English.

Filbon. I shall obey sir. 15

Enter M. Auditor in a Marchants
habite, with Tabitha.

Auditor. Fairest of beauties, loue her seemely selfe,
For thy two eies are *Cupids*, which doe shoote
From thy inamor'd bow, shafts all of gold,

10. offices] offices, *Q*. 13-14. *Q*. *prints*: "Were...in/ English."

Headed with mettall of immortall proofe.

In thy faire bosome liues two hearts relenting, 20

Thine penetrable, through attoning pittie,

Mine longing by desire to scale the fort

Of loues faire presence, make me happie,

Signe to my sute, but ye, for tis thy censure

Makes me thus bold, pronounce faire iudgement, 25

Either of life or death, I that plead loue,

Doubly deuoted, challenge from thy dietie

A maiden answere, let it come bright fire,

To trie the substance of my loues resolue.

Tabitha. Sir, in sooth and veritie beleeue me, 30

That I am faire tis credible, but to shoote

Arrowes, whose heads haue such immortal proofe,

Tis most erroneous and false.

[Auditor.] Sfoot your a puritane,/

A cittizen Ime sure, her canuas curran bags, 35

Stuft with sweete sinnomon and cloues,

[Tabitha.] Good sir you are deceau'd in me, Ime country plain

Without this nicetie, and do you loue me, yes?

Then craue an answere without ceremonie,

Fetcht from proud Ouid in his Arte amandi. 40

I doe not like it I.

Tutch. Ples you Latie.

33. false.] false, Q. 36. cloues.] cloues, Q.

Tabitha. Sir, and you tell me of _Cupids_ eies,
Shot from inamord bowes with hearts relenting,
Doubly deuoted, and I know not what. 45
Tutch. Ples you firgen.
Tabitha. No sir no, giue me plaine curtesie,
Drawing on loues white hand a gloue of warmth,
Not cheuerell, stretching to such prophanation,
You ouerthrow loues dietie in this, 50
And putrifie his altars with bad breath.
I am a dairy huswife, no such wanton,
So easily flatter'd with farre fetcht replies.
Yet I esteeme this worthlesse person free,
And tho not faire, yet something fortunate. 55
Tutch. Harg ye now Latie.
Tabitha. Sir cry you mercie.
Tutch. Was a knight, marg you, of Englise in Wales,
welse blood, and tis no mock in en to marrie in
welse blood, is it? 60
Tabitha. Sir all the smiles a modest maid,
Can in this kinde make proffer of, are youres,
In your faire welcome, blame me not,
Though his vnkindnesse made me negligent

43-45. _Q._ _prints_ _as_ _prose_: "Sir...eies/ shot...de-/ uoted ...what." 43. Sir,] Sir _Q._; you] you, _Q._ 61-65. _Q._ _prints_ _as_ _prose_: "Sir...this/ kinde...welcome,/ blame...negligent/ in...entertaine."

In your kinde entertaine. 65

Auditor. Neglect me so.

Tabitha. Wiues vnto Citizens are trades-mens daughters,

I am a blood of gentle composition,

My minde dos equall it, I must be coacht,

Banckqueted euery where, courted abroad, 70

At home flattered, for my priuate vse,/

I must haue fancies, playfellowes, as apes,

Monkies, baboones, mufs, fannes, receits,

Costly abilliments of seuerall suites,

Wil ye giue this? twil breake you sir, 75

And crack your credits faire condition, no,

Citizens would, but cannot answere so.

Tutch. Harg you, marry with her, and God dudge me, all is yours, was a knight haue land, and a great deale of rishes, wil maintaine you well, say you. 80

Tabitha. This gentleman or this, before a Citizen,

You sir pardon me I wil ha none.

Auditor. Then whom you will,

Call you this modestie to be so waspish?

Giuen to slight men off with inciuillitie, 85

Giue me leaue to remember.

81-82. Q. prints as prose: "This...sir/ pardon...none."

83-86. Q. prints as prose: "Then...to/ be...giue/ me... remember."

Tabitha. What you please.

All the world except one or two,

My eie motes that trouble but my sight.

Filbon for me, man else but meere 90

Illusion and idolatry, vaine worship,

Images of molten mettall,

Which to drosse dissolud, appeare as nothing to

My iudgement, but his worth beyond compare,

Gentle and suffring as the silent aire, 95

That tho it brooke the buffets of base breath,

Yet in it selfe tis heauenly, free from earth.

Tutch. Harg you, was knight in house cald _Sir William Perger_.

Tabitha. _Verger_ sir? 100

Tutch. Morris was say true, giue a ducket, looke you tucke it, is marke, marke you that, and marke is 13 shillings foure pence, good currans money, and how doe you? well, whan was sir _Robert Morgan_, mik you latie, grace a God. 105

Auditor. You sir.

Tutch. Was I lye pray you?

Enter Sir William, Sir Rafe, Henry,
a Priest of Putney.

87-97. _Q. prints as prose_: "What...or/ two...for/ me... worship,/ images...appeare/ as...com-/ pare...brooke/ the ...free/ from earth." 87. please.] please, _Q._

Sir William. Thinke you Master Auditor knew nothing
sir.

Sir Rafe. Vpon my soule I thinke it. I did
Winde him subtilly as hounds the game,/ 110
New got on foote, for instance he lamented
Oft his sonnes proceedings, neglecting his owne
house,
Lest you in quest of her should search it,
Beleeue me sir I tell you what I know.

Sir William. Tis likely, sonnes in these doting daies 115
Wil from their fathers alienate, differ stil
From loues obedience, and in hearts affection,
Ioyne hand to hand, though beggery neighbor it,
And let them go.

Henry. Sir I am free then from your feare. 120

Sir William. I good sir Henry I was wrong inform'd,
I am your patron in all loue.

Henry. Long may ye liue, so sir I find you gentle,
And a good benefactor to poore schollers,
We ha few such, many we rather haue, 125
That sell the Church rights, then maintaine them,
And in my next stanze, I shall tickle them.

Sir William. Speake conscience and no more.

108. Auditor] Auditor, Q. 109-114. Q. prints: "Vpon...it./ I...game,/ New...sonnes/ proceedings...quest/ of...I/ know."

Henry. Nay as for that sir pardon me,
I seldome exercise without that thought, 130
What my text leads me to, I wil pronounce,
Mauger the diuel of iudgement.
Sir William. Soft.
[Auditor.] Blesse you gallant knight, a marchant sir,
Of London am I, my estate secure, 135
And so it please you couet this faire maid
In marriage, nothing else.
Sir William. Know you him Sir Rafe?
Sir Rafe. Not well sir, but by guesse,
He is indifferent rich, has broke three times, 140
Made his head hole by meanes, & that say I,
As this world shapes, is secure policie,
What think you sir?
Sir William. I doe not thinke it so,
Though common practice finds it furthering shifts, 145
Like it not, doe the diuel resemble,
And banckrout bacenesse makes good credit tremble.
Tutch. Plese you Aunt, harg you now, knight was loue
this firgin, and God wil, must make her wife, shall

134. Auditor.] Tutch. Q. 135-137. Q. prints as prose: "Of ...co-/ uet...else." 139-143. Q. prints as prose: "Not... rich,/ has...that/ say...you/ sir?" 144-147. Q. prints as prose: "I...practise/ finds...banck-/ rout...not." 146-147. Like it not] Q. prints after "...credit tremble,"

be her laty,/ go in Wales, great worship God willing. 150

Sir William. O know this knight, he was created tother day.

Sir Rafe. Sir Robert Morgan, O sir, such a one,
Whose reputation reacheth to the best,
Merits a good coniunction, wer't my daughter,
She should haue him. O beware 155
When maiesty shines in a mans estate.
They long stand firme, spread wide, regenerate
And though base borne, yet honour makes them swell,
Like clustered grapes, till mature sweetnes brings,
Lussious conclusion. 160

Sir William. I haue some mind to him, sir you receiue
Kind welcome, let it store your thoughts with
Those sweet motions louers wish to enioy, she may,
Perchance, all things concluded on, be for ye.

Tutch. Was a clad man, Morris fetch trunck of parrel 165
Was lye here a foure weeke, will not out now.
Was welcome, plague on you, was loue ye.

Sir William. Sir, as for you, being citty proud,
My daughters looke sits on a Courtiers brow,

152. Robert] Rober Q. 152-156. Q. prints as prose: "Sir ...reputati-/ on...my/ daughter...shines/ in...estate." 155. him.] him, Q. 157. wide,] wide Q. 164. Perchance,] perchance Q. 166. Was] was Q. 168-170. Q. prints as prose: "Sir...looke/ sits...girle?"

What saist my girle? 170

Tabitha. O sir, a Courtier on my life,

I loue to sit vp late, ly long i'th morning,

Rot with sweete meates, and to play at shuttle-cock,

Me thinkes the games now in myn armes,

In any hand a Courtiers wife and why not? 175

His black iet shewes best about beauties necke,

And I am proude of such a suter,

If I vnderstand not his welche.

Like a good peece of ord'nance,

I shall ly fast vpon the bulwarke, 180

And discharge my obedient English.

Must be a Lady sir.

Sir William. Yet welcome sir, let it not grieue you.

Auditor. Signior no, you'r welcome to the wife *I* wooe.

Henry. And mistres, might *I* be the man to strike the stroke. 185

Tabitha. You, or else none, sir *Henry*.

Sir William. Troth she saies true, but listen me for that,

Come gallants enter with me, we will feast,

171-181. *Q. prints*: "O...late,/ Ly...and/ To...now/ In...and/ Why...about/ Beauties...such/ A...like/ A...the/ Bulwarke... English/" 172. i'th] it'h *Q.* 174. myn armes] my narmes *Q.* 178. welche.] welche, *Q.* 181. English.] English *Q.* 190. *Q. prints*: "Troth...come/ Gallants...lost,/ where...coast."

Theres little labour lost,

Where tryall bids presumption scyrre the coast./ 190

[*Exit*.]

Henry. Right to a haire, tis mine, and I must do't.

I see my fees, my rich aduantage, sirha boy,

Shall wee haue worke, in faith and shall we? *Exit*.

Auditor. Conclude, ile busie him, Sir *Rafe*.

Sir Rafe. Sonne, you see to what a happy issue this disguise 195

Speakes faire, you know the plots, boldly proceede,

Tis ours in action, but your owne the deede,

I must shunne all suspition

By my presence, looke to't boy.

If thou failest now, for euer loose thy ioy. *Exeunt*. 200

Tutch. Ha, ha, master, I a Welchman, a Hangman.

[*Discards his disguise*.]

Tabitha. A tricke now on my maiden-head,

I did mistrust it, come leaue the rest to me,

This Priest shall marry vs incontinent.

Filbon. I, if I were the Welchman. 205

Because your father gaue him light thereto.

Therefore come sirha, weele shift clothes, meete vs

At Putney as my father shall mistrust ye.

191. do't.] do't *Q*. 196-198. *Q*. *prints*: "Tis...must/ Shunne ...boy." 202-204. *Q*. *prints*: "A...it,/ Come...incon-/ tinent." 207-208. *Q*. *prints*: "Therefore...Putney/ as...ye."

Sir Rafe. I will, excusing your departure till anone.

Filbon. Do gentle loue. 210

Heauen on our venture smiles, this to approue.

Tabitha. O it cannot choose.

Fathers are fortunate in this good newes.

Go ye drones, ye do not loue the hiue,

Theres hony in't, tis a sweet thing to wiue. 215

Tutch. I must breake the ice for ye, if I slippe vp
to the chinne, now you will pull me out, saue mee
from drowning mistresse.

Tabitha. Feare it not. *Exit*.

Tutch. I would bee loath betwixt Welch and English, 220
to bee hanged, mistresse, I cannot liue on the
bargaine, come sir, Ile shift with them, and now
I must shift with you.

Filbon. I clothes, good *Tutch*.

Tutch. And vse me no worse being your man, then I 225
vsed you, being mine.

Filbon. O better, better.

Tutch. O loue, thou art a begger, yet I am thy debter.

Exeunt./

209. anone.] anone, *Q*. 210. Do] do *Q*. 215. wiue.]
winne. *Q*.

[Scene XVII]

Enter [_Toures_, _Master_ _of_ _a_ _ship_, _and_] _two_ _sailers_
with _a_ _truncke_, _wherein_ _is_ _Mistresse_ Mary _in_
her _winding_ _sheete_, _others_ _with_ _a_ _pick-axe_
and _spades_, _as_ _on_ _the_ _sands_.

Toures. Set downe the heauiest load
That euer true affection vnderwent,
To you tis like the Anchor of your ship,
Heauy at first, but easly waied seemes light,
To me, that not supports her bodies waight, 5
Tis heart deep in the burthen, & too ponderous
Sad, heauy is that load, whose leaden poize,
Is as a sullen sorrow, too, too pressing.

Master. Sir, I would wish you to be briefe.

Toures. Dig ho this golden beach, whose glittering
sands 10
Shewes with the sunne as Dyamonds set in gold,
Fitly intombs a iewell of much worth,
Whose liuing beauty staind all lapidary.

Master. She was most gentle which was worth all
riches.

Toures. And this nights tempest did a cruell
deede, 15
To take from me a vallue of such price.

Master. Sir, though our seas kill women with their
frownes

[To] vs their bug-beare threates are womanish,
And so we leaue 'em.

Toures. Leauing your selfe and all, somtime. 20

Master. Euen so, no safer in our beds,
Or on the land, but vnder deaths black stroke,
And he that is the surest, sits in state,
Dyingly tended by the hand of Fate.

Toures. And yet me thinkes death should not 25
Take her from me, being scarce mine owne.
But newly wed, neuer bedded yet.
So that the Ceremony burning bright,
Himen yet hath his tapers flaming red.
And the bold boastings of that good mans breath, 30
That all religiously made one of two,
Hardly disgested in the freezing cold.
Little I thought the priests word, being euer,
Should find his period in so short a time./

Master. Sir, but the gift was giuen ye on condition, 35
Till death d'ye part, better or worse,
Me thinkes this Catechizing little needes,
To humane guiding, and to you the lesse
Knowing what openly you do confesse.

18-19. *Q. prints*: "vs...e'm." 20. somtime.] somtime, *Q.*
31. two,] two. *Q.* 32. cold.] cold, *Q.* 33. word,] word *Q.*;
being] being, *Q.* 36. d'ye part] depart *Q.*

Toures. Beare wi' me maister, he that pines in griefe, 40
Liues as you sailors doe, thinking at sea,
Euery storme ends, when flattery flouts ye,
So to our loue-sick sorrow comes a calme,
By ease of fancies, when tis furthest,
And many times the weapon that doth wound, 45
_Is_ salue, and Surgeon both, to make all sound.
Master. Are ye ready sir?
Toures. All fitted, let me take my last farewel,
I am all gelly in my teares and sighes,
Wasted by wailing her vntimely losse, 50
So long _I_ did consume in drops of woe,
That contrary _I_ laugh to thinke it so.
He that weepes much, hauing no teares to spend,
Smiles out the rest, but inwardly does rend,
O God that _I_ ventring so hard a chaunce, 55
Should loose my dice, before my hand be out,
Tis euen so, in all things man intends
The losse is ours, the winnings not our friends.
Master. For charity be briefe, should the wind
Turne his beake into the southerne side 60
Our ship would leaue vs, dally not with griefe,
Once and no more, let sorrow rule as chiefe.
Toures. Then thus, and this the last,
Moll, _I_ take leaue yet on thy hersed selfe,

40. wi'] w'e _Q_. 50. wailing] waiting _Q_.

Dead selfe, and selfe slaine, Moll decest 65
I am thy morning musike, call thee vp,
To wedded rights, I leade thee to the Church,
And there receiue thee, dine with thee at noone,
Daunce all the after day, bring thee at night
Into the wedding chamber, this is it./ 70
And here I leaue thee to thy virgen slumber,
Neuer attempted, as thy birth bestowd,
Madam beginning, take it in thy end,
So liue thus die, onely my married friend,
And nothing else, gone art thou to a power, 75
Which will with welcomes take thee, left I am
To the worlds crosse, thy father who inrag'd,
Will bitterly reuenge thy death on me,
But I will proue his martyr, pre-thee Moll,
Foole that I am so say so, here is all, 80
Gownes, tire, all abilliments of thine,
No rag shall rest remembrant in my viewe,
To stirre the imbers of thy dying fire,
I kisse thy key cold corse, and with this key,
Lock thee for euer vp, farewell, farewell, 85
My mouth the Church, my voice the parting knell.
All eares that liue and heare this bell to toule,
Christian-like bid peace vnto her soule.

79. pre-thee] se-thee Q. 86-88. Q. prints: "My...the/ Parting...heare/ This...vnto/ her soule."

Master. Amen, be speedy mates, see ye not, looke
The blewnesse of yon cloud dos threaten winde, 90
If it rise faire, we shall be lodgd in France,
But not where please the fates. Dispatch.
Within. Aboard, aboard, heie. *A crie within.*
Master. Hollo, linger no time aboard, you heare
With me ho, will the rest stay? how a yeare? 95
[Toures.] O God that man should leaue behind,
And liue, the loue of soule and minde.
Exeunt, and leaue the pikax and spades behind.

[Scene XVIII]

Enter Gouernour and a Gentleman.

Gouernour. Sir welcome to Scillie,
Where I command my brothers friends haue welcome,
But now my flattery gets you on this beach,
Where you prospectiuely see many countries,
Learn this of me, where danger shootes her string, 5
We in our neighbour neerenesse ought to feare:/
But arm'd by our foresight, make bold resist
Against the brags of forraigne enemies.
Gentleman. I haue not seene a better glasse to looke in,
What country call you yon, whose cliffes are as 10
The cloudes smoake, and all shadowing mists?

10-11. *Q. prints as prose*: "What...cloudes/ smoake...mists?"

Gouernour. Sir that is _France_, a faire beseeming
friend,
On yonder continent stands _Ireland_,
On this side _Brittaine_, and on that side _Garsie_,
Ilands besides of much hostillitie, 15
Which are as sun-shine, sometimes splendious,
Anon disposed to altering frailtie.
We that all neighbor must so strength our being,
As fearelesse we may frolicke yet not seeing.
Gentleman. I vnderstand ye sir. 20
Gouernour. Now let my longing haue content in you,
With the report of them you lately saw,
My brother _Vergir_ and his children,
Is he a widower stil at _More-clacke_?
Gentleman. Married sir vnto a London cast away, 25
One whose decaied husband left to liue,
(Though poorely) yet your brothers Lady.
Gouernour. It is his choice, and I subscribd to't,
But for his daughters sir?
Gentleman. Alas, in them is he vnhappy, 30
One is haild from him by stolne practises,
The other liues as though she were not his,
A goodly gentlewoman, but her owne in heart,
She will be gone to, for her gouernement
Stands vpon will, as men stand on the beach, 35
Seeing the sea wherein they must be dround,
Yet fearelesse venter on the ruthelesse maine,

She will regardlesse of her father, marry,
And dos as most, long for the miserie,
Signd to them in their cradles. 40

Gouernour. Sorry am I.
Ha, what scrambled ends heape vp confusedly?/
New digd and ript vp is this plot of ground,
Some Shipwrack on my life, hid to deceiue
The Queene and me of our aduantages. 45

Gentleman. Likely sir,
And see our sodaine comming scar'd from hence,
In the new ending, such as pil'de this heape,
Behinde them haue they left their implements
Which did the theft, what thinke ye sir if we 50
Redig the ground, should we depart & leaue it?
At midnight wold they fetch their borrowings.

Gouernour. I like your purpose, ile make one.

Gentleman. What doe you thinke it is sir?

Gouernour. No bodie buried, it is sure some goods, 55
Wrackt on the sea, money or rich commoditie.

Gentleman. Tabacco then.

Gouernour. Tis likely, for with vs men smoke ther lands
Thorough their nostrels, shall I tell ye sir,
Tis a commoditie may well be spared. 60

56. Wrackt] wrackt Q. 58-60. Q. prints as prose: "Tis... lands/ thorough...commoditie/ may...spared."

Gentleman. Good lucke a gods name, sir it is a
truncke.

Gouernour. Lift sir. *They lift it out*.

Gentleman. Tis quicke, it heau'd as I heau'd it.

Gouernour. Yfaith *I* thinke so to, in heart of hope
I will be all so bold as to breake way. 65

Gentleman. Ha.

They breake the Truncke open, and she sits vp.

Mary. If you be men and borne of that weake sex,
Which I my selfe professe, being woman,
Pittie the liuing sorrowe of a maide,
Buried for dead, but backe againe recal'd, 70
By the diuinitie of heauenly power,
Amaze not, I am creature, flesh and blood,
Not as I seeme, a pale and earthly Ghost,
The story when you heare it shall make plaine,
The wofull chance of life so lately slaine. 75

Gouernour. I had acquaintance with this voice, my
cosin.

Gentleman. Tis she, sir, tis Mistres *Mary Virger*, I
know her./

Mary. My name recalles my memorie,
And I am such a creature, oh,
My vnckle, where am I? returne againe, 80
Death thou art wanton in a louers paine.

64-65. *Q*. *prints as prose*: "Yfaith...all/ so...way."

Gouernour. Cosin I will not question the particulars,
The time calles on a present comfort,
And your life halfe spent,
Makes true necessitie delay no longer, 85
Therefore come, at leasure we shall heare,
The dying story of your miserie.
How euer, glad I am that such a chance,
Landed in Scilly not in neighboring France. [*Exeunt*.]

[Scene XIX]

Enter Filbon in welch attire, and Tutch in seruingmans, like one another, with them Sir Rafe, M. Auditor & Tabitha.

Auditor. If euer you vs'd speede, be swift as lightning,
Shoote as the starres in their celestiall sphears,
Go and returne as *Paris* did from *Greece*,
With that immatchles *Hellen*, tell the Priest
It must be done, he will beleeue your haste, 5
Because twas quickned with the former grant,
And promised by the knight himselfe.
Sir Rafe. Let me alone to make the way, follow you sonne. *Exit*.
Filbon. And if I doe not let me loose my prize.
Auditor. Wheres the knight? 10

86. at] as *Q*. 0.1. *Enter*] *Enter in Q*.

Tabitha. Busie with one, who comes as coniur'd vp
From _Cupids_ quiuer, stroken deepe in loue,
He is a Pothecary.

Tutch. I know him his mother was a.

Auditor. Peace. Him will I busily attend, go you dispatch 15
While I detaine the father, if this proue,
Tis comicke pleasure in the schoole of loue. _Exit_.

Filbon. We must be quick and sodaine, come.

Tutch. Slip like your Eele.

Tabitha. If any man know any lawfull cause 20
Why these two may not marry, now speake,
Or else euer mumb, I am gone yfaith./ [_Exit_.]

Tutch. Master, remember, you ha my tongue.

Filbon. Yes, and thou mine, let me alone to counterfeit. _Exeunt_.

[Scene XX]

Enter Sir William with Humil, like a Pothecary.

Sir William. Thinke on your oth.

Humil. Sir, if I do not, let me dye.
When I haue poison'd her with this confection:

11-13. _Q. prints_: "Busie...from/ _Cupids_...Pothecary." 15-17. _Q. prints_: "I...Peace./ Him...the/ father...of/ loue." 20-22. _Q. prints as prose_: "If...these/ two...I/ am...yfaith." 24. Yes,] yes _Q_.

Be you cloudy kild with sorrow, tis a skin,
Will draw to purpose on the straitest gloue, 5
But then your promised reward.

Sir William. My daughter and my goods,
I haue no other sonne but you, all is thine,
Question not the reason, why this is,
For I haue many, and amongst them one 10
Hides all the rest, that knowne to thee,
Will rather hasten death, then pitty it.
Go, I will bid my guests, for to this feast:
Shal she haue noble poison, twill cause feare,
Vselesse suspition, and my mortall hate 15
Shall it selfe kennell in the pride of state.

Humil. Giue order for the banquet.

Sir William. Within there. *Enter Lady.*

Lady. Sir, what is your will?

Sir William. To murder thee. *He speakes aside.* 20

Humil. [Aside.] She dies sir, if I liue, I am a
Pothecary.
And can knead the paste to purpose, she is gon
Had she a thousand liues laid vp in one.

Sir William. Wife, I must haue thee paint,
And set a glosse vpon this louely front, 25

11. Hides] Sites *Q*. 15. hate] hate, *Q*. 16. kennell] kenuell *Q*. 17. Giue] giue *Q*.; banquet.] banquet, Q. 18. Within] within *Q*. 20. thee.] thee, *Q*.

To moue, and to attract all eies. Looke as the
sommer,
Which glads all hearts with his bloud-creasing
spring:
Vse thy best graces, though most proudly
I will haue it so, sit thee to all state,
Deck't in thy choisest ornament, shine glo-worme, 30
In the noone of night, for at this supper
I will haue more then all our friends,
Musike seuerall, Masques and Reuellings,/
In which thou shalt be mounted as the bride,
And I the iolly Bridegrome, will tend on thee, 35
As duty and the time commands me.

Lady. Whereof comes this cost?

Sir William. Examine not, but lay your best end now
to't,
Councell with this Pothecary which I sent for
To the businesse, pray ye vse your art: 40
For I am bent to this consumption,
Wheres our seruant _Iames_?

Lady. Within sir, shall I call him?

Sir William. No, I wil waite on him, for tis my duty.
Such as would spend in feasts, are but the slaues, 45
To attend the pleasures of consuming knaues.

26. eies. Looke] eies looke _Q_; sommer] sonmer _Q_.
31. supper] supper. _Q_. 33. Reuellings,] Reuellings. _Q_.
38. to't,] to't _Q_.

And I am one of those, he is the flower
That I must crop too in this fatall hower.
Pray ye appoint sir, she will fit you well,
My purse shall puruey what you shall determine, 50
What we will be wastful sometime, & our owne,
We vncontrol'd may dispose of: tis our loue,
Rather our destinie hath ioin'd to this brow,
A horne that drawes on death, no matter how. [*Exit*.]

Lady. Sir, in my closset serue your selfe with sugers, 55
There are spices of the purest,
Vse them in this cost, what else you want,
Please you command, they shall attend you.

Humil. I want vertue in a mother, are you one?

Lady. *I* am a mother to an absent sonne. 60
But not to vertue wanting, wrong me not.

Humil. Wrong not yourselfe.

Lady. *I* neuer will. *He discouers himselfe to his mother*.

Humil. You haue.

Lady. Humil, O my shame and not my sonne. 65
By thee a mother is made miserable.

Humil. By my blacke sinne? no by thy owne neglect,

53. destinie hath] destinie, hate *Q*. 54. *Exit*.] *Exeunt*. *Q*. 55-58. *Q*. *prints as prose*: "Sir...there/ are...you/ want... you." 67. my] me *Q*. 67-70. *Q*. *prints as prose*: "By...made/ perfect...cunning/ masqu'd...knew/ not...bed."

Made perfect by my true intelligence,
And who euer cunning masqu'd and don'd the vissard
That so muffled me, _I_ knew not who was in the bed./ 70
Lady. Your eies were witnesses.
Humil. And holy ones.
Lady. Found you the man you look't for?
Humil. No, twas a subtill straine, so hudwink't truth,
_I_ am a traytor if I did not see 75
Iames your man fast in your armes.
Lady. Thou art a traytor then, if any _Iames_ were there,
Hee was no man of mine, he was thy father.
[Humil. My father.]
Lady. Maruell not, at leasure _I_ will tell thee all. 80
His late returne, the tricke to place him here,
My stay, and his continuing in this house, which knowne,
Thou wilt no sin account, to keep our owne.
Humil. O you prophetique Fairies, how dally you,
In concaues of our hearts, sham'd at my errour 85
I thought for euer to be from your sight,

69. who] how _Q_. 73. look't] loo'kt _Q_. 75-76. _Q_. _prints as prose_: "I...your/ armes." 77-78. _Q_. _prints as prose_: "Thou...hee/ was...father." 82-83. _Q_. _prints_: "My...which/ knowne...owne."

But thinking truth was blinded, _I_ forethought
Some following businesse, thus _I_ altered
Comming as one disguised to saue her life,
Dam'd for that fact. 90

Lady. My life?

Humil. You must be poisoned at this feast,
Tis I must do the deede, O mother,
How are you blest in my returne from trauell,
_I_ that to light bring your offence, so thought, 95
Must be the pardon at your iudgement brought.

Lady. Ah me.

Humil. No more, much secrecie calles on vs,
Acquaint me with my father, plead my guilt.
We shall with cunning so vnfold this businesse, 100
That our hopes shall strengthen as they flourish,
No idle practise, but a serious toile,
Must bring home conquest from this long wisht
spoile. [_Exeunt_.]

[Scene XXI]

Enter _Henry_, _Filbon_, _Tabitha_, _Sir_ _Rafe_, _Tutch_.

Henry. If I lock vp this treason, let me perish,
No sir, my breath is yet an vncorrupt

87. thinking] thinking, _Q_. 101. flourish,] perish, _Q_.
103. _Exeunt_.] _Q_. _prints_ _at_ 1. 2-5. _Q_. _prints_: "No...house/
That...do/ This..._fidem_."

And holy house,/ that harbors in it nought
But honestie, and to do this wrong to my patron,
Per deum atque hominem fidem. 5

Tabitha. No matter if you tell it now, tis done,
Finis men say, concludes the auncient worke,
And this though newly done, cries so be it.

Henry. If keept, secrets can be but offence,
And so tis now, may be, I loose my place, 10
But theres a friend which turning calles detraction,
At his heeles liues hope, whose cunning quickens
Euery fault to fauour.

Filbon. Why true, and we shall as we may excuse it,
Twas a deede done in welch, you vnderstood it not. 15

Tabitha. Let me alone to buckler thee sir *Henry*.

Henry. Can ye ward your selfe?

Tabitha. This was a passe, twas Fencers play, and for
The after venny, let me vse my skill.

Sir Rafe. How euer girle, thou art my daughter now, 20
What thou shalt loose in father, from thy owne,
Thou vncontrold shalt find as much in his,
And I am he.

6-8. *Q. prints*: "No...men/ Say...this/ Though...it."
9. keept,] keepe *Q*. 9-13. *Q. prints*: "If...now,/ May...which/ Turning...hope,/ Whose...fauour." 12. quickens] quicknes *Q*. 18-19. *Q. prints as prose*: "This...the/ after ...skill."

Tabitha. And I acknowledge both this in my Lord,
My head, my husband, at whose bed I am obedient, 25
At whose board I am obedient: all in all,
I am the wife of Filbon, whose rough Welch,
Hath got a constering English, parse it boy,
Nounes, Pronounes, Verbs, Aduerbs, and God giue
thee ioy.

Tutch. With vocatiue O, your father heares it. 30

Tabitha. And ablatiue caret, takes his daughter.

Henry. Then in pluraliter, ha has a sonne.

Filbon. So singular and plurall all is done.

Enter Auditor, like a Merchant still.

Auditor. If euer you were swift be nimble now,
What ha ye married, tide this knot? 35

Tabitha. I, and the earnest blow giuen, feare it not.

Henry. Sir, I haue set my hand to't, seal'd the
deed,
Pray God it cancell not in me.

Auditor. Then part, and euery one be silent.
There is a feast appointed at the knights./ 40

Tabitha. Our marriage dinner, is it?

Auditor. A gallant one, much cost is threatned.

24-29. Q. prints as prose: "And...my/ head...board/ I... rough/ Welch... Nounes,/ Pronounes...ioy." 32. ha] ah Q. 34-35. Q. prints as prose: "If...ye/ married...knot?"

And the good old knight vnbuckles from his backe,
The liberall loade of honour, dos proclaime
Triumphs and welcome vnto all, 45
Calles for his wife, charges her care,
Commands his seruant Iames to inuite his guests,
Which in a rolle stands quoted,
Theres a new come pothecarie, and he bribes,
Euen grace her selfe in this assembly, 50
And dos promise his furtherance in
The businesse, on the sodaine you are mist,
Daggers and diuels the knight cries wheres my
daughter?
One vp ascends to search the chambers,
Another runs to seeke for this lost daughter. 55
I knowing more then much in this her absence,
Singled my selfe to warne you of his search,
Hether will he come, for he feares yong Filbon,
Missing the suters, calling for the marchant,
I answered not (being absent) 60
In this heat: the welchman, where is he?
None can be found, cries out he knowes not what,

43-63. Q. prints as prose: "And...libe-/ rall...welcome/ vnto...his/ seruant...quo-/ ted...grace/ her...in/ the... di/ uels...ascends/ to...lost/ daughter...absence,/ singled ...hee/ come...calling/ for...heat:/ the...he/ knowes...a/ plott."

And all his word is now, a plott, a plott, a plott.

Sir Rafe. What will ye do?

Tabitha. Kisse and part, 65

Till fit occasion of our next salute,

Filbon farewell, my husband thinke on me,

I am thy treasure but thou bear'st the keie. Exit.

Sir Rafe. I will home.

Auditor. And I will see the rest, what will you sir 70
doe? Exit.

Henry. Nay I ha done enough, I am vndone in my selfe,
Hei mihi quod nullos, I must doe this deede, twas I
pauca the rest, Ile home sir, I. Exit.

Tutch. What rests for welch sir Robert Morgan, by God 75
was cragge de pen, and the hangman calles to me, da
hum a, da hum a?

Filbon. I will be at this feast in some disguise.

Tutch. Ile fit ye sir, tis here, I am tutch right, hic
& vbique, euery where. Exeunt. 80

[Scene XXII]

Enter Sir William Vergir.

Sir William. Now smiles the instant, & wrathes
wrinckles seeme,/

As smoothed curles vpon a wanton streame,

My hopes grow big, and their diliuery,

67-68. Q. prints as prose: "Filbon...treasure/ but...keie."

Is by our midwife time brought to true birth,
I will not be a pointing stocke to th' world. 5
No, if this gossip rumor publish it,
It shall be christned with reuenge and death,
Why when, are we growne sluggards now?
Tardy in bountie, shall we niggard it?

Enter Humil in white sleeues and apron, and others posting ouer the stage with boxes.

Humil. Be quicke, carry those sweete meats in, 10
Bid them that in this businesse haue to doe,
That they attend this rich confectionary,
With no common care, the cost comands more loue
And duetie, sir we are fitting to occasion,
Would all your guests were come. 15

Sir William. Tis the feasts duetie to attend,
Thou art a willing mischiefe, hast thou fitted
Our purpose to the proofe?

Humil. Haue I, thinke you I am slacke?
Pusht on with hope of beautie and reward, 20
She dies had she a life more deare
Then the last spring, sole comfort of the yeare.
But I will couer and prepare. *Exit.*

Sir William. Doe, doe, my daughters thine, my goods, my all,

5. to th' world.] tot'h world, *Q*. 18. Our] our *Q*.

Blessed beginning to my sorrowes fall. 25

Wheres my Lady?

Lady. Here.

Enter Lady gallant and braue, while

Humil and others prepare.

Sir William. That one so heauenly faire should earthly be,

Slaue to misfortune, bace in luxurie.

Lady. Sir for to please your eie, I am thus quaint, 30

Good faith I am asham'd in my selfe.

Sir William. How and a woman.

Come blaze thy affections to immodesty,

And tho thy vertues contradict the deede,/

Be Venus wanton, smile, with Helens eie, 35

For I will haue it so.

Lady. I was not so brought vp: I shall endeauor,

Tho my cheekes put on sensuable die

Of other bashfulnesse.

Iames. Sir your honourable guests are come. 40

Sir William. Nay then you wrong me most of all,

Shew not these signes of feare, all's past,

And I am dead in old remembrance,

Troth I am, forget it, as I doe, say on.

Iames. Coches so fill the pauements of your dore, 45

37-39. Q. prints as prose: "I...my/ cheekes...bashfulnesse."

That scarce can passage giue the footemen way,
Tis not amisse you goe to meete them sir.
Sir William. Why well said, spoke with courage, & I wil,
Iouiall like a bridegroome, Lady you see,
They waite on vs, and all attend on thee. 50
Lady. Worthlesse I am, but since it is your will,
I borrowe light from sun-shine of your beames,
Who glisters so, giues splendor nothing proud,
Dark'ned by feare, halfe hidden in a cloud.
Sir William. Nay hand in hand, in faith *Iames* pardon
me, 55
That dally with the darling of your heart. *Exeunt*.
Iames. Euen so, but little thinking such a thing,
Small gaine springs from that toile, where industry
Sweats in the browes of others victorie.

Enter Humil busily still.

Humil. Father be mindfull, this presuming knight, 60
Plaies with the flame, burnes in the candle-light,
When we shall furnish to disfurnish him,
Of what he yet enioies.
Iames. *Humil*, tis cunningly contriu'd, and I attend
it. *Exit*.
Humil. For charitie be swift. 65
Place your plate, and pile your vitriall boales
Nest vpon nest. These for wines and beare,

67. nest.] nest, *Q*.

The other tend the call of altering diet,
Sirrha, quoth he, we shall fit I trow,/
The pleasant purpose of loues appetite, 70
At hand yfaith and welcome to the feast,
Whose foode is pleasure, dainties but a iest.
And I prouide it for ye.

Enter Earle, Lords, Ladies, so many as may be,
Sir William and His Ladie in complement.

Sir William. Right noble & my hearts indored friends,
To preach your welcome, were to drowne the sea 75
With floods of water. Be it knowne vnto ye,
That your comming solemnely inuited,
Hath that attendance appertaining as the Gods
In their selected Bacchinels command,
Mary, the Nectar wants, and the Ambrotia 80
Smiles in the presence of such earthly wines,
As the worlds compound furnishes with all.
Though it come short of lushius surfetting:
Yet willing furtherance makes the value meete,
In her best suite of entertaine, sit then, 85
And let our musicke rellish to the eare:
Such care and cost as loue and welcome giues,
Not to prophane the best except the least,

71. At] Ad *Q*. 79. Bacchinels] Bacchiuels *Q*. 80. Ambrotia] Ambrotia, *Q*. 82. all.] all, *Q*.

As prolog to begin this worthlesse feast.

Earle. Sir we are easily won to fawn on frendship, 90

Spanniel-like, yet with the smiles of men,

Which redeliuers loue for loue,

What we receiue are treasures safely stor'd,

And shall with intreest be repaid againe,

Your free, yet frugall, without lauishing, 95

Nor come we to make boote of curtesie,

But value kindenesse in her best of loue,

So wee dwell in your bountie.

Sir William. Rent-free welcome.

If you thinke this your receptacle, then 100

Landlord I am, and shall so soundly proue,

As fines forgiuen, you leese, free borne our loue.

Welcome our tenants Landlady./

Lady. I do, my duty tenders it,

Sit then and frolicke, for to my hearts liking, 105

Is this day consecrated, blest the meanes,

That added to it, such prosperitie,

While we sate sighing on the bancks of bale,

Blisse kist her cheeke, and bids her ioy, al haile.

Sir William. I such a storm as when the shower is past, 110

It driues destruction to thy soule,

Morral in faith, enigmaies riddles so,

89. prolog] prolong Q.

Musike fal too, wife I will seate thee heere.
With pardon of thy betters.

Earle. In yours she is the best & does command 115
Place and periority i'th vpper hand,
Besides, her beauty merits as the best,
To ouer shine starres, were they here possest.

Lady. Well mock't my Lord.

Earle. No, not a whit. 120
My iudgement erres, if otherwise I censure it,
Sit sirs, for I, although inuited, chalenge here
Ful flowing welcome, from his lippes that lends,
As vnto me, so much to all my friends,
And I begin vnto ye. 125

The Earle sits, and all do follow him.

Sir William. Theres a cockrel right,
That learnes to crow from others, good my Earle,
If that my boldnes may, chalenge thy owne,
Engadge vnto thy noblenes for euer,
I promise whose performance lightly giues, 130
Heart willingnes to boote, cods me fill wine.

Filles two glasses,
giues her one.

Skink & carouse, wife charge this common shot,

126. Theres] theres Q. 130. lightly] lighly Q. 132. shot,] shot Q.

Leauell point blanke, see who thy pearsing eye,
Can marke to hit, if they be bullet free,
They scape the vnder daunt of courtesie. 135

Earle. They say hees curst that by a cannon dies,
May I be blest in such a destiny,/
For of all other, I were onely happy,
Being the ey-marke of so faire a shot.

1. Lord. Discharge bright beauty, & shoot home, 140
Make me the man so happy.

2. Lord. I, or me.

Earle. Or any, mongst so many, liues free choice
To one as principall, to each a voice.

Lady. Then to the worthiest, to your selfe my Lord. 145
By figure of the rest, tis vnderstood,
By the kings nod, he greets his subiects freely,
Though his eye settle vpon one.

Earle. Euen so to me, I answere & acknowledge
Receite of complement bestowd about 150
On euery willing, and right welcome guest.
Pray ye all memories.

All. We do so, and he giues a duty
To gratulate such seeming courtesie.

Enter Filbon, & Tutch, in blew like nurse,
and Iohn ith Hospital.

140. home,] home *Q*. 153. duty] duty. *Q*. 154.1-154.2. *Q*. *prints after line* 156.

Sir William. Nurse, _Iohn_, vnlook't for better welcome, 155
This is kindly visitation faith.

Filbon. Sir, tis my duty, and my beggard boldnes
Makes me presume to trouble ye,
Knowing how you affect this ignorant,
I brought him to giue welcome to your guests, 160
Hearing at London of this preparation.

Sir William. At London, is it got so farre abroad?
You see a niggards bounty how it spreades,
Like to a nine daies wonder gentlemen:
And much the more, because tis seldome seene, 165
That couetous misers are so plentifull,
Faith, tis much in me.

Earle. We find it so, sir _William_.

Sir William. Now my suck-egge tell me, what's the newes at
London, you heare all. 170

Tutch. That honest men want,
And knaues get money,
I ha nothing,
Nurse has some,
Dogs are let/ loose, 175
And the beares vndone.
Ha, ha, ha.

168. Now] now _Q_. 171-177. _Q_. _prints as prose_: "That...get/ money...let/ loose...ha."

Sir William. Came ye by foot _Iohn_, or by water?

Tutch. A horse-backe ith boat.

Sir William. Art not gal'd with riding, _Iohn_? 180

Tutch. No, but weary with sitting, nurse shall sing a _Geneua_ psalme, and bids these beggers welcome.

Sir William. How beggars, _Iohn_?

Tutch. All the world is so, ha, ha, ha.

Earle. He saies true, chide him not, we are no lesse. 185

[_Enter_ _Tabitha_.]

Sir William. Daughter welcome, Nurse all day, at night be your bed-fellow.

Tabitha. My nurse, indeede my bed-fellow for euer,

[_Speaks_ _aside_.]

My _Filbon_ welcome, welcome as my husband,
My last, and for euer best beloued. 190

Sir William. _Iames_, to season this good meeting,
Take hand in hand with our faire wife and dance,
Gallants, my man can trick it with my Lady,
You shall see else, make not squeamish, to't,
It is my will, and what I will shal be. 195

Iames. Beseeke ye sir.

Sir William. Befoole ye sir wilt be, wife make not coy.

Lady. Since you command it, I am ready.

Sir William. [Aside.] I trow so, but I trust a

179. A] a _Q_. 180. not] no _Q_. 188. My] my _Q_. 191. to] To _Q_. 197. coy.] coy _Q_.

potion pleades

By this time to true purpose, dos it not? 200

Humil. I would not be so sped, for all the world,

Tis done too late, tis past.

Sir William. Good its beginning, let her dance her last

Who fronts me with a Cornucopian wreath,

Were she a wife sprung from the race of kings, 205

Such bitter breathing followes, now ye lamps,

Of spotted Nemmisis, burne blew, let the light

Fall on mischiefes selfe, that dallied lately

In our wretchednes, tell her sad sorrow,

Tombs and epitafes tend her amazing obsequies, 210

& then liue free thou wrong'd soule from slanders cruelty.

Lady. I am not well sir, pray ye leaue the daunce./

Sir William. Not well, Iames be gone.

Iames. Sir, you shall pardon me, vnles with her being not well. 215

Sir William. Ha.

Iames. Thinke you I will, what leaue my country, sir.

Vpon a slight, a trifle, tis more deare to me.

Sir William. Wast not thy promise?

203. its] ith Q. 207-211. the light/ Fall] Q. prints: "the fall,/ Light...our/ wretchedness...epi-/ tafes...free/ thou ...cruelty."

Iames. Pughe. 220

Sir William. Pughe.

Tabitha. Madame, leane on me, Ile bring you to your
chamber.

Lady. Pre-thee daughter, faith I'me passing ill,
Your honour and the rest must beare with vs, 225
Tis nothing vsual, a queasie fit.

Earle. The mother.

Lady. No, the husband.
Good faith I am not woman sick, though woman
But earnest ill, clog'd at the very stomacke with 230
A sodaine calme, I feare me tis my death.

Sir William. Nurse help to bring her to her closset,
do.

Filbon. Excellent fit, supported by vs too. [Exeunt.]

Tutch. Plague on't, shall I be left alone, master
make haste? But tis my deede, I am author of this 235
shift, hees where hee would be now, Ime where I
should be too, but not wel back't, yes now I am.

Enter Sir Rafe.

Sir Rafe. Beseeke ye pardon me.
Sir William, I am wrongd, and to this company,
I make it knowne by comming of thy daughter: 240
Is my sonne made her indored husband, shall I
Suffer it, call you this curtesie?

242. curtesie?] curtesie, Q. 242-246. Q. prints: "Suffer ...craft?/ Cloak't...vn-/ knowne...all,/ and...daughter?"

Tis simple craft cloak't vnder thy denial.
Is this wel to ingraft with vs unknowne,
And so to ioyne yonkers to heirs? he is 245
My onely all, and married vnto thy daughter.

Enter Filbon and Tabitha.

Sir William. Ha, married? Nurse, how is't within?
Filbon. Shees very ill sir, and I feare.
Sir Rafe. That your disguise is knowne, come iuggle not,
Call you this Nurse? O thou dissembling boy. 250
Sir William. Are you married?/
Tabitha. Sir I must needs confesse it, he's my husband, & the reason.
Sir William. No matter for the reason, I ha done, God boy ye,
Conicatcht by a tricke, and so perswaded, good. 255
Sir Rafe. I am abus'd.
Sir William. Yes questionlesse you are, I haue all right.
Filbon. You haue no wrong sir, I to affirme your word,
When I was woman, and from man I should, and now,
I trust my shape dos challendge but your promise. 260

243. craft] craft? Q.; denial.] denial, Q. 245. heirs?] heirs, Q. 247. married] Married Q. 253. reason.] reason? Q.

Tutch. I plaid but "*Iohn* come kisse me now" saies she,
I am *Tutch* your quondam seruant sir, thrust out to
thrust them in, a lawfull marriage is no mockery
sir, I counterfeited welch, to ioyne this constring
English. 265

Enter Auditor and his sonne Toures.

Earle. What at a gaze sir *William*? cannot be recald.
Sir William. No, no, more mischiefe, nay come all
together,
Welcome.
Auditor. Thanke ye sir.
My sonne return'd, surrenders to your doombe his
life, 270
For yours so lately lost, deputed in your daughter,
For she is dead sir, buried in the ile of Scillie.
Sir William. Not amisse, what the next *Pagan*?
All the craft of this is knowne.
Toures. Sir had I too hearts to melt, 275
This frozen feare would thaw with passion,

268. Welcome.] welcome. *Q.* 270-272. *Q. prints as prose*: "my...for/ yours...dead/ sir...Scillie." 273-274. *Q. prints as prose*: "Not...of/ this...knowne." 275-279. *Q. prints as prose*: "Sir...feare,/ would...torme-/ ted... knowes/ how...dide." 275. melt,] melt *Q.* 276. feare] feare, *Q.*

The drops distil'd from our tormented braine,
Witnessed by these sailers that inter'd her,
Knowes how I parted with her when she dide.

Earle. Is mistris Mary dead? 280

Toures. She is.

Sir William. Well, shall I haue Iustice for her death?

Earle. Command it sir.

Sir William. To prison with him then, for she is murdred,
Sir cause you knew your rapine and your theft, 285
Tied to your runnaway legs that clog,
You were vncertaine of her portion
And our loue, therefore to rid that feare,
You rid me thus of her (to me) most deare,
My owne, my onely eldest of my/ daughters, oh. 290

Auditor. Ile be his bale.

Sir William. Sir tell not me of bale,
For my assurance pleads in his life,
And he shall die.

Earle. You haue no president for that. 295

Sir William. Yes, remember Donningtons man, Grimes,
Who for an heire so stolne and married,

284. then] them Q. 285-290. Q. prints as prose: "Sir... your/ runnaway...portion/ and...of/ her...my/ daughters ...oh." 292-294. Q. prints as prose: "Sir...pleads/ in ...die."

Was hanged, and the sergeant at armes
For assisting them, did loose his place,
If this were done, your theft will hardly scape. 300
Earle. I thought of that indeede.

Enter Iames and Humill disguised still.

Iames. Murder, murder, murder.
Earle. Ha, by whom?
Iames. By this faire counterfeit of husband, heres my
witnesse, and the deputie in such a mischiefe. 305
Sir William. Nay then.
Iames. My wife is made away, poison'd here,
And you that should be iust are witnesses.
Earle. We follow, speake, explaine this mystery.
Sir William. Your wife sir. 310
Iames. Yes, supposd for dead, as risen from my graue,
I came to More-clacke, but a little late,
Euen when the lying Priest did call her thine,
She knew it, and deuised with her gloue,
To repossesse me of the house she chalengd. 315
So honourd, I slept with my owne, but thought
The contrary, you know what happened,

307-308. Q. prints as prose: "My...that/ should... witnesses." 316-323. Q. prints as prose: "so...contra-/ry...betraid/ his...wrought/ by...biding,/ therefore... and/ yet...you?"

That sonne that so betraid his parents thus
disguisd,
Fearing insuing mischiefe, wrought by you
To haue poison'd his deare mother, twas your bidding, 320
Therefore murder, but the will of
Heauen bad otherwise, and yet she liues,
Wife what say you? *Enter Ladie.*

Lady. That al is so.

Humil. And I affirme it true. 325
My shape cast off dos answere sir in few.

Sir William. Prettie infaith, no maruell you forswore my bed,/
When you had substance for a property.
Sir you must haue your owne, who can deny it?
And I must as the story runs be mum, 330
Foold in my selfe by my owne slights vndone.
But whats this to my daughter, where is she?

Mary. [Offstage.] Here sir.

Enter Gouernour, Mary and others.

Gouernour. Brother *Vergir*.

Sir William. Brother *George* from *Scillie*, what the newes? 335

320. bidding] biding *Q*. 325-326. *Q*. *prints as prose*: "And ...answere/ sir...few." 328. property.] property, *Q*.

Gouernour. That your deare daughter dead and buried
sir,
By miracle was thus preseru'd,
Which at more leisure I shall manifest:
Pray ye forgiue her fault, come theres some wanton
blood
Left yet, saies I, ye will I know, 340
And wrongs past all remedy, the world must vndergo.
Mary. My _Toures_, the dead dos liue, I am thy wife,
Mary.
Toures. Or her ghoast, a shadowe or a substance.
Tabitha. Sister I will teach ye a medecine
To make a shadow substance, ly with him tonight, 345
As I will with my _Filbon_,
& by the morning thinke but what is past,
And you will reckon rightly you,
Hele hold you three to one my medicine's true.
Sir William. Methinkes I haue a tickling in my blood 350

336-341. _Q._ _prints as prose_: "That...buried/ sir...I/ shall ...some/ wanton...wrongs/ past...vndergo." 344-349. _Q._ _prints as prose_: "Sist...sha-/ dowe..._Fil_-/ _bon_...will/ reckon...medi-/ cine's true." 350-370. _Q._ _prints as prose_: "Methinkes...crosses/ all...Feare,/ this...welcome/ is...&/ yet...know/ not...general/ ly...gallants,/ and...pray/ ye... resolue/ to...per-/ swasion...worlds/ fond...prodigious/ to ...thank-/ lesse merit."

Crosses all anger, malediction hence, hence,
Thou ill temper'd Feare, this comicall
Euent seasons the true applause;
Since welcome is the word, y'faith,
I know not what to say, faine I would 355
& yet a lazy lagging apprehends with doubt,
But well I know not what, in me,
It lyes to punish or to pardon.
I wil be generally laught at,
Once insooth I will. I am a widdower, 360
Gallants, and you meete at marriages,
And funerals, so thinke it pray ye,
I abridge all complement, barre all opponents,
& resolue to fauour you, you, you,
And challenge from your lou, perswasion to this
purpose, 365
Since our fate makes vs the worlds fond Idiot,
Be it so youth,
And your fortune was prodigious to it,
And my best of spirit,
Binds vp in this, all is but thanklesse merit./ 370

Earle. Then Epilogue am I,
Imagine all the world were in your house,
And hearing this report with wondring braine,

I thus excuse it, Gentlemen you see
How fortune fauours in extremity, 375
If any botcht vp ill, haue shew of good,
And is not in thee sequell vnderstood,
Yet beare with all, as this old Knight has done,
Loosing a wife redoubled in a sonne,
What you shall want in iudgement, seeing this, 380
Thinke euery act is subiect to amisse,
So said, so done, will bring to true delight.

[All join hands.]

Hands meeting thus, to signe this blessed night.

FINIS

374-383. Q. prints: "I...fortune/ Fauours...haue/ Shew... vnderstood,/ Yet...done,/ Loosing...shall/ Want...euery/ Act...will/ Bring...thus,/ To...night."

EXPLANATORY NOTES

The following notes are intended to aid the reader by (1) providing definitions of archaic and obscure words or neologisms (most of the definitions are taken from <u>OED</u> or dictionaries of the period, but some are simply inferred from the context); (2) offering interpretations of passages rendered obscure by reason of unidiomatic expression, ellipses, figurative language, or textual corruption; (3) pointing out confusions or contradictions in the action and the characters' motivations; (4) tracing literary and historical allusions; (5) suggesting parallels of thought, language, action, and theatrical convention in other works of the period; and (6) displaying the limitations of the editor's own comprehension of the play in hopes that the reader will be challenged to bring further illumination to it.

Scholarly sources are referred to by the author's name and, where required by the existence of more than one relevant work by the author, by short titles. Full bibliographical information on each work can be found in the "List of Works Referred to in the Apparatus," which follows the notes. All notes beginning with lower case letters are intended as direct paraphrases or synonymous equivalents.

Editorial comments or observations are distinguished from straight definitions and paraphrases by beginning with capital letters.

[To the friendly peruser]

1. quis non] whoever.

3. boyes of the Reuels] The Children of the King's Majesty's Revels, as indicated by the title page, who performed at Whitefriars from 1607-1608.

3-5. which...hole] which was sometime acted, perchance in part if not in the whole, more naturally in the city. naturally] It is not clear why we should more reasonably expect the play to be performed in the city; cf. line 17 where "naturally" seems to mean "convincingly" or "in person." in...Citty] In the "private" theaters, Blackfriars or Whitefriars, presumably the latter. hole] Probably "whole," antithetical to "in part," but the phrase could be jocular self-disparagement since, as Sugden (p. 253) reports, "the hole" was a name given to a section of the debtor's prison, reserved for the poorest prisoners.

7. crancke] lively, high-spirited.

7-8. passe...currant] be admitted as fashionable.

8. againe...selfe] Chambers (III, 210) points out that Armin, being an adult, could not have performed with a children's company; the phrase therefore implies an earlier, unrecorded production of the play.

9. Tempora mutantur [nos et mutamur] in illis] Times

change and we change along with them. I...would] Grosart (p. viii) and nearly all subsequent commentators infer from this and "it may not be" (lines 17-18) that Armin's health prevented him from performing in the play, but see pp. 9-10.

11-12. whose...likely] Armin presumes that his audience will not have forgotten John's odd appearance.

Title.] "More-clacke" is a common corruption of Mortlake, in Surrey, ten or fifteen miles southwest of London. A tapestry weaving factory was set there during the reign of James I, as a result of which the town won some poetic recognition (cited in OED) by Cowley--"Mortclakes noble loom" (Several Discourses, 1680, p. 110)--and by Oldham--"a rich suit of Mortlack tapestry" (Imitations of Third Satire of Juvenal, 1684).

[Scene I]

0.1-.2. The ritualistic stage action referred to is described by Percy MacQuoid, Shakespeare's England (p. 146): "The bride's gloves also formed an important item of her costume, and these with some other pairs were generally presented to guests and the two bachelors who led her to church. The bridegroom was often conducted by the bridesmaids along the path strewn with flowers and rushes. In his account of the wedding of John Winchcombe, the wealthy clothier of Newbury, Thomas Deloney says: '...next there was a noise of musicians, that played all the way before her....' At the conclusion of the service a cup of muscadel with cakes or sops in it was drunk by the bride, the bridegroom, and the company." MacQuoid goes on to quote the stage directions of Two Maids but does not explain the reference to perfume, apparently thinking it sufficient evidence of a country custom. Flowers are strewn before the marriage of Theseus and Hippolyta in the opening scene of The Two Noble Kinsmen (1613), but I have found no other references to perfuming except in The Valiant Welshman (1615), which I believe to have been written by Armin (see Appendix A).

2. Muskadine] muscatel wine. stayes for] awaits.

9-12. The speech is Euphuistic in its employment of cumulative analogy. The lady is not as poor as Job but as devoid of ornament and wealth ("bare") as January, which is a time when trees are bare of color and when the cheeks of girls are made pale by the cold, which also freezes milk and causes the frost to come and go in milk as color comes and goes in the girl's cheeks.

14. false] OED gives no useful definition, but the context seems to indicate an ellipsis for "but now the expectation has proved to be incorrect."

15. How...poore.] Those who have honor are rich no matter how poor they are.

18-19. if...pray.] I wish a rich knight were fooled or deceived ("gulled") enough to marry me.

20. waits] A small body of wind instrumentalists maintained by the city at the public charge. They played for

the daily diversion of the councillors on ceremonial and festive occasions. They are referred to in Nashe's _Almond for a Parrot_, Jonson's _Silent Woman_, Fletcher's _Captain_, and Beaumont and Fletcher's _Knight of the Burning Pestle_, and many other works.

24-26. Humil calls for music and joy in heaven to match the harmony and unity betokened in the wedding ceremony. The speech implies the following analogies: music is to disorganized sound as weddings are to ordinary human relationships and as heaven is to earth. Fundamentally, however, he is drawing on the Platonic conception of "the music of the spheres," which, according to the _Timaeus_, is produced by Sirens, each of whom, in her particular sphere, sings notes whose pitch is conditioned by the velocity of the revolution of her sphere. The totality of these notes produces that world harmony which is inaccessible to human ears, and which is willed by the demi-urge, the world spirit.

27-28. Humil is personally triumphant because he believes that the wedding seals not only the marriage of his mother and Sir William but also the future union of himself with Mary, one of Sir William's daughters. Then his bride's blood will "sympathize" (_OED_ gives "agree...or contrive harmoniously") with his.

29. ours] Throughout the play the "gentle" characters refer to themselves in the first person plural, apparently in pompous affectation of the royal "we." It is probable

that Humil is so indulging himself here, since it is unlikely that he could mean that Mary will be "mother's and mine."

29-30. some...riualship] there are some competing suitors.

30-31. sure...ours] His mother's marriage is a "sure card" (i.e., trump or guarantee) that will assure his taking the "trick" (i.e., triumphing over Toures in the rivalry for Mary). Cf. Lyly's Euphues, A. IV., "a cleere conscience is a sure card" (cited OED).

34. seasond] spiced, unusually pleasant.

38. Good...starres] Though the phrase sounds as if it may be an allusion to a proverb or other stock idea, I can find no parallel. Undoubtedly there is a pun on "rich" (preceding line), since Kokeritz (p. 82) has shown that Shakespeare used reach and rich as rhymes. Furthermore, in A Nest of Ninnies (p. 15) Armin refers to those who "reach at stars, ayming at honour" but are rewarded with a whipping. Humil and his mother, too, are "ayming at honour" (i.e., social status) and will later suffer for it.

42. just...she] Grosart suggests that James points to her.

44. Rellish...them] I have altered the syntax but not the sense by my emendation (Q. prints "Rellishes in them"); "relish" means sexual pleasure, especially the anticipation of it, as when Troilus (Shakespeare's Troilus and Cressida, III.ii.17-19) thinks of his imminent meeting with Cressida:

> I am giddy; expectation whirls me round.
> Th' imaginary relish is so sweet
> That it enchants my sense.

If Q.'s reading is allowed to stand, the phrase is elliptical: "By this the blessing of the holy rights, and by the rellishes implied by them, they are married."

44-45. at...it] at least, almost so.

46. pleades nonage] indicates youthfulness.

47-50. tis...know] The difficult part of the passage is the restrictive clause, "Whose nature challenges right property/ Of perfect being." Ignoring that clause for the moment, we understand the passage to mean that if Humil were like the lion, he would know his true father. The allusion seems to be to the belief in the lion's capacity to see through disguises, which, according to A. R. Humphreys (I King Henry IV, II.iv.265-267n.), "is traceable back to Pliny." Falstaff defends himself against the charge of cowardice for not having attacked Prince Hal by claiming that instinct forbade him: "should I turn upon the true Prince? Why, thou knowest I am as valiant as Hercules: but beware instinct--the lion will not touch the true prince." This example, like the one in Thomas Lodge's A Margarite of America, and the others cited by Humphreys, involves the lion's recognition of royalty. I find no evidence that lions were thought capable of penetrating all disguises, and there is no indication in the play that James is wearing any disguise. Therefore the allusion is not as apt as one would like it to be and does not clarify the restrictive clause describing the lion. In what sense does a disguise-penetrating lion "challenge right property of perfect being"? If "challenge" means "defy," as it often does in the play, and if "property" means "propriety," Armin may be alluding to another belief about the lion. It was widely held that lions copulated backwards, surely a defiance of propriety. Sir Thomas Browne, in _Pseudodoxia Epidemica_ (ed. Keynes, III, 134) observes:

> if in the Lion the position of the pizell be proper, and that the natural situation, it will be hard to make out their retrocopulation, or their coupling and pissing backward.

He also notes (II, 249-250) that the lion, like the hare, does not have his "part designed unto the excretion of urine" in the "common position": it is "aversely seated," so that, apparently, the animals have to back into one another, making it difficult to distinguish male from female. It is curious that James, who is comparing the unnaturalness of retromingent creatures to his son's unnatural failure to recognize a briefly absent father, should say, "Tis _not_ the lyon's kinde."

53-54. thanke...funerall] This is the first of two crucial but cryptic allusions to letters James wrote prematurely announcing his death; the second appears at VI. 6-7. They are crucial because they provide the only exposition for Lady Vergir's assumption of widowhood (for a discussion of James's motives for the falsification, see VI.6-7n). They are cryptic because they both imply, absurdly, that James wrote to say that he was dead; in this passage he refers to "my letters," not to "the letters I had sent," and he implies that they dealt not with his impending death but with his funeral. At VI.6, the Lady asks "Why writ you dead?" The question is less absurd when one recalls that the Elizabethan idiom enabled Hamlet and other dying characters to say: "I am dead, Horatio" (Hamlet, V.ii.364).

55. follow it] consider the effects of it.

56-57. divide...hand] sever that bond ("band") which was formalized by the Lady's and Vergir's mutual hand clasp at the wedding.

[Scene II]

0.1. watermen] Watermen taxied small boats up and down the Thames; water-bearers carried water from the conduits to the houses in tankards or hooped wooden vessels. In this scene the men's remarks would seem to identify them as watermen, but in Scene X they are associated with a conduit. The speech tags, Wat and Fer, would seem to be abbreviations for waterman and ferryman, but Wat is used in line 2 in direct address as a name (perhaps short for Walter) and at X.23. the speech tag "Ferris" is given, thus indicating that Armin was ingenious enough to provide his characters with names which were also abbreviations of their occupations.

2-3. suit...bridegroomes] Pun on "suit," meaning

"request" and "apparel."

5-11. The ferryman argues that they are asses because, like animals carrying the hay which will be fed them, they are carrying money which will be used to buy their food.

12. by a figure] figuratively.

16. No...good.] is that the only similarity you can find? You're not so witty.

23. Obscure mock-logic. There may be a proverb lurking here or perhaps a pun on "prouender" (more proven, i.e., that you are an ass).

24-26. thinke...him] Wat's reference is to the frequent disappointment that arose when a waterman saw a prospective fare but was beaten to him by a hustling competitor.

30. officer] anyone who is charged with a duty to perform. The question seems to mean, "What, do you have an errand to do?"

31-32. _salue...salue_] hail, may you be in health.

33. _Iubio...aue_.] "I wish you health. Hello!" They are teasing Tutch for being "bookish" by being bookish themselves.

35-36. He is making out a shopping list.

37. Meaning us] I.e., the last, woodcocks (fools).

39. water-squirts] As watermen they occasionally splash water.

42. ha...doo't] do you have money to buy a drink with?

43-44. The ferryman's reply is an intricate double entendre, the words "do," "stand," and "spend" meaning one thing in terms of compotation and another in terms of fornication. In the first set of terms the statement means, "we have enough money (in the trunk) to stand (the word is still used today to mean "treat") all of us to a drink, if we were allowed to spend it." In the second set of terms it means, "we have the copulatory apparatus to fornicate and stand erect before a woman, if we might 'spend' an orgasmic emission. For "spend" and "stand" see Partridge's Shakespeare's Bawdy (pp. 191, 194).

45. beare in] carry the trunk in.

48-49. tutch...suckets] Humil directs Tutch to provide the waterman and ferryman with drinks from the cellar ("seller"), which may be either a store-room or a case of bottles. The context suggests that "suckets" is probably slang for "mugs," but none of the relevant dictionaries list it.

51. baste] moisten.

52. ierk't the cat] Partridge's Dictionary of Slang lists "jerk the cat" as a synonym of both "whip the cat" (to get intoxicated) and "shoot the cat" (to vomit). whippes] tongues.

53. tis ended] I.e., the wedding ceremony. The following lines are obscure, perhaps in imitation of a verbalized, ill-flowing stream of consciousness or perhaps through corruption of the text. Q. prints the first line of the speech as verse, ending with a dubious period, and the rest of the speech as prose. The crucial and ambiguous words are "pull,"

"fleece," and "golden." The context for "pull" seems to demand "turn" or "opportunity," which could refer to a "turn" at the wine bottle invoked by Tutch in the preceding lines or which could be borrowed from the jargon of card playing, as when one "pulls" for a high card. In either case, Humil avows that it is his turn at the eldest daughter, whom he refers to as the "golden fleece," "fleece" because she would be a prize illegitimately got (and perhaps because he is thinking of her pubic hair, which Partridge in DSUE gives as a synonym for "fleece"), and "golden" perhaps because she has a dowry or because she is a blond and certainly in allusion to the golden fleece which Jason sought for so cunningly in Greek mythology.

56-57. These two lines are rendered obscure by Armin's failure to provide clear antecedents for "it" and "'t," though "What then rests in it" may mean, "what remains to be done?" It is tempting to speculate that a line has been dropped between lines 49 and 50, which would contain a reference to a nest holding the heart of at least one of the maids; the golden, fleecy nest would be the referent for the impersonal pronouns which follow. O...to't] Lyly, in his "Epistle Dedicatory" to Euphues and his England (p. 4) confesses: "In this I resemble the Lapwing, who... flyeth with a false cry farre from their nestes." And in his Campaspe (II.ii.8): "Wherein you resemble the lapwing, who crieth most where her neast is not." Shakespeare makes similar allusions in Much Ado (III.i.25) and Measure for

Measure (I.iv.32). These examples indicate that the lapwing tried to mislead any who would attack its nest by pretending greatest concern when the would-be attacker moved away from it. In order to protect what was precious, it acted as a decoy. Humil may mean that the girls are only pretending an interest in his competitors, Toures and Filbon, to conceal their real interest in him. He may be consoling himself that the girls retreat fastest when he comes closest to their hearts.

58-59. Quando...amores] Professor John O'Connor suggests that this is probably a quotation, or misquotation, from a piece of pastoral poetry. In light of some irregularities in the Latin, he offers the following as a tentative translation: "When the herd grazes in the shade, we name over our loves."

[Scene III]

1. Whether the initial "it" refers to the wedding or to his return home, clearly James is bemoaning the fact that it is too late to repair the damage.

2-4. Tardie...pretious] Due to his belated intrusion, he is merely taking up space in the household, like a cipher (zero) placed before a whole number, while Sir William's wealth ("substance in the other") has persuasive value with his wife ("makes number pretious").

4-6. I...mone] He imagines himself a "round O," a cipher, a nothing, which, sadly, recognizes its loss too late.

8-9. To...danger] He admonishes himself that by exposing his identity, he will also expose Sir William to ridicule, thus further exposing himself to Sir William's dangerous wrath.

9-12. O...am] In his strained, extended metaphor he is over-ripe fruit, over-zealous tree, and negligent pruner. The conceit is reminiscent of the one employed by the player King in _Hamlet_, III.ii.202-203, who speaks of purposes

> Which now, like fruit unripe, sticks on the tree,
> But fall unshaken when they mellow be.

13. indeede] an intensive, also a pun: "in fact."

14. These...words] The words he had written in the letter announcing his death.

16. stand] position.

18. what she was] I.e., his wife.

19. picture] image, face.

22. attempt] act, undertaking.

23. second choice] new husband.

24. witnesse] glance of recognition.

24-25. my...ioy] Paraphrased, the Lady's speech means, "Having witnessed my first husband's reappearance, my disloyalty to him has slain my hopes for those joys which normally are concurrent with marriage."

26. Euen...look't] The phrasing indicates that the Lady believes she has seen only something that looks like James, not James himself but probably his "spirit" or ghost. It

was an Elizabethan theatrical convention to have characters express wonder and skepticism at the appearance of ghosts (cf. Hamlet, I.ii.44) but scenes in which living people are thought to be ghosts are rare.

27. estranged] alien, unexpected; or she may think of James's death as one which estranges her from him.

29. To...vndo] The same estranged death which gave her license to say "I do" now requires her to "vndo" her vow.

30. Weake...sect] I who am weak in the duty of my sex (i.e., to remain faithful to my husband).

33. losse] i.e., of the glove.

35. purchase] gain. crosse] burden, loss.

37. constant] Grosart's gloss is: "somewhat unusual use of the word, but as 'fixed' may have meant 'intentional'!" But perhaps James means that the "accident" indicates her "constancy."

38. subscribes] reinforces, confirms.

41. late...life] lately or recently lived life.

45. difference] indifference.

46. president] precedent.

48. Who] Which.

49. destiue] Either a neologism or a misprint for "destined."

54. In...wretchednesse] With the memory or consciousness of the shame she would experience as a bigamist.

56. buckler...wiu'd] James must contrive to defend his reputation against the charge of being married to a weak

woman or a woman weakly tied by marriage.

[Scene IV]

4. triumph] tournament. helme] helmet.

5. approue] prove.

6. owes] owns.

7. challenge...account] defy or disprove your version.

8. by my friend] Incoherent as it stands; perhaps the line should read, "To find it, my friend, by my industry."

9-10. Grosart notes that they are referring to the sport of "Running at the glove" which was similar to "Running at the Ring." Curuet] to execute a leap in which the horse's forelegs are raised together and equally advanced and the hind-legs raised with a spring before the forelegs reach the ground. course of armes] the rush together of two combatants in a tournament.

11. curious] expert, skillful.

[Scene V]

5. Arch...votaries] Create an arch in the brows of the two young men devoted to the Goddess of Love.

10. el] ell, a measure of length (an English ell is 45 inches). Tilley (I, 56) cites: "As good is an inch as is an ell." "Give an inch and he will take an ell." "He prefers an inch of his pleasure before an ell of his profit." In this line and the next Tabitha humorously reveals her vain, contradictory, jealous, feminine nature, jeering at the men for (1) seeking disproportionate rewards

("kisses," "amorous glances," and "modest curtesie"), and (2) working too diligently for "little pay." At the same time she satirizes and belittles her stepmother, who, having a son presumably the same age as the suitors, would look ridiculous indulging in such coquetry.

13. Mary scoffs at her sister's outburst of trumped up scorn for their suitors, saying that Tabitha is like all those girls who say "Go to, _etc_." to the men who make passes at them, even though they are actually delighted.

15. To...haunce] "English rash" may refer to a smooth textile fabric made of silk or worsted, but since the context implies that "rash" is something abrasive or unpleasant, it is not clear how this definition would be appropriate. _OED_ supports Grosart's belief that "rash" was a variant spelling of "ratch." A "ratch" was a fire-lock, a kind of musket which was ignited by the abrasive rubbing of flint on powder. A "Dutch snap haunce" was a kind of wheel-lock gun. Thus Mary seems to saying in later vernacular, "The man who marries you marries a hot pistol"; i.e., a tough, fiery, violent, passionate woman with a tongue so flinty it can strike a fire.

18-19. Mary interrupts Tabitha, correctly filling in the thought (see Tabitha's response). this light] Apparently Mary is holding a light, a candle of some kind, which Tabitha points to; "wincke" suggests blinking, as does "simper" (line 21). See also notes to lines 34 and 36 below.

20-23. The difficult words in the passage are "simper" and "quantitie," which I cannot satisfactorily explain, but the sense seems to be, "It's hard to outwit you, you devil; we sisters are so sensitive to one another's rhythms and thoughts that it's as if we knew the new fashions before they were even devised." Perhaps she also implies that they are so foresighted that they actually already know what marriage will be like, so they may as well forswear or disavow their suitors.

24. Again Mary completes Tabitha's thought and seems to agree with it. just...so] Exactly!

25. The question indicates that she has already changed her mind, however.

26. Tabitha recognizes that if Mary must speak honestly, she will have to refuse to forswear her lover.

27. I] Aye. You are right.

28-29. Quibbles on I-aye and no-know.

34. folding] enfolding? misprint for "holding"? Mary probably fondles an object, perhaps the candle suggested in the note to line 18.

35. as...yearely] Here and in lines 39-44 Tabitha seems to be teasing Mary for insufficient ardor, for wanting her lover only once a year. But she also puns on the homonym of "yearely": "yarely," meaning "quickly."

36. such...sort] Again she apparently gestures suggestively.

37. A double entendre: Mary's embraces are as meaningless

or passionless as a child's playing with stones, but "stones" equals "testicles" (see Partridge, _Shakespeare's Bawdy_) and "sport" may be pronounced "spurt."

38. She blushes at the bawdy pun.

39. Tabitha says, "You blush not at my words but at your own desires."

40. A woman who does not like sex is like a cat that doesn't like fish and milk.

41. pictures] imitations, images. faine] fain or feign. Tabitha's idea here and in the next line can be interpreted in at least two slightly different ways: "We women all appear to be maidens; yet fain (gladly) would we yield to our desires though we kittenishly tell men to go away when it is _we_ who should go away (either out of shame for our hypocrisy or to protect what we claim to value)." Or, "We all feign (pretend) to be pictures of maidenhood; yet we merely tell men to leave us alone rather than leave them."

44-45. Tabitha claims she has "never yet" slept with Filbon but will ever be doing so when "our matters fit." The latter phrase can be read in three ways: (1) "matter's fit," meaning the situation is suitable (i.e., when we are married); (2a) "matters fit," i.e., plans jell; (2b) "matters fit," genitals are joined.

53. Filbon's answer, as it stands, is gibberish, but a simple transposition supplies a meaningful one: "By finding you that lost not what we sought." The sexual symbolism in referring to the women as the men's "gloves" is patent.

54-55. Tabitha points to the paradox that to lose or give up something willingly is to gain the receiver's or finder's pity, affection, or gratitude.

56-57. The passage is probably deliberately obscure, suggesting by means of archly cryptic rhetorical structures the speaker's hesitation to reveal her concerns too baldly. The ambiguous badinage of Shakespeare's witty lovers sometimes aims for the same effect. Perhaps the passage can best be paraphrased this way: "I will not say the finder _enjoys_ the loser's pain; on the contrary, he will not, because the giver (Tabitha) protests against ("cries out on") her father, who tries to prevent the gift-giving by obstructing the marriage." There are other possibilities as to which of the mates feels pain or enjoyment and which cries out on the father, but the central thought of the extended quibble involves equating the glove with maidenhood.

58-59. Tabitha admits that if she dared defy her father and give herself to Filbon, she would, but until the time when marriage is possible, they must disjoin their hands and gloves to symbolize their celibacy.

67. Punctuate, "I take it on me. Musicke! Triumphs come!"

70-72. James gratefully accepts his duties and privileges as governor (a kind of master of ceremonies), saying, "I am only a citizen, who came unthinkingly, not looking for welcome or honor in a statesman's room."

73. addresse] direct my attention to.

77. Prooue on] Strive on! He is challenging fortune to test him, believing himself fortunate, regardless of whatever luck he may have, as long as he has Mary.

80-81. And...love] The sum of the fairest fortune I could hope to experience ("prove") is only this: to enjoy my fairest love.

83. thy] Tabitha's.

84. hers] Mary's. Humil is seeking Mary.

84-46. Humil wishes Tabitha and Filbon well but not Mary and Toures; on them he wishes mischief and horror unless he himself receives (participates in) a freely delivered offer of his choice.

88. his] its.

[Scene VI]

2-4. A strained and strange metaphor. The "all wondring eies" are evidently stars, whose "fire[s] flame," but what are the stars' "eie-balles"? And what is "moist imagination"? If James means that the stars should drop tears, like eyes, how are they to flame at the same time? Armin seems to begin with the metaphysical conceit that stars are the eyes of heaven (a notion pursued in Herbert's "Ode Upon a Question moved..." and Carew's "Song: Ask me no more") and then move on to suggest that they should have eyeballs and shed tears. Perhaps the word "tears" has been omitted after "drop" and "imagination" is a catachresis for "recognition."

6. In I.53 James referred to "my letters"; the Lady's phrasing here again perpetuates the bizarre and absurd implication that James himself wrote to say "I am dead."

7. Sick...life] Q. assigns this line to the Lady; if Q. were correct, the line would have to be interpreted either as her jeering paraphrase of his letters (a reading rendered implausible by her use of the past tense) or as a description of her reaction to the news of his death. Neither of these seems as likely as the probability that James utters the line to provide his only explanation for writing or sending the letters.

8-10. Grosart attributes these lines to the Lady, arguing that James "counterfeited to be dead, while she could in no way be said to have counterfeited." This argument creates more problems than it solves. The threat to "make it knowne," which begins with the word "no" on line 9, must be assigned to James, since this is the position he takes in regard to disclosure throughout the play, so that if Grosart is to have his way, he must argue that the compositor misassigned three different speeches. The word "counterfeiting," which is such a hurdle to Grosart, can sensibly be applied to the Lady since in James's eyes she, like King Hamlet's Gertrude, has shown herself to be a "false wife" (i.e., a counterfeit) in her haste to present herself as a marriageable widow.

12. All...yours] She denies she has done him injury,

claiming the opposite to be true.

13. Putting...weakenesse] Even if James were telling the truth in line 7, when he says he believed that he was dying, Lady Vergir is quite justified in looking for another motive for his precipitate necrology; he could have followed it, after all, with notice of his recovery. He does not deny the accusation she makes here that he was testing her fidelity as Walter did Griselda's in Chaucer's "Clerk's Tale."

14-15. Which...ill] The syntax is unclear, but the sense seems to be that, "the letters being believed, the woman, in her decision, is a guiltless causer of the ill."

16-17. but...speede] This is an interruptive phrase and would today probably be set off with dashes.

19. Baud...misdeede] She charges that the effect of his death announcement was to oblige her unknowingly to prostitute herself; thus he acted as a pimp to his own wife and brought on his own misfortune.

20-21. Furthermore, she claims that he is three-quarters responsible for their difficult position, since he could have avoided the risk.

22. She asks if he will further compound their troubles by miraculously returning to life.

23. worse...note] more publicly infamous.

24. bauins blaze] punctuate, "blaze?" A bavin is a bundle of brush wood; cf. _I Henry IV_, III.ii.61, "bavin wits, having a quick and short-lived blaze."

26. water-course] a bed or channel for the conveyance of water.

27. I...myself] The clause probably means here, as it does elsewhere in Elizabethan literature, "I am beside myself" (out of my wits). But it is also possible that James is here, as in I.54-55 ("blame her not, Tis my owne proiect, thanke my letters"), accepting responsibility for their misfortune, saying "I am in this difficulty from my own misbehavior."

28-29. mischiefe...purpose] mischief, unaware of our honorable intentions ("unwitting of all purpose") and therefore blind and crushing, menaces us.

31. stickler] governor, moderator, or umpire at a tournament.

32. a...practise] Grosart suggests "a point-prevailing practice" but does not explain what such a practice would be. Two more reasonable readings are: (1) that "prevailing" means "exceeding" and the Lady is regretting that she gave him power to a point beyond the usual practice, or (2) that we have a misprint for "appoint [the] prevailing practice," meaning that the Lady ordered that the prevailing practice of rewarding finders of lost objects be acted upon.

33. A non-sequitur. She has asked "why," not "how." His reply may be elliptical, meaning, "I know not how to solve our problem."

35. wits-charter] _OED_ cites no other examples of this combination, but the Lady is expressing the notion that

women in trouble have been granted a charter by the gods that authorizes them to use their wits to avoid suffering. Such a notion is clearly enunciated in Chaucer's "Merchant's Tale," where May, the adulterous bride, is enabled to lie her way out of a compromising situation. As Queen Proserpine says in her defense:

> Now by my moodres sires soule I swere
> That I shal yeven hire suffisant answere,
> And alle wommen after, for hir sake;
> That, though they be in any gilt ytake,
> With face boold they shulle hemselfe excuse,
> And bere hem doun that wolden hem accuse.

36-37. that...Which] to digest that which.

40. ly with] pun: have sexual intercourse with/deceive.

44. simply] innocently.

47. salue] save from loss. taint] coloring, dye.

48. build on] put faith in.

49. Some moneth] Perhaps elliptical for "I need about a month." Another possibility is that "moneth" is a variant spelling of "moaneth," by which the Lady might mean either that other women in her situation would moan and give up or that she will be moaning inwardly during the time that she retains her new name in order to marry off her son.

50. glory...name] the power that comes of having Sir William's name through being his wife.

51. Attendances according] attendants, retinue appropriate to my rank.

53. ioynter] jointure, a covenant whereby the husband assures his wife, in return for their marriage, lands or

tenements for the term of her life.

57. single] unmarried instead of bigamous. blame] exposure and condemnation.

58. Behooues] It behooves us to.

61. noble...expects] May refer to the Earl of Tumult, or perhaps verb and subject should be made plural.

62. does...itself] is neglected by its central figure, the bride.

65. commanding] exalted.

66. retaines] preserves, or malapropism for "sustains."

67. ours before] a pun referring to her health and her first husband.

68. yeeld] yield to.

69-70. Will...yours] Perhaps elliptical for, "if you would serve my marriage best, begin your own properly." "Begin" may be a misprint for "being," but the syntax would be no clearer.

[Scene VII]

3. pardon] freedom. presume] be presumptuous.

4. challendge] demanded. Lines 2-4 are difficult, partly because the subject of "doos proclaime" may be either "we" or "deity." Of the three following readings, I prefer the first: (1) "we, to whom Love has given pardon to presume and speak (that is, to leave the banquet unconventionally and exchange love-talk), demand our liberty"; (2) "we, who proclaim love's deity, beg pardon to presume

and speak and demand liberty"; (3) "we, whom love's deity proclaims pardon to, presume and speak and demand liberty."

6-10. Sir...curiositie] Paraphrased, this yields: Sir, I _will_ swear, and till I lack my liberty and maidenhead (_via_ marriage), no matter what you say, nothing shall stop me; I would rather feed on the delights of lovers' fantasies than be gagged with the attention of others in whose presence I would have to be excessively careful to hide my thoughts. In _As You Like It_, IV.iii.101-102, Orlando, the stereotype of the romantic lover, leaves Rosalind "chewing the food of sweet and bitter fancy." Spurgeon (pp. 146-147) confirms that conceits equating love with food are common in Elizabethan literature.

22. by rule] with propriety.

24. Drest] cooked, prepared to eat. to my hand] close by, accessible.

25. maids modicum] a pun: female pudendum. _OED_ cites Cotton, _Scoffer Scofft_, 1675, "Such knees, such thighs, and such a bum and such a, such a Modicum." In _A Nest of Ninnies_ Armin uses the word twice with the apparent meaning of "small repast," but the context of one of the two usages indicates that the bawdy pun was intended.

29. Mot] Not? Moot? The context provides no good clue as to what is meant. If the line were emended to "Not I, as I am of Louers union/ Contracted...," the statement would mean: Not I (i.e., _I_ won't be the one to "feed" your "dish"), because I am contracted to a solitary or celibate

life by the rule of our lovers' union (engagement vows). If the word "moot" is meant, the sense would be, "Doubtful as I am of lovers' unions, being contracted to the solitary life, and thus retaining singleness of heart...." The most reasonable explanation is that "mot" is a form of the archaic verb "mote," which, according to OED, was occasionally spelled as we have it here. The verb is akin to our "may" and "might," in some cases expressing necessity or obligation; thus the line would be paraphrased: "Obligated as I am to (or 'by') a lovers' union."

29-31. Mot...heart] Regardless of the syntax of these lines, the words "union" and "Contracted" along with "sollitarie" and "singlenes" suggest that Toures is reaffirming some vow of chastity he has made with Mary. The phrase "singlenes of heart" (apparently meaning "bachelorhood") is echoed by Filbon at XII.24-25, where he replies to the question, "seest thou yong Toures?" by answering, "Not since our last repulse in loue, since when I stand affected vnto singlenes of life."

32-33. Changing] The word may be equivalent to our "exchanging" or it may mean something more like "experiencing" or "enduring." If "exchanging" is meant, the passage, in context, would be paraphrased as "by retaining singleness of heart (i.e., bachelorhood and undivided affection) I exchange all doubts which arise from the whims of passion for the one certainty of our mutual love." If "experiencing" is meant, a paraphrase would leave, "by maintaining celibacy I experience all doubts that arise from my fears that our love will never be consummated, but I am still certain of your goodness and faith."

34. idea...thoughts] Toures draws on the Platonic conception of the beloved as pure objectification or symbol of the ideal.

35. reconciled amitie] contented friendship.

37. his] its.

38. alienates] separates us from. At this point in the play the audience has no reason to believe that Sir William seeks to separate the lovers from their choice of one another. Hints and suspicions of his rejection of Toures and Filbon are developed as this scene progresses, but his position is not made explicit until Scene VIII.76-80.

39. sunne-shine...raine] The implied metaphor is ambiguous. Toures may mean either that Sir William is hypocritically pretending to be like hope-inspiring sunshine while he is actually a hope-quashing rain cloud or that the father is simply a sunshine-threatening rain, inimicable to the brightness of their love.

41. which...cleare] i.e., evidence for which impression is that *etc*.

41-42. honourable...regard] Probably uttered in an ironic tone.

43. past...attention] Perhaps, "surpassed their normal rate of attention to us." Sir William is being overzealous.

44. their] The pronoun lacks a logical antecedent since what follows seems to demand that the pronoun refer to the lovers' attempts to marry.

44-46. Toures expects Sir William to respond to their pressure for his approval as a soldier responds to a battle, enjoying it and bidding it come even while resisting it.

55. other...merriments] Structurally, the place of this phrase in the sentence is that of a final element in the series of things that are "made free." The grammar of the phrase itself is ambiguous, however; "dues" may be, generally, "matters owing or owed to time's merriements" (i.e., all things arising from the celebration of the occasion), or "dues" may be an allusion to the practice of the bride's selling ale and food to guests, who paid what price they chose for it (see Jonson's *A Tale of a Tub*, I.i.95n).

66-90. The text for these lines, which are printed on the lower half of signature B3, is quite ragged if not corrupt. Speech prefixes are missing at lines 70 and 77, for instance. Of thirteen full-length lines only six (66, 71, 72, 77, 82, and 87) are quite regular iambic pentameter, but these are enough, I think, to indicate that Armin intends the passage to be in verse, though there is cause for wonder. The seven remaining full-length lines present various problems. Line 79 has an initial trochee followed by five iambs, which is no cause for alarm. Line 84, however, is either prose or very irregular poetry; it has nine syllables, the last four making two iambic feet. _Q_. prints lines 85-86 very oddly: "Yeeld...there./ Musique...round"; if this is meant as prose, why is it broken into a short line and a long one? I have recast them to provide an extremely irregular (actually prosaic) line followed by a rhyming regular iambic pentameter line. Line 87 contains an initial trochee followed by four iambs and seems to be meant as verse. _Q_. prints the next lines: "Select... Labits,/ Turne...may/ partake...sports." I have recast this metrical anarchy to provide an iambic half-line ("Select...does"), followed by a line made up of an initial trochee and four iambs and another containing an initial trochee and five iambs.

67. excuse...so] Toures tells Mary to pretend to be absorbed in dancing as an excuse for ignoring Humil.

69. in againe] step into the dance again.

78. Brainford] Brentford, a town outside London, a resort and playground for the frivolous. Thus the expression means "go get some brains, you need them."

82. by...hence] A strange idiom; perhaps "slaves to violence hurry hence (i.e., to their deaths)" or "slavish people are hurried hence violence."

85. Yeeld...it] yield to your obligations as wedding guests to remain at peace. hall...there] clear a space on the dance floor.

86. round] of dancing.

87. cul...bucks] pick out your gay young men.

89. Labits] Neither Grosart nor I am able to identify this term; perhaps it is a neologism taken from the French _lapin_ (hare) and English "rabbit." toiles] snares, traps.

91. woodman] huntsman.

94-97. Sir William begins his speech by apparently reassuring the two fathers that he agrees that his daughters will make appropriate brides for their sons, but, assuming "these giddy gamesters" refers to Toures and Filbon, he then shifts at "the bucks..." to muttering a denial of their eligibility; the muttering cannot be a conventional aside, however, since Toures overhears it, as indicated by his next question. It is also possible, of course, that "giddy gamesters" refers not to Toures and Filbon but to the younger generation at large and from which Toures and Filbon, by way of a compliment, are being excluded. This latter possibility, it must be admitted, is not supported by the ensuing dialogue, since the young people read an unfavorable meaning into Sir William's remarks.

99. Mary indicates that Sir William's words are the warning flash before a heated family quarrel.

100. Filbon fears that Sir William's demeanor foreshadows opposition to their marriage.

101. coate] daughter, female symbol.

103-104. James calls for another couple to dance, the measure (a grave or stately dance) requiring at least three couples.

108. were] Emphatic.

112. The obscurity of the line is largely due to the absence of antecedents for "It" and "his." Perhaps the Lady means that her dancing brightens the luster of James's honorary position.

113. warrant] the authority granted to James by Sir William. James is pointing to the paradox that Sir William has given him the right and power to command Lady Vergir, so that he can better win her while Sir William loses her.

115. heres...loue] Sir William remarks that he has several love-intrigues to iron out.

116. One] i.e., Toures. challenging] demanding.

117. And...vnknowne] and with reason, Mary, since your fate is yet unknown.

118-119. Shifting his attention to Humil, Sir William acknowledges that his stepson's future is unknown, too; his past words have hinted it, but his subsequent deeds will cement it.

121-122. what...friending] The text is apparently corrupt, but a reasonable paraphrase might be "what justice exists that is not partial ["friending"] to her own?" The unusual word "friending" is used by Hamlet (I.v.212), who expresses his "love and friending" to Horatio and others, though Shakespeare uses it as a noun while Armin uses it as an adjective.

125. Stations] Though I can find no authority, the context indicates that the word means "steps through." measure] i.e., of the dance.

127. Saturne] Humil is identified with the remotest, and therefore coldest, planet known in Armin's time or with a less attractive god than Jove (line 125).

131. 't] her glance.

132. Guilding...hope] making my torture more bearable by offering hope of pleasantries to come. Compare "after hope" with "after deedes" (VII.119), "after ioy" (II.25), and "after venny" (XXI.19).

133. moroliz'd] interpreted.

134. challeng'd] demanded.

134.1. blew coates] Nares notes: "Blue was a colour appropriated to the dresses of particular persons in low life," including servants, law officers, beadles, wards, and patients. For the historicity of John and his conversation, see pp. 62-63.

137. Tardi venientis] Probably intended to be Latin for "You arrive late."

138. Quaso...quid] "Quaso" is probably an error, either Armin's or the printer's, for "quasi." Thus Sir William, after telling John he is to be whipped, says, "As your teacher, [I can] not [do] anything for you."

140. Vtters...gaine] Probably elliptical for "utters much that would lead one to hope for matter (sense), but offers small reward for that hope."

141-144. This same biographical sketch and much of the dialogue appear in Armin's Nest of Ninnies (Works, pp. 50-53).

149-150. caret nominatiuo] "the nominative is missing."

151. reddish] radish, picks up the pun on caret-carrot.

156. Deane Nowel] Sir Alexander Nowell (Nowel or Noel), Dean of St. Paul's (1561-1589), died in 1602 at the age of ninety-five. The allusion provides strong evidence that the play is set in Elizabeth's era, though not necessarily before 1589 since Nowel, who preached the "Spital sermons," held a sinecure in the neighborhood until his death and could have been seen by John up to that time. See p. 16 for the relevance of the allusion for dating the play.

161. point] a strip of lace used to hold clothing up.

164. fooles head] the head at the end of the stick often carried by professional fools.

168. whose] who's.

169. In _A Nest of Ninnies_ (_Works_, p. 51) Armin writes that the sexton of Christ's Church "would often set John aworke to toull the bell to prayers or burials, wherin he delighted much." The dialogue to line 174 also appears in _A Nest of Ninnies_ (pp. 51-52).

177. ries] I can find no parallel for this spelling of "rise," if that is what is meant; perhaps the printer made an error by inversion of the last two letters or he may have omitted the "t" from "rites."

181. her] i.e., the Court, Queen Elizabeth, see p. 16. Grosart would punctuate, "We will attend her. Kind Sir William Vergin [_sic_],/ Our time is bride-groome to yourself and you;" I quite agree that we would require a full-stop

after "her," but I take "Our times bridegroome" (meaning, the bridegroom of the moment) to be in apposition to "Sir William Vergir."

183-188. amends] powers to change matters. The Earl is saying, in effect, "if there's ever anything I or my office can do for you, let me know. Having acknowledged my benevolent intentions toward you, I bid you adieu as an infrequent visitor but loyal friend."

190-192. The Earl assures Auditor that whatever his son lacks in wealth to assure his success in love, the Earl will supply.

193-196. These lines are important for providing a motive for Sir William's plot-thickening rejection of Toures and Filbon as sons-in-law, but they are not clear. In the preceding speech the Earl has used a conceit involving balance scales in which Filbon's worth as a potential mate is matched with Tabitha's. The Earl has said that he would provide Filbon with sufficient gold to match Tabitha's worth. In this speech Sir William continues the conceit but seems to reject Filbon even with his newly promised wealth. Perhaps "theirs" (line 189) refers to his daughters, in which case the speech means, "It won't take much gold, my daughters' dowries will grow less if they don't judge better than to marry Toures and Filbon." I can find no authority for this use of "poize," which is obviously drawn from the balancing conceit, but "weie," of course, is a familiar metaphor for "evaluate" or "judge."

198-199. make...legge] make an elegant bow.

201. Queene] More evidence that the play is set in Elizabeth's era. See p. 16.

[Scene VIII]

4. looke...way] Since Sir William has ruled out Toures, he must have no specific substitute for Humil in mind.

7. Grosart would punctuate the line as a question, saying "yet" means "nevertheless." He may be right, but the line may be an imperative statement, a threat.

10. accord] The context requires that the word mean something like "opinion," but OED gives no parallel for that meaning.

12. selfe] self-same. dye] mould, die. wee] emphatic. The Lady tells him that a father cannot be condemned for marrying his daughter into the same family he has chosen.

13-17. her...stroke] the value of her beauty, which in the minds of others has been made more stunning by my boasting ("vantings"), entitles her to look to a higher peak of social standing ("promintoria"), which, should your son look down from it, would make him dizzy, moon-struck.

24-25. when...death] Armin invents the conceit that a word or vow, like a body, can be said to have a posture and that posture would be base should the word lie (down); furthermore, the posture of a lying word is an imposture, a deception. If his promise (word) to allow Mary to marry Humil and her promise to refuse him her bed are broken, if they lie (pun: tell untruths and cohabit), she will die (sexually and spiritually).

29. lists] scenes of tournament combat. He means, "all right, let the battle between us be joined."

31-32. keepe...mine] I will break my vow of abstinence when you keep your promise to my son.

34. Haue...thou] He demands to know if, after he has picked her up from the gutter, an indigent widow, and made her a respectable lady, she will have the ingratitude to deny him his marital rights.

35-39. She replies that since he has cavalierly broken ("loosely fractured") oaths and vows, it is lawful for her to shun the bed that would normally make peace by bringing them together.

40. Exit Lady] Since the Lady does not speak again in the scene and since a quarrel has just ended, I think it likely that she exits here, but Sir William remains on stage and there is no scene division required.

43. next] i.e., next to be married.

44. past it] Probably "past thinking about it" or "past allowing them to marry."

45. praid vnto] pleaded with; i.e., by their sons to arrange their marriages.

48. past] passed.

55. auouchments] guarantees, declarations.

56. ye] Grosart recommends "yea."

57. Vnder...of] of lesser rank than.

58. toule...on] draw them on by enticement.

59. choice] eminent gentlemen.

61-66. Looke...hand] Puns on "reach," "richer," and "reaching." Sir Rafe has argued that the higher nobility values the honor of a good match (i.e., rank) more than Sir William's money. Sir William replies: "Let [those men of] honour look to heaven, my money ("earthly reach") is so great that it takes level aim at that noble, heaven-looking eye, and with the attractiveness of that money I'll buy the nobility who have only rank ("imprisond scope of reaching blood"). What cannot money do when its possessor is determined enough?

68. quaint] fashionable.

69. earths...starres] The phrase reminds one of Shakespeare's sonnet 130 ("My mistress, when she walks, treads the ground"), in which there is a thematic contrast between the earthly real and the heavenly ideal, but Armin's phrase is illogical because the bright stars (presumably, ethereal aristocratic types) are made to tread the earth.

77-78. Armin imitates a riddling formula often used in medieval romances, and subsequently, for example, in _Macbeth_: X will occur only after Y, Y seeming to be impossible. I can find no source for Sir William's specific oracular pronouncements, though this is the common formula for prophecies.

82-83. when...woman] when you make a woman of yourself.

84-85. Filbon is understandably bemused by an admonition

to sexual transformation; thus he speaks in fragments: "if I marry her after I am 'from myself a woman,' we will be joining woman to woman, a cause for wonder which I refuse to participate in."

89. scandall] disgrace.

94. shine] Grosart would emend to "shrine," but the text is sensible as it stands: Toures' eyes shine with adoration of Mary's heart.

96-97. hie...eie] high, out of the reach of a gentleman.

100. except] accept.

103-104. One "with" is redundant.

[Scene IX]

2. hudwincht] hoodwinked, deceived. pertaking] sharing; thus sympathetic.

10. are...possest] I.e., by demons; but also "in possession of a woman by means of sexual intercourse."

14. challeng'd it] demanded that he keep his word.

15. maine] Q. prints "morne," which is senseless, but James compares their troubles to a "maine" (i.e., ocean) in line 43 below. choller] choleric.

16-17. pause...contrarie] Dictionaries give no clue as to the meaning of this phrase; perhaps it is an inkhorn expression used by James to imply that Sir William said something like "Oh no you don't, just hold on a minute."

18. subscrib'd too] agreed to. which...doe] The phrase would *seem* to mean "which to do else (otherwise)," but such

an interpretation does not fit the context, which probably demands that we read it as an elliptical expression for "about which there was nothing else to do."

18-20. sooner...challenges] sooner should earth presume to travel ("a progesse") to heaven than the granting of Sir William's promise should yield to and affirm ("make firm") what the Lady ("the [thy?] antecedent," mother) demands ("challenges").

23-24. such...purchase] "such a cloze to day" and "such a wedding night" are in parallel construction. never... practise] was not customary. We would probably use "precedent" as a synonym for "practise" here.

25. purchase] At III.35 and IX.49 "purchase" means "gain," so James may mean that such a wedding night has never been profitable up to now. agree] reconcile.

26. attone] attune. iarre] discord.

33-36. For press variants, see Appendix B. Humil compares James's treatment of him to a king's treatment of a seldom-seen servant who receives much praise but little of use, e.g., money.

36. in...necessitie] Perhaps "out of necessitie," but more probably "at the mercy of cruel forces beyond my control," "necessitie" being the medieval equivalent of our "determinism." di'de] died.

38. wants...proofe] remains to be seen. stand by] This verb lacks a subject unless it is hortatory and addressed to time's "minion" and inconstancy. Time's "minion" might

be her daughter, "Truth," the opposite of inconstancy, or Fortune, its equivalent.

41-45. The passage is important for explaining Humil's petty viciousness and ambition as the result of his bitterness over his father's abandonment of him. tickles] As is common in the play and elsewhere in Elizabethan literature, a singular verb is used with a plural subject.

52. scatter...intents] disrupt and lay waste our plans.

53. idle purchase] a gain got without work. He fears that beachcombers may profit from their misfortune.

54-57. my...flood] the injury to my position ("state") may be healed ("salu'd") by a wise response to and handling of the situation ("occasion"), thus turning to advantage ("make good") this unexpected misfortune ("sudden overflow of tide and flood"). foil'd] defeated, trampled upon.

[Scene X]

2. crow] John is apparently fond of attributing events to a non-existent crow; see line 19 below.

5. counter-hole] I can find no allusion to this game in the literature or scholarship of the period.

6. counter] Presumably the toy used in the game, perhaps a kind of top (see note line 12).

7. point] The boy may mean a lead in the score of the game, a point advantage, but John takes him to mean the string or cord which holds up his trousers.

8. hose] pants.

8-10. O...too] This may be either the nonsense talk of a "natural" or a kind of incantation used in such games.

12. lagge] last (in my own childhood we yelled "larry" when we wanted to take our turn last). hoblies hole] Grosart notes, "Halliwell gives 'Hobler-hole,' the hinder hole at a boys game, alluded to in Clarke's Phraseologie Puerilis, 1655, p. 255. From our passage the 'boys game' was Counter-hole."

17. muckender] handkerchief.

19. crow] See line 2 above.

20-22. John's cries in line 22 seem to be in response to a whipping; therefore, "him" (lines 20 and 21) may refer to John, as she picks him up to whip him, or to his breeches, which may be falling down due to the lost point, or to the point itself. Armin frequently uses personal pronouns to refer to inanimate objects (see pp. 46-47).

23. suck-egge] Partridge's Dictionary of Slang gives "silly fellow."

24. moueable matron] The ferryman is engaged in hauling--in transportation; hence he speaks of the nurse as "moueable," perhaps suggesting that she is a piece of baggage (a saucy or wanton young woman). tugegge] Grosart says this is the same thing as "suck-egge," but he does not say what "suck-egge" means or how he knows the two words mean the same thing. More probably, "tugegge" is the ferryman's comic coinage, modeled on luggage and baggage.

28. Lothbery conduit] A conduit is an artificial pipe or

channel for the conveyance of water, usually for sewage. Watercarriers picked up their load at the conduit. Sugden (p. 319) reports that Lothbery Street was "in London, north of the Bank of England, running east from the corner of Moorgate St. to Throgmorton St.... There was a conduit at the corner of Lothbery and Coleman St."

30. Sternigogilus] A nonce word meaning, as the boy indicates, "a goggle eye, a madcap."

33-34. The waterman responds to a pun on what/wat.

35. Partridge, in _Shakespeare's Bawdy_, gives these entries: "trim" alludes to sexual intercourse; "boat," he says, "may be the female body..., a rich prize that a man is ready to board; or it may be a shape-allusion to the female pudend"; "turn" may mean "to seek sexually"; and "head" may refer to maidenhead. muscherumpe] mushroom, which is shaped vaguely like a male organ and which might be said to be "at hand" if John were given to naughty, childish habits--Shakespeare says "the bawdy hand of the dial is jump on the prick of noon" (_R. and J._, II.iv.119).

38-39. The lines are made up of popular songs of the day. Since John's part was played by Armin, who was a singer, it is likely that John sang far more of the songs than is indicated here. I can find no reference to "Haue ore the sea to florida" in the literature or scholarship of the period. "Was not good King Solomon" appears in J. P. Collier's _Old Ballads_ (I, pp. 25-28) and was used by Shakespeare in _LLL_ (I.ii.180). "Tom Tyler" is requested as a dance tune in Heywood's A Woman Killed With Kindness (ii. 36).

40-41. a boord...there] They call for a water-taxi.

[Scene XI]

0.1-0.3. The tinker (an itinerant repairer of household articles) and his budget (a leather sack which might contain his tools, clothes, or even the liquor referred to in line 1) were a common sight. Frank Aydelotte gives evidence that tinkers ordinarily used their trade as a cloak for thieving (p. 27); that they were named along with actors, rogues, and sturdy beggars in the Poor Laws of 1572 and 1597 (p. 68); and that they frequently appear as type characters in the literature of the period, notably as Christopher Sly in The Taming of the Shrew and in stories by Greene (p. 42). In 1596 Edward Hext wrote a letter to Lord Burghly recommending stronger enforcement of laws against them: "And yf some lyke course might be taken with the wandrynge people they wold easely be brawght to ther places of aboade, and beinge abroade they all in general are receavers of all stolen things that are portable, as namely the Tynker in his Budgett the pedlar in his hamper the glasseman in his pasket..." (p. 170).

2. renst] rinsed.

7-8. clout...cauldren] Probably a bawdy double entendre.

11. Toures, as the tinker, is pretending to be drunk and is thus speaking quite incoherently; here, in response to

the boy's reminder of their destitution, he suggests they should pawn their budget, or at least pretend to, since "ring in" can mean "substitute fraudulently by exchanging something bad for something good."

11-12. ha...tinker] A street cry used by tradesmen. Compare to the title of Martin Marprelate's tract, Hay Any Work for Cooper.

14. Twitnam] Twickenham. Toures is remarkably fortunate that Madge and, later, Humil should mistake him for another tinker. But see lines 25-26.

15. flowre...pan] Probably a jocular compliment meaning she is a flower among the frying pans. I can find no evidence that it is a proverbial expression, as might be suspected. stops holes] I.e., as a mender of pots and pans; also a bawdy pun.

19-20. vpon...end] There may be a mistake here, as the line would make more sense if printed "a long staffe with a picke i'th end," since all of OED's examples indicate that a staffe was a stick up to six feet long and a picke was a spike or sharp point. I have been unable to find other references to a tinker and his stick, but Armin may have in mind a "hooker," who used a stick with a hook on the end to "pull out of a window any loose linen cloth, apparel, or else any other household stuff whatsoever" (Judges, p. 172).

23. dainty...me] "Dainty Come Thou to Me" is a ballad printed in Roxburghe Ballads (I, 628-631).

25. Draw boy] In light of Toures' feigned drunken state

this phrase might be assumed to be an instruction to draw a draught of ale, but homo armatus means "armed man" and Toures may be mimicking a sword fight (perhaps with the aforementioned pick with a staff in the end); on the other hand, he may have originally meant the former and then taken the opportunity for a pun with the latter. pepper] beat upon.

26. dogge] In the light of further references to a dog (lines 28, 32-33) in connection with the tinker from Twitnam, it may be that Toures deliberately designed his disguise to promote the false identification which Madge and Humil make.

27. him] I.e., the dog. Putney] a village in Surrey on the south bank of the Thames about two and a half miles from Mortlake. Since this is the place the lovers elope to, it is likely that the boy looks meaningfully at Mary as he says the line, intending it as a clue.

28-29. whats...dogge] Thomas Harman, in A Caveat Or Warning for Common Cursitors (Judges, pp. 92-93), says, "These drunken tinkers...never go out without their doxies. ... I was credibly informed...that one of these tippling tinkers with his dog robbed...six persons together."

31-36. I...Querester] The fictitious exaggeration implies the existence of a local legend about the Twitnam tinker. Masty] mastiff. Querester] chorister.

37. stop, mend] stay, rest; or, stop up holes and mend our pans.

38. tickle...holes] clog up leaks; also bawdy.

42. Relish] sing, warble (the word is used quite differently at I.44 and XXII.86). note above ela] Grosart notes that this is "a common saying (in Shakespeare and others), meaning 'sing your best, sing above your usual,' ela being the highest note of the gamut."

44-66. I can find no source for the song, which seems to me a splendid one. It is not clear whether the girl is lamenting an unfulfilled love or a fulfilled one; she may be either frustrated or pregnant, but see lines 48, 60, and 65.

50. stone] testicle. Is she protesting what stones have done to her or lamenting their inubiquity?

59. by...slipper] A bizarre oath for which I have found no parallel.

61. greene sicknes] Partridge, in Shakespeare's Bawdy, says, "The Elizabethan dramatists emblemized it as a sign of a girl's love-sickness, or of vague desire for a man." The "old wiues" say it "was dangerous," which may mean she is now suffering the consequences of it, or they may only be warning her.

62. oate-meale eating] Partridge, in Shakespeare's Bawdy, points out that oatmeal in several phrases (e.g., "to sow one's wild oats") is associated with profligacy. Thus to eat oatmeal is to be profligate.

67. chopping] large, lusty. The line is quite firm evidence that the maiden has been pregnant.

68. _Omne bene_] all is well.

69. diet] food intake.

70. Layes] Context seems to require the sense of "imposes."

71. Lingers] Evidently, "lingers in."

72. Swelters] Another instance of a singular verb with a plural subject ("meanes"). surfet] surfeit.

73-74. I...drinke] I would be running contrary to my own principles and beliefs to think that a man is helpless before the drinking habit.

76. cusse] kiss.

77. busse] kiss. neb] nose; therefore, as a verb, kiss.

79. in...straits] His arms are around her.

83. y'faith] in faith, a common oath.

84. shals] shall we. Cf. XI.7, "shal's."

85. in] go in. seller] wine cellar.

86. dept] debt, a pun.

86-87. black iacks] leathern drinking bags (Cunliffe cites _Taming of the Shrew_, IV.i.52), probably stored in the cellar.

87-88. shake hands] I.e., in imitation while holding the neck of the bag to one's mouth.

99. what...message] He spies the letter as Tutch passes it to Tabitha.

104. bone-lace] bobbin or pillow-made lace.

106. lace...bones] handwriting; a pun, "ten bones" being the fingers.

108. tri'd...tutch] A touchstone was a key tool in the goldsmith's trade, in which Armin was a practitioner (see pp.2-3); it was a smooth piece of black quartz or jasper used for testing ("trying") the quality of gold and silver alloys by the color of the streak produced by rubbing them on it. Thus the line means that he is tested by his own standards.

109. true...other] true or loyal to Tabitha and Filbon but false to Sir William.

110-111. These lines, like Jonson's in Every Man In His Humour (I.v.57-58), burlesque the notorious hyperbole and bombast of Kyd's The Spanish Tragedy (III.ii.1-5):

> O eyes! no eyes, but fountains fraught with tears;
> O life! no life, but lively form of death;
> O world! no world, but mass of public wrongs,
> Confused and filled with murder and misdeeds!

118. Tutch is being stripped of his livery.

119. fall off] Either his coat is in tatters or he pretends that it is in order to mock the ceremony.

119-120. if...leafe] It is not clear whether Tutch is complaining that without a coat he will be cold in the present and coming seasons or that his coat, like leaves from a tree, is about to fall off because this is the time of the year when he is normally paid his wages, with which he would buy a new coat. In any case, there is a play on the word "fall."

121. seruingmen...coates] Certainly servingmen would not drop off their coats in the fall if they did not expect to

put warmer ones on.

123. carrier] I.e., of the love message.

124. mercurie] messenger.

125. my...owne] my own servant betray my own daughter.

126-127. your...decke] As at I. 30 and II.47, Armin draws on the language of cards: you are a rascal ("knave"), they (Filbon and Tabitha) misguide ("shuffle") you; I'm in charge here (i.e., the "dealer") and I'll throw you out ("cut ye from the decke").

129. Gang...worst] "gang" is dialect for "gone"; the phrase probably means, "it is bad to be told that one must go, but it is worse to be told that one must hang; therefore, I consider myself lucky."

129-134. Tutch, confronted with unemployment and poverty, responds in confused doggerel; winter nights are not short, especially when one is out in the cold, but Tutch has some consolation: he can go to "spittle fields," which were fields belonging to and adjoining the Hospital of St. Mary. Sugden, perhaps following Stow (I, p. 168), notes (p. 483) that, "the clay from the field was made into bricks, and the warm kilns were used for sleeping places by tramps." brickill] brick-kiln.

135. ginnie hen] Partridge, Shakespeare's Bawdy (p. 124) gives "A wanton; a whore."

136. treading] copulating. gossip] a close acquaintance; here Lady Vergir. closset] private sitting room.

137. Filbon...will] Sir William seems to be about to

warn himself that if he lacks the will to prevent it, Filbon will elope with Tabitha; apparently he is interrupted by some indication that the Lady is about to speak.

139-141. Tabitha begins boldly to denounce Filbon so as to mislead her father, but after "dangle" she probably stalls, stutters, and meekly admits the impossibility of even pretending to deny her lover. "iustifie" means "verify," but I cannot explain how "actions" can be like "apricocks" or how they can be said to "dangle" unless there is some sexual innuendo in the passage.

148-149. Christmas...mare] Grosart notes: "shooing *etc*.= a Christmas gambol or sport." But he neither gives nor can I find any supporting evidence. I suspect, rather, that Tabitha means, "All the excitement of the elopement, with people running about and shouting, is like the festivities at Christmas time, father, and your trying to restrict (tame or domesticate) Mary is like shoeing a wild mare."

152. I...race] An odd idiom; perhaps: "I am a match for you in racing."

157-159. who...gold] Danae was an Argive princess, daughter of Acrisius, King of Argos. He, told that his daughter's son would put him to death, resolved that Danae should never marry and accordingly locked her up in an inaccessible tower. Zeus foiled the king by changing himself into a shower of gold, under which guise he readily found access to the fair prisoner, and she thus became the mother of Perseus. Douglas Bush, in his *Mythology and the*

Renaissance Tradition (passim.), shows that the allusion was a very common one.

161. Etiam, ita, ego.] This is probably gibberish, but it may be a version of pig latin, putting an "ee" sound before the word intended. Dropping the initial e's and i, the line sounds like "time to go," which would be very appropriate since the boy is beginning to realize that he will be caught as an accomplice.

167. price] prize.

170-171. since...second] since the devil drives me on, I will follow.

173. counsellor] Ironic epithet for the boy.

178. cabbinet] secret place.

179. Putney] See note XI.27.

181. my parsonage] Sir William provides the benefice and house for the parson, Henry, at Putney.

182. hospitall] place of shelter for those in need. shadowe] cover, protect, conceal.

182-184. my...me] my own beneficiary shall fraudulently deprive me of my own daughter. Sir William's phrase echoes his earlier response to Tutch's betrayal at XI.125.

185. Richmond] A village about two miles from Mortlake.

186-187. No...selfe] The passage is made difficult by Q.'s indiscriminate use of the comma, preventing the reader from determining with certainty which phrases modify which clauses. A possible paraphrase is this: "No sir, you shall go with me; that's the next thing to be done, because you tend to act for your own interests; delaying what ought to be done while ready in all other things, you then serve yourself."

188-189. nor...appetites] neither Filbon nor you will be allowed to manipulate the situation to suit your own desires.

[Scene XII]

5-6. ball...stoole] An allusion to stool-ball, a game frequently referred to in Elizabethan literature (see citations in Nares and Wright) but about which, according to the _Encyclopedia Brittanica_, very little is known.

9. crum...porrage] put crumbs in my porridge.

12-13. take...stoole] Percy McQuoid, _Shakespeare's England_ (pp. 121-122), writes, "joint-stools of the last half of the sixteenth century resembled tables in miniature....being the furniture most commonly encountered, [it] lent itself to jocular reference." Such jocular references occur, for example, in _The Taming of the Shrew_, II.i.196-199, and _King Lear_, III.vi.55. The joint-stool, then, was a commonplace object that one sat on; thus, "to take one for a joint-stool" might mean "to take one for granted" or, metaphorically, "to sit on," as we sometimes say today that an offensive person should be "sat upon," or squashed.

16. molesting] A humorous catachresis, a malapropism.

25. stand...vnto] am favorably disposed to.

26. stable...thoughts] The phrase is ambiguous. Sir

Rafe may be remarking humorously that Filbon is better off for having accepted bachelorhood or that the young man is demonstrating admirable reserve in his resignation.

30. got...court] gone to court to complain (of the abduction).

32. Here Tutch tells us that Tabitha is as impressionable as wax, whereas in line 11 above he had pronounced her "firm." Elsewhere in the play Tutch is meant to be respectably witty, not ridiculously contradictory; furthermore, the contradiction in Tutch's thought could not be underlined for comic effect since his speech is here interrupted and ignored. If the contradiction cannot be explained as a comic device, it must be due to Armin's carelessness.

35-37. Filbon protests that Toures stole the tinker-disguise stratagem from him. For a discussion of the ethos of shabby morality and petty, self-serving social climbing among the second-rate nobility in the play, see pp. 79-85.

38. But himselfe] I.e., no man but Toures could take priority over him.

39. <u>ipse</u> <u>facto</u>] the grounds of the fact itself.

40. And...me] Filbon suddenly shifts his attention and seems to be musing to himself, though not in a conventional "aside," since Tutch must overhear him in order to interrupt him with such an appropriate song; Armin also used the device of an overheard "aside" at VII.98. The referent for "thou" in the speech raises difficulties since Filbon has been talking <u>to</u> Tutch <u>about</u> Toures and surely "thou" does

not refer to Tutch, but it could refer to Toures, who may be said to have "stept beyond" Filbon by taking the initiative in securing his beloved.

43-46. Tutch's song is a parody, perhaps an original one, of a popular ballad, which appears in Percy's Reliques of English Poetry (II, 175), entitled "Mary Ambree." Ten of the song's twenty-two stanzas end with the refrain: "Was not this a brave bonny lass, Mary Ambree?" Although the original ballad portrays her as chaste as well as courageous ("Ile nere sell my honour for purple nor pall:/ A mayden of England, sir, never will bee/ The whore of a monarcke, quoth Mary Ambree"), Armin's irreverence toward her is not singular. Charles Felver, in his "Robert Armin's Fragment of a Bawdy Ballad of 'Mary Ambree,'" says (p. 15) that she was probably a "camp-follower of uncertain reputation" who has been characterized in many ballad accounts as a noble, moral, somewhat masculine woman. Felver adds that her name "became a byword in the theater for some thirty years," the name being customarily associated with "(1) any woman who masqueraded in men's clothes and did things that men normally do....or (2) with any woman who has a shrew or morally loose." Jonson treats her as a valiant wench in A Tale of a Tub (I.iv.21-22), but implies a baser interpretation of her in Epicoene (IV.ii.123-124).

47. resign'd] assigned.

48-51. of] off. Filbon says he seems near to having Tabitha but that this seeming proximity is like that of an arrow which, to the archer from afar, seems to be on target but which is actually, upon closer inspection, off-center.

52. mark] target. white] the central part of the mark.

52-54. Change...black] There is an intricately bawdy logic behind Tutch's advice. The "white" of a target is its center and is so named for its color, but when the target is a woman, her white (central part) is black (pubic zone). Shakespeare puns similarly in Othello (II.i.132-134):

> Desdemona. How if she be black and witty?
> Iago. She'll find a white that shall her
> blackness hit.

See also LLL (IV.i.120-134). But the locus classicus of the penis-arrow pudend-target metaphor appears in "On Black Hayre and Eyes" (available in Grierson's edition of Donne, I, 460-461), a popular poem of uncertain date and authorship (though ascribed by Edwin Wolf, who dates it between 1615 and 1620, to Walton Poole). As Wolf says (p. 836), the speaker is defending "a brunette complaining of her complexion in days when the blond standard of beauty, adopted as a tribute to the red-headed Elizabeth, still prevailed." Toward the end of the poem he says:

> Nor hath kind Nature her black art reveal'd
> To outward partes alone, some lie conceal'd,
> And as by heads of springs men often knowe
> The nature of streames that run belowe,
> So your black haire and eyes do give direction
> To make me thinke the rest of like complexion:
> That rest where all rest lies that blesseth Man,
> That Indian mine, that straight of Magellan,
> That worlde dividing gulfe where he that enters,
> With swelling sayles and ravisht senses enters
> To a new worlde of blisse...

. . . .
The rover in the mark his arrowe sticks
Sometimes as well as he that shootes at prickes,
And if I might direct my shaft aright,
The black mark would I hitt and not the white.

53. clout] a pin in the very center of the target.

54. tis] I.e., blackness is.

54-55. wenches...up] We are asked to assume that rolled-back eyes are a sign of passion as well as death.

55-57. custard...hot] John Earle, in his character of "A Cooke" (Microcosmographie, p. 85), says, "Hee seemes to have great skill in the Tactikes, ranging his Dishes in order militarie: and placing with great discretion in the fore-front meates more strong and hearty, and the more cold and cowardly in the reare, as quaking Tarts, and quivering Custards, and such milke-sop Dishes which scape many time the fury of the encounter." One gathers from this that a custard, which was then a kind of pie, often filled with meat, was served at the end of a meal. Perhaps Tutch felt that it was not uncommon for the custards to be placed on the table while hot in anticipation of their being eaten last, in which case the impatient and greedy diner might be burned if he tried the dish early in the meal. Pies are notoriously long in cooling.

60. key cold] very cold. Cf. XVII.84 and Richard III (I.ii.5): "Poor key-cold figure of a holy king."

64. The...man] The phrase may be elliptical for "I am the only man" (i.e., to help him), or "man" may be a printer's error for "means."

72. beshrow] curse. right...it] I have right (justice)

due to me from Sir William in acknowledgement of my disinterested treatment of my son and his mistress Mary.

73. stricter] more conservative, more legally or morally acceptable.

81. mone...comfort] Sir William's protest and complaint will require the Earl and other nobility to do something to comfort him.

83. meanes] power.

84. adde...purpose] Probably elliptical for "add their power and means to achieve the present objective."

85. discharge] rejection by Sir William.

86. his] Sir William's. allay] quell, reduce the effectiveness of. Auditor has said that Sir William's protests against the elopement will arouse the Earl's displeasure with their two sons; Sir Rafe replies that if the Earl were to know of Sir William's disdainful ("careless") rejection of Filbon, it would beget a cold response from the Earl to Sir William's hot pleas.

89-92. Filbon takes the blame for their predicament, saying, in effect, "It's my problem, let me worry about it; if the sunshine of my hope is dimmed and blinking like a troubled meteor, well, that's my bad luck, and nothing can remedy it."

93. vantings] boastings, affirmations.

94. custome...me] custom demands of me no duty to *etc*.

97. you] Emphatic; in contrast with Toures.

98. hurry] commotion, tumult.

100. lessoned] taught.

101-102. As...rule] Tutch asks, with proper skepticism, "As schoolboys do the opposite of what they are taught?" Note also the conventional scene-closing rhyme.

[Scene XIII]

1-30. For a discussion of Humil's speech as a parody of Hamlet's soliloquies, see pp. 73-74.

4. hold...stearne] The antecedent for "her" may be either "imagination" or "Lady Vergir" understood. If "imagination" is meant, the phrase would mean "keep it at bay," as Humil is admonishing himself not to think about what he has seen. If Lady Vergir is referred to, the phrase would mean "remove her from society's good regard" by holding her over the stern of a ship, dropping her, and letting her sink. Although the latter is a more sensational reading of the metaphor, the rest of the sentence supports the inference that it is the Lady who is referred to by the pronoun, since it is she who will never again win or recover her honor.

6. _Honours_] Grosart originally suggested the emendation of _Honours_ for _Q._'s _Homers_, but he did not incorporate the emendation into his text. _Homers_ makes no sense and Humil is clearly concerned with her reputation.

8-9. Haue...sleepe] Humil asks himself if he is not talking nonsense, being in a daze after having been roused from bed.

9-11. rose...dead] He presents himself with another reassuring possibility that he may be in a somnambulist's dream.

11. flattering feare] The fear that he may be walking and talking in his sleep flatters his desire to believe in his mother's innocence.

16. twind brazings] entwined embraces.

19. harould out] proclaim publicly.

20. quarter'd scutchin] An escutcheon, often quadripartite in design (thus "quarter'd"), was a shield ornamented with emblems of its owner's proud heritage.

21. one] I.e., of the lovers.

22. turne hilles] Grosart suggests that "hilles" may be a misprint for "eieless," which seems quite plausible, but "hilles" appears again in an equally baffling context in XV.89. More probably Humil means that to turn up hills of earth and cover up the truth would make him an accomplice ("baude").

24. content...equity] happiness permitted by law.

[Scene XIV]

1-10. Since the difficulties in this speech are as much syntactical as verbal, a full paraphrase will clarify more than the rendering of some isolated words. "You, Sir William and men like you, who are bound up in nocturnal intrigues, your normal daily pleasures, like peaceful birds lodged in a sanctuary, being put temporarily to rest, smile (in pleasure and gratitude) at the cares and efforts of us Courtiers, whose industry rules in silent, darkening night on those suits that would be quiet even on a troubled day and that make their existence felt in our cares at night, being adjudicated with difficulty ('hard censur'd') and resolved ('atton'd') only by long-lasting reflection ('advice'), and by means of which we are salving the world's scars, as we would <u>your</u> care, if we knew the main theme of it." Line 9, "worlds scares" puns on "scares," "scars," and "cares."

11. morn...moone] day is indistinguishable from night.

12. retrograde] opposite or contrary; the Lord is contrasting courtiers' activities with those of other men.

14. Challeng'd] Commanded.

15. blood...free] rank endows us with the privilege of being free from labor.

16. It...industry] The line, as it stands, makes some sense: "It (i.e., <u>your</u> blood), being of more plebian origin, requires that you do more work." But the line would fit more logically into its context, which is a "though X, yet Y, therefore Z" construction, if "thee" were changed to "us" and if "It" were construed to refer to "our blood."

18. extremities] extreme bad fortunes.

19. But...contrary] But if we were ungrateful, we would not deserve your aid.

20. Thinke...kind] And you would justly think it a lack and a weakness in our nature.

23. dull past] dull-paced.

23-24. houres...me] the hours of the slowly passing night are eclipses of the sunshine that interfere with my mission.

26. Seeking...owne] An exclamation or question: "What do you mean, you are 'seeking your own,' who is lost?"

31. A rescue] to the rescue!

32. right] I.e., right the wrong. challeng...benefite] command whatever gift I can bestow upon you to aid you in your search.

34. Restraints...Cinck-ports] Restrain all ships from leaving the five port towns on the southeast of England.

37. Draw...meanes] Draw up the documents which will enable you to effect the means needed to achieve your purpose.

38. let...act] let the conscientious attendance to your purpose ensure the early satisfactory completion of the act.

42. misery seeking] Elliptical: the moral of my misery is that I am seeking too late...

44. in each] I.e., losing and seeking. indifferent] the same.

45. I must] Another elliptical phrase which could be completed in several ways: (1) I must stand by passively and helplessly ("indifferent") until I am strengthened and advised by you; (2) I must experience either a loss in this late phase of my life or a timely victory; (3) I must

recover what I fear is past recovering. perfected] advised, instructed.

47. aduantage] opportune moment.

48-49. things...mend] Probably, the comma after "worst" is misleading: things, at [the] worst season in their decay (i.e., at their most decadent) mend as children [do]. Or, "season" may mean "palliate," as it does when Polonius tells Reynaldo to "season" his charges against Laertes (Hamlet, II.i.30).

49-52. as...ill] The argument seems to be that children mend even though, in a rebellious phase, they may seem to have their eyes bent on ruin, yet they pause at a moment of grace and recover their good sense just when the general opinion judges them rashly and deems them ill.

61-62. is...steept] have you forgotten what you came here to tell me?

62-63. all...all] His remaining daughter, being all he has left, is all to him.

65-68. Sir William's badgering of the messenger, commanding him to speak while interrupting him when he does, seems to be virtually a theatrical convention of the time; cf. Shakespeare's Antony and Cleopatra (II.v.24-29).

70. talles] The word "tales," meaning summons, is still used today in legal circles.

77. iauntings] jaunts, journies.

[Scene XV]

1-4. D. J. McGinn (p. 158) cites these lines as allusions to Hamlet (I.i.150ff.). See pp. 74-75.

2. parture] departure.

3. sleetie] icy.

4. earnest] an assurance or token of something that is to come.

7. idolatrie] A misprint for "adulterie"?

8. Blow...battlements] The line, so strongly remindful of Lear's "Blow, winds, and crack your cheeks!" (III.ii.1), is discussed on page 75. battlements] indented parapets on a castle.

9-13. Humil begins by calling on the winds to rouse and frighten the lovers, then checks himself ("No, *silent* aire *fan* on them" [my italics]), realizing that it will be more advantageous to him and Sir William if they sleep on undisturbed until Sir William can discover them sealed in a devilish pact.

16. stands...desteny] It is not clear how Sir William can be said to be in debt to his destiny, but perhaps Humil means that the lovers stand in debt to Sir William's determination of their destiny. The common Elizabethan disregard for consistency of number in verb-subject relationships makes it quite plausible that "stands" could have a plural subject understood.

18. period] end, conclusion.

22. vengeance...iust] Humil clearly accepts the vengeance

code that underlies much Elizabethan tragedy.

27. bale] sorrow.

34. desperat...prioritie] fearful of my heritage or beginnings.

37. front] forehead or face.

38. distemperature] ill-humor, discomposure.

39. sanguinitie] blood relationship, ancestry.

51-52. I...misdeede] I have been robbed of an honorable name by her misdeed. (Perhaps because it argues other misdeeds--one nine months before _his_ birth.)

53. report...flye] call a spade a spade, tell the unpleasant truth.

57-58. How...dwell] The scandal will make a strong impression in a Christian community.

59. I...base] I will test the truth of the report, perhaps it is false. This is one of several images in the play which may have occurred to Armin because of his experience as a goldsmith's apprentice. See pp. 2-3.

61-63. Scarlet...hand] The idea that even the whole ocean cannot wash clean some vile dirt is pretty much a cliche; it is used often in the French version of _Amadis de Gaule_ and takes this form in _Titus Andronicus_: "For all the water in the ocean/ Can never turn the swan's black legs to white,/ Although she lave them hourly in the flood" (IV.ii.101-103). Nevertheless, an echo of _Macbeth_ (II.ii.59-62) here is quite strong:

Will all great Neptune's ocean wash this blood
Clean from my hand? No, this my hand will rather
The multitudinous seas incarnadine,
Making the green one red.

63-65. Is...yes] Humil is asking himself tautological questions ("Is my hand my hand? Does a fire that dissolves melting ['relenting'] metal deserve to be called fire?") in order to emphasize or confirm his conviction that he must proclaim his mother a stranger to his blood. Again Armin uses an image from goldsmithery.

67. fall off] McGinn (p. 158) cites this phrase as an analogue to Hamlet, I.v.47, where a similar phrase is used in a similar context but in a very different rhetorical frame. The cuckolded Ghost condemns Claudius,

that adulterate beast
[who] With witchcraft of his wit, with traitorous gifts--
O wicked wit and gifts, that have the power
So to seduce!--won to his shameful lust
The will of my most seeming-virtuous Queen.
O Hamlet, what a falling-off was there!

In line 71 below, Humil says James "Plotted, contriu'd, and woon her with deuise."

68. in...blisse] Partridge, in Shakespeare's Bawdy, gives "in heat" and "in rut" for "in pride"; also "extreme delight in sexual intercourse" for "bliss."

69. attempts] Cunliffe gives "tries to seduce."

71. woon] won. deuise] trickery.

72. She...now] She has never been disloyal or "two-faced" before.

73. single singler] The words suggest "having a single object of loyalty," "behaving like a single (unmarried)

person," and "having a uniquely sincere character," but I can find no other instance of this particular phrase.

74. Euen...her] Vesta, in Roman mythology, was the goddess of the hearth and hearth-fire, the protectress of the home. The syntax is ambiguous. Probably, "modesty her selfe" is in apposition to "she" (line 72), and Vesta is being said to resign or surrender her role to the Lady, but "Vesta" may be in apposition to "modesty her selfe," in which case the idea would be that Vesta gave up her crown of modesty to the Lady.

75-77. hand...kennell] "Barley-break" was a game, similar to our "hide-and-seek," in which a couple who were "it" joined hands and chased the others, trying to bring them back to home base, which was called "hell." Humil seems to be arguing that formerly Lady Vergir had played hand-in-hand with virtue, but James, the "hound of hell," has brought the Lady, or "fawne of fortune," to his kennel.

78. degree] rank, station.

78-81. mother...disgrace] My mother, by the practice of this one deed, having captivated (made captives of, in keeping with the "barley-break" meatphor) love, life, and liberty, has brought not only a wicked but a fatal disgrace upon us.

81. honours...course] The phrase is obscure and ultimately indecipherable because it contains so many variables: "course" could be, as Grosart suggests, a misprint or obsolete spelling for "curse" (thus the phrase would be

in apposition to "disgrace," meaning that "disgrace" is the opposite or curse of "honour"); "created" could be a misprint for "cheated" (thus the phrase would mean that honor had been cheated in the game and prevented from following its normal course, leading to disgrace); or "course" could be a reflexive reference to the "swift course" (playing field and action of the game) of line 76 (thus the phrase would be an ironic summation of the dishonorable course the Lady has followed in her game of love); "honours," lacking either a capital initial or an apostrophe, could be a verb, a plural noun, either a singular or plural possessive, or a contraction for "honour is." Unfortunately, none of these possible combinations of the variables provides a satisfactorily meaningful phrase.

84-86. Sir William pretends to be chastizing himself for believing Humil's "slander." He cannot be speaking to Humil because he curses a "fond eare" rather than a "fond tongue" or "eye," which would apply to Humil. He calls himself a "light bubble" because he has been empty-headed. Humil, of course, has been telling the truth and Sir William knows it.

89-90. cast...selfe] In charging Humil with desecrating his mother's honorable name, Sir William allusively equates his act with the proud heresy of the builders of the tower of Babel and with the mythological twins, Otus and Ephialtes, who strove to overthrow Zeus and threatened to pile Mount Pelion on Mount Ossa and scale the heights of heaven, as the Giants of old had piled Ossa on Pelion. A similar allusion occurs in Hamlet at V.i.249-251.

96. respect] respectability, worth.

99-100. waking...vnto] The phrase "true requir'd" is odd; the sense seems to be that mischief seeks to undo that which requires truth as a guardian.

103. cutted] The word does not appear in any of the dictionaries of the time. The word "cut" is frequently used as a term of reproach in reference to short-tailed or castrated dogs and horses; as a noun it can mean (a) harlot or (b) pudendum; as an adjective it can mean "drunken." I do not believe that any of these meanings is relevant here. Grosart suggests, plausibly, that "cutted" may be a misprint for "cursed," a word which would make sense in the context and could possibly though not very probably be misread in Elizabethan manuscripts. My own suggestion is "'culted"; Hamlet (III.ii.82-84) says, "If his occulted [i.e., hidden] guilt/ Do not itself unkennel in one speech,/ It is a damned ghost that we have seen." Two lines later he refers to "Vulcan's stithye," which Armin uses later in this scene at line 154.

105. iugling] Probably a pun as the word has, apart from its normal meaning of "trickery," a bawdy connotation of sexual intercourse.

107-110. I...ouerthrow] The passage is made obscure by its diction, syntax, and allusiveness. Nares cites a passage which indicates that "giddy" means not merely "dizzy" but, more specifically, "made dizzy out of terror of one's hunters." The lines state that the leopard, in defense against man's mischievous plot to destroy him, flings poisonous foam in his path; this is an allusion to the still current belief that the leopard is an especially filthy beast whose claws and saliva contain toxic germs. By the same token, Sir William will resort to ignoble strategies to protect himself from those who would rob him of his reputation.

111. that...so] Sir William, seeing the irony in his use of the word "true" (the facts about the Lady's untrue behavior are true), regrets that he has lived to think "untruth" true.

112. Or...thought] He also regrets that the lovers should have been so wretchedly dishonest as to deserve and require such bitter puns to be made about them.

113. Soundly...waking] In his distraught state the paradoxes give him grim pleasure: the lovers' serenity in bed begets his anguish, since it indicates the emotional depth of his wife's betrayal.

115. Done...practiseth] I have done what works ("practiseth") to my purpose.

117. kick at] In this context the phrase seems to mean "overcome" or "defend itself against" but I can find no analogue.

119-120. Fortune...too] If good fortune is with me (and my deception is successful), I will recover that good name the loss of which the devil himself admits to being responsible for ("cries guilty too").

120-121. my...renowne] The syntax here is indecipherable. The antecedent of "it" (line 121) may be "fame" or the deceptive practice he is using to preserve his reputation (lines 114-116). It is even possible that a line was dropped between line 120 (last line of sig. E2^{v}) and line 121 (first line of sig. E3), the possibility of such an omission is supported by the lack of a subject for the verb "imps" (i.e., grafts feathers onto an imperfect wing), unless the subject is, again, the deceitful practice referred to earlier. Despite these grammatical and syntactical difficulties, the passage, incorporating a metaphor from falconry, seems to mean that Sir William is attempting to protect his threatened reputation by denying his wife's guilt.

122. That...lost] The relative pronoun refers to his "fame" or "renowne"; "left" may mean "left behind" or may be a misprint for "lost." In either case the meaning would be the same.

124-125. These lines must be spoken either aside or to himself or in an ironic tone to Humil.

128. transiue] Citing this passage only, OED offers "of the nature of a trance" as a definition.

132. Argos] A mythological hero with a hundred eyes, originally a personification of the starry heavens.

137. your...torture] you must judge what my punishment should be.

139. Sorrow...least] my sorrow is inadequate punishment; death is the least I deserve.

140. challenge] In his present mood he does not <u>defy</u> cruelty but <u>demand</u> it; Armin uses "challenge" to mean either of these (see pp. 43-44).

143-162. <u>Q</u>. assigns the whole passage to Humil; to justify my assignment of lines 146-150 to Sir William I must offer an interpretation of the passage. In lines 136-140 Humil has expressed deep shame for having "murdered innocence" and has demanded cruel punishment. In line 142 Sir William has expressed his dismay that a son could so besmirch his mother's honor. In lines 143-144 Humil announces his intention to depart rather than remain and be forced to look upon the damage he has done his mother. Line 145 <u>could</u> be part of Sir William's reply to Humil's announced departure (i.e., "go then"), but I think it more likely that Humil is repeating his invitation to Sir William to "go ahead, do your worst to me, then." Sir William then replies to that invitation by saying that he will try to appease the devil who tempted Humil to such a sin and that Humil should devote all his disturbed thoughts to appealing for mercy from his mother's sex. Lines 148-150 mean, "To her spotless innocence freely confess all your treachery, say that you build on slippery ice (?) and are icily cruel." In lines 151-152 Humil repeats his appeal for stern punishment, saying that if Sir William fails to insist on "black torture" for the wrongs done him, it will be a greater hell for Humil. Lines 153-156 may be paraphrased as follows: "Oh you sons, whose true obedience shines in majesty, while mine (i.e., _dis_obedience), which is more ugly than Vulcan's stithy, smells ranker than despised hemlock, curse and ban him (i.e., me); I am your subject in this."

154. _Vulcans_ stithye] Vulcan was the blacksmith of the gods; his "stithye" was his smithy or anvil, a frequent symbol of dirtiness. D. J. McGinn (p. 158) cites the phrase as another parallel to _Hamlet_: "And my imaginations are as foul/ as Vulcan's stithy" (III.ii.88-89).

157. as...palme] The _Salix caprea_, called "palm" in England because of its use on Palm Sunday, has downy golden catkins.

161. 'hem] every mother.

163. the] thee.

166. Catiue] poor, villainous wretch.

168. still] Sir William puns; "still" can mean "cease," "even now," and "always"; Humil would naturally take it to mean the first, but Sir William would believe the latter two to be more just.

169-171. was...honor'd] McGinn compares Humil's question to one Hamlet asks of Gertrude (III.iv.76-77), "What devil was it/ That thus cozen'd you at hoodman-blind?"

176. exasperates] increases the violence of pain.

179. dalling] dallying.

180. gauds] children's toys, pieces of festive finery.

181. Respectes] The verb seems to have two objects:

(1) mother, and (2) womb. See p. 46.

182-184. The grammatical relationships between the phrases and clauses in the speech are very obscure, but it is clear that Sir William is marveling over a son who is so devoted to a new stepfather that when he finds his mother in a wanton fault, he scorns his natural respect for her and broadcasts her shame.

186. challenge...right] demand or claim some rights in compensation for injury done me.

187. confine] Grosart, following Nares, gives "banishment as the synonym for "confine," thus referring to Humil's exile. But it is not clear in what sense "banishment" would be "added" to adultery. The word more probably means "confinement," since Sir William intends to limit the Lady's freedom and confine the knowledge of her treachery.

191. Giue...yet] Sir William is probably sarcastic when he suggests that his "discontent" over his wife's adultery could be "allayed" by having reasons for it.

194.1. unready] undressed.

194.2. garterles] Nares cites several passages to show that "it was the regular amorous etiquette, in the reign of Elizabeth, for a man, professing himself deeply in love, to assume certain outward marks of negligence in his dress, as if too much occupied by his passion to attend to such trifles; or driven by despondency to a forgetfulness of all outward appearance. His <u>garters</u>, in particular, were not to be tied up." But James is not a foppish young lover; he is a middle-aged, married man, and the stage direction is probably meant to convey not his affectation but the unseemly haste with which he was forced to withdraw from his "twind brazings."

196. looze] I can find no authority for Grosart's note, "'looze'--misprint for 'leese'=lie, falsehood." As synonyms for the substantive "lose," Nares and OED give "reputation," "renown," "fame"; thus Armin may mean "report." Or the word may equal our own "loose" and mean "release" or "getting free"--i.e., "don't 'acknowledge all,' do something that will get us a more beneficial outcome or escape."

197. adde...torture] The Lady seems to imply that, by telling all, James would add the crime of mental torture to the mischief they have already done. If this is, indeed, what the Lady and Armin mean, she must be either insincere (in an attempt to quiet James so that she may pursue her goal of winning one of the girls for Humil) or making strange assumptions about Sir William's psychology, since it seems natural to suppose that he would rather know himself to be married to an unintentional bigamist, capable of love and loyalty to at least one man, than believe himself married to a casual nymphomaniac capable of seducing a stranger on her wedding night. It is also possible that the references to fear and torture, both here and line 201 below, allude not to the mental suffering imposed by their past acts upon Sir William but to possible future retribution imposed by him on them. Neither of these readings is

quite satisfactory, and, since in lines 200-201 James seems to acknowledge that Sir William is already enduring torture, we are perhaps justified in assuming that the line in question is corrupt and should read: "This will but adde mischiefe to torture." If this correction is allowed, "torture" would refer to the shame Sir William is already enduring and "mischief" would refer to the damage that would be done to her plans for Humil's eventual marriage to one of the girls.

197. that] I.e., the truth or explanation.

200. brand...brow] A reference to cuckoldry.

201. exclaime] Though OED gives merely "exclamation" and "outcry," the three pre-nineteenth century citations seem, as here, to carry connotations of explanation and confession.

202. scar'd] James may be admitting that he is scared lifeless, or he may be claiming that his brain (i.e., forehead) is metaphorically "scarred" (or, as Grossart suggests, "seared" by the "brand" (line 200) of wickedness that is upon him. Again, it is not absolutely clear whether he is afraid of his own torture at Sir William's hands or suffering in sympathy with Sir William's pain.

205-206. No...bed] The syntax is unclear, but Sir William is apparently saying that, "It is no wonder that you vow sexual abstinence with me and shun my bed, when you have been deputized (appropriated) by him. It is conceivable that Armin uses "deputed" in a basic sense, to mean "be-whored." "Puta" and "putain" are Spanish and French for "whore" and both derive from Latin for "rot" and "decay."

207. You...well] Sir William is ironic.

208. fellow] person of humble station.

211. alleadge] make excuses. This meaning of the word is still current, according to the Funk and Wagnalls _Standard College Dictionary_.

215. be...pleasure] There is some bitter ambiguity in his admonition to her to feign merry serenity: each of the operative words ("tickling," "sportfull," "topt," and "pleasure") has sexual connotations; see Partridge's _Shakespeare's Bawdy_.

216. that] emphatic. me concernes] is what is of importance to me (i.e., because it will work to dispel any suspicions injurious to his reputation).

217. To...guise] Sir William seems to begin to contemplate the advantages of assuming the role of a madman, as did Hamlet, but he apparently rejects the scheme on the grounds that, having acted as he already has, the time is past when he could convincingly pretend to be the crazed, indignant husband.

218-219. Since...supportable] Since what is done, is done, and wishing is of no avail, my position is, by virtue of my good reputation ("for credit sake"), endurable ("supportable").

220. senseable] capable of feeling, conscious of my

predicament.

221-222. such...base] I.e., other cuckolds.

223-224. I...repent] It is clear enough that Sir William should want to allay their fears in order to trap them more easily when he is ready to do so, but why should he expect them to believe it when he says he knows they repent, since they have not even pretended repentence in any way.

228-229. Go...confounded] It is not clear whether "neuer till now possest" refers to a sense of shame or, in the sexual sense, to his wife; his wife is the cause of his shame because she has been possessed by another but not by him. Neither is it clear how his shame could be "in a breath [moment] confounded." As a verb, "confounded" means either "destroyed and "undone" or "wasted," and neither meaning seems applicable to his shame. Two possibilities present themselves: (1) Sir William pauses and interrupts himself at "breath" and "confounded" is an adjective modifying "sir," meaning that James is "confused" at being caught in the compromising position, or (2) after "possest" Sir William shifts his attention from his shame to his honor, which has been suddenly and easily ("in a breath") destroyed.

229-231. you...others] There are several puns in the passage and probably some allusions to the last scene of _The Merchant of Venice_. horne] Both lantern and the horns a cuckold supposedly sprouted; thus "your wrongs are revealed by the light of the lantern" and "your wrongs are manifest in the horns you put on me." Sir William says, "your wrongs shed light on others," whereas Portia says (V.i.91-92), "How far that little candle throws his beams!/ So shines a good deed in a naughty world." Later in the scene Bassanio uses the phrase "candles of the night."

234. spight] injury.

235. next] next opportunity.

237. second] second chance to cuckold me.

239. Fashion...frailty] the tendency to moral laxity in the face of temptation. About to launch into an abstract sermon, Sir William interrupts himself and begins anew on the next line.

247-248. It...guiltinesse] It may be that other reasons will restrain me from exercising my "power of mischief," such as whims ("causeless motives") or a sudden blindness to your guilt.

249-250. In...mischance] Perhaps in consideration of the consequences ("needy sequences") to me my heart will reconcile itself to the injustice done me.

251. spleene] ill will, resentment.

254. giue...countenance] mask your faces in contented expressions; do not reveal your disquietude to others.

257. reason] I.e., cause of my suffering.

258. closet] I.e., heart or bosom.

259. The...reuenge] Sir William makes it clear that all his future behavior will be determined by his desire for

safe, appropriate revenge.

261. consume] is consumed.

266. Phoenix] In Egyptian mythology, a bird of great beauty said to live for five hundred to six hundred years in the Arabian Desert and then consume itself by fire, rising from its ashes young and beautiful to live through another cycle. The term is often used to refer to a person of matchless excellence. Sir William's point is that if any man can be sure of his wife's fidelity, he is, like the phoenix, one of a kind, "unfellow'd."

[Scene XVI]

3. Tailer] He asks for his servant, a tailor. dudge me] No dictionaries give an appropriate definition; the expression seems to be an equivalent for "damn me!" will...pad] Tutch's Welsh for "I will knock his pate."

4. What...done] "Is the jerkin with the gold button done?"

7. Saucebox] impudent person.

12. fortie...time] Grosart notes: "An allusion to the time of payment of wages when his year is up, when, of course, if he desired to be retained, he would be especially 'owing in his duty.'"

16-29. This seems to be a set speech, having, like a sonnet, fourteen lines, but only some partial rhymes; it is also exceptionally clear.

18-19. shafts...proofe] Arrows ("shafts") that were

tipped ("headed") with gold were thought to be able to penetrate any armor.

20. relenting] melting, softening. She has two hearts because he has given her his.

21. attoning pittie] Pity melts the heart, thus making it penetrable, so that it can be "attoned" or reconciled with his.

24. Signe...sute] Give a sign of acquiescence to my suit. censure] judgment, opinion.

28-29. let...resolue] let your answer be fiery, to try the metal of my love.

34-36. Q. assigns these lines to Tabitha, but Auditor has not been talking like a Puritan, though he might naturally ridicule her for her puritanical and literal-minded rebuke to his use of the conventional language of courtly love.

34. Sfoot] God's boot, a mild oath (cf. "swounds," God's wounds); it appears in The Reverger's Tragedy (III.iv.10) and The Valiant Welshman (D4^{v}) as well as in plays by John Marston.

35. canuas...bags] "Currans" are raisins, introduced in England during the Elizabethan era, but I can find no mention of canvas curran bags elsehwere. Auditor is teasing her for being a caricature of the wholesome, domestic, solid middle-class "cittizen" (i.e., city-dweller).

37-38. Ime...nicetie] Tabitha, evidently attempting to live up to her father's image of her as a "homely milk-bole thing" (VIII.68), insists she is a country girl, not a city-type and rejects the polite formulae and Ovidian ceremonies.

39. craue] beg to know.

42. Ples...Latie] Stage Welsh for "Bless you, Lady." Here, as in lines 46 and 56 below, Tutch is appealing for her attention and interrupting her. Elizabethan stage Welshmen substituted unvoiced for voiced consonants "f" for "v," "t" for "d," and "p" for "b." In _The Valiant Welshman_ (see Appendix A) a character named Morgan says "God plesse her" and "I prought you a calves head." In Thomas Heywood's _The Royall King and the Loyall Subject_ the Welshman says "Heaven plesse thee from all his mercies." Fluellen, in _King Henry V_, says "There is a auncient lieutenant there at the pridge." Parson Evans in _The Merry Wives of Windsor_ does the same.

46. firgen] virgin.

49. cheuerell] kid leather. Being of a very yielding nature, a very flexible conscience was proverbially compared to it: "which gifts...the capacity/ Of your soft cheveril conscience would receive/ If you might please stretch it" (_Henry VIII_, II.iii.30-33).

54. worthlesse person] myself.

56. Harg] Hark.

57. cry...mercie] I beg your pardon.

58. Was] I am. See also line 78 below.

59. tis...blood] it is not deserving of mockery in one

to marry into Welsh blood.

64. his] Auditor's.

65. entertaine] entertainment.

66. me] emphatic. Or the line could be a querulous question.

67. Wiues...daughters] Merchants' daughters are the appropriate wives for city-dwellers.

68. gentle] of a rank able to receive knighthood; or perhaps merely "genteel" and "aristocratic."

69-74. I...suites] Tabitha offers her satirical portrait of what city girls would like to demand of prospective husbands.

72. fancies] light ballads, airs. as] such as.

73. receits] Grosart notes: "recipes for cosmetics," but more probably receptions and accommodations are meant.

78. her] The Welsh were thought to use "her" for any personal pronoun; here it means "me," as it does in this line from <u>The Royall King and the Loyall Subject</u> (1602): "I pray where apout stands <u>Pauls</u> Church, can you tell her?"

79-80. was...rishes] I am a knight, have land and a great deal of riches.

81-82. This...none] There are two possible interpretations of these lines, depending on whom Tabitha addresses herself to. If she is replying to Tutch's proposal: Shall I choose this gentlenan (Tutch) or this (Auditor)? I would take you (Tutch) before a mere citizen, but I will have neither. If she turns to Auditor: I would choose this gentleman (Tutch) or this (Filbon) before a citizen like yourself.

87. Apparently she interrupts him and speaks in fragments; perhaps there should be punctuation after "world," so that "except one or two" would refer to "eie motes."

89. eie motes] specks in the eye. Grosart suggests that "my" is a misprint for "are."

99. Perger] Berger.

101-104. Tutch lapses into his clownish character, talking nonsense for the sake of rhymes and puns.

104-105. whan...latie] I am Sir Robert Morgan and will make you a lady.

106. You sir] Uttered in contempt and disbelief.

107. Was] do.

110. Winde] Draw forth his secrets by gaining his confidence.

112. neglecting...it] avoiding his house so that it cannot be searched.

116. alienate] be alienated.

118. though...it] though early, unsanctioned marriage will make them nearly beggars.

119. And...go] and good riddance.

120. free...feare] innocent of those crimes which you fear.

126. sell...them] Probably a reference to the abuse of selling church benefices.

127. stanze] stanza, probably jocular for sermon.

130. exercise] celebrate or perform a religious service.

132. Mauger] in spite of.

140. indifferent] tolerably, fairly. has broke] has been broke, bankrupt.

141. made...hole] reunified his forces; i.e., recouped his losses. Since Sir Rafe vouches for the imposters (Auditor here and Tutch lines 152-153 below), he must recognize them and be in league with them in order to avenge Sir William's peremptory rejection of his son as a suitor.

142. secure policie] safe or cautious expediency and cunning.

145. shifts] ingenious and expedient devices for effecting some purpose. doe] Could be either "it does" or "that do."

147. banckrout...tremble] bankruptcy undermines faith in the credit system and makes businessmen fearful.

148. Aunt] Like "cousin" the epithet may merely suggest an informal relationship, or it may have an insulting connotation of "light woman or procuress." In either case, Tutch is no doubt enjoying his role as a foreign knight, since it enables him to deal flippantly with those who ordinarily have power over him.

149. firgin] virgin.

149-150. God...willing] if God wills it, I shall make her my wife, she shall be my lady, we will go to Wales, where she will receive great worship, God willing.

151. O...day] This line could mean a number of things. First, "O" may be a misprint for "I." Sir William may suddenly have misremembered hearing of the recent bestowal of knighthood on the Welshman; or, his statement may be a sarcastic aside, meaning that such a preposterous character as this must be only a very few initiate into knighthood. It does not seem to be an indication that Sir William recognizes the fraud as a newly self-made knight, for if he did, he would not allow the scheme to reach its planned conclusion. In any case the remark is ironically ambiguous since Sir William is closer to the truth than he suspects. If the line were reassigned to Tabitha and understood to be an expression of her recognition of Tutch and Filbon, it would explain why she seems to forget her recent declaration of fidelity to Filbon and consents to the arranged marriage. In the passages of bantering between Tabitha, Tutch, and Auditor, before the entrance of Sir William (line 107), she gives no indication of recognizing their true identities, but after Sir William leaves, her remark (lines 202-204) indicates that she knew and "mistrusted" the plot and that Auditor and Tutch knew one another throughout the scene. Perhaps she, Tutch, and Auditor go into a huddle on stage during lines 108-133.

154. coniunction] connection, marriage.

155-156. beware...estate] Sir Rafe apparently denigrates those whose "maiesty" or dignity stems from their birth into a social class ("estate"); "estate" may also refer to pomp and display.

157-158. They...swell] In contrast there are those who, though "base born," may be reborn ("regenerate") and become strong, firm, and powerful by virtue of their personal honor.

165. Was...man] I am a glad man. parrel] apparel.

166-167. Was...ye] I will stay four weeks, will not leave now; I am welcome, a plague on you, I love you. The comic bumptiousness of "Morgan" is reminiscent of Harold Ross, a Welsh-American, who bid farewell to John McNulty with, "Well, God bless you, McNulty, goddam it."

168. citty proud] I can find no precedent for this phrase, which would seem to mean "proud as one from the city, sophisticated." If that is, indeed, what it means, it is in contradiction to previous descriptions of Tabitha as domestic and "homely"; perhaps it means "too proud to be associated with the city." In any case, Armin probably uses it to pun with "sits on" (line 169) and "sit vp" (line 172).

169. My...brow] She has her eye on a courtier, "brow" being a synechdoche.

175. in...hand] in any case.

176. black iet] a ring. "Jet was a favorite material for cheap rings owing to its electrical attraction" (Hereford and Simpson's note to EMIH, II.iv.35, in Ben Jonson, IX, 365).

179. ord'nance] The word generally referred to a battle

arrangement, but Armin seems to think of it as artillery equipment, which forms part of the array. The military imagery here and in the following lines is used, as it frequently is elsehwere in Elizabethan literature, to suggest sexual matters.

180. ly...bulwarke] entrench myself upon the rampart or fortification.

181. discharge] fire, as a cannon. obedient] compliant or conventional? OED lists no precedent for similar usage. The use of battle imagery for her anticipated linguistic difficulties seems a bit strained.

185. strike...stroke] Presumably a reference to the priest's gesture in the marriage ritual but perhaps carrying a bawdy implication.

187. listen me] listen to me?

189-190. Theres...coast] The passage is obscure because the words "tryall" and "presumption" can both mean two quite different things, and even if we knew which definitions to apply, we wouldn't know whom Sir William is applying them to. The first, "tryall," may refer to some test of the Welsh knight's authenticity or to the endurance of suffering (presumably Tabitha's, over the loss of her preferred lover); "presumption" may refer to an assumption or inference about Morgan's genuineness or to Tabitha's willful insistence on marrying Filbon. Professor Dunkin suggests: "where testing [or a trial run] encourages one to be bold and go ahead." skyrre] scour.

194. him] I.e., Sir William. This is the first direct indication we have that Auditor is part of the conspiracy to bring about the marriage of Filbon and Tabitha. The purpose of his disguise is never explained and his motive for helping the lovers is not explicit, but he is presumably prompted by indignation at Sir William's rejection of his son as a husband for Mary.

201. I...Hangman] Tutch, apparently dropping his assumed identity, exults in his successful deception, saying that the idea of his being taken for a Welshman is as absurd as if he were mistaken for a hangman.

202-203. A...it] The line could be an expression of surprise at the unmasking. The stage convention of the successful use of the most patent disguises renders unnecessary the re-creation of the excited protests and questions which such an unmasking would provoke in real life. Nevertheless, we cannot rule out the possibility that Tabitha has known about the deception and is here exclaiming over the success of a trick which she "mistrusted" (had misgivings about).

204. incontinent] immediately.

205. I...Welchman] Filbon's remark indicates that Henry is not aware of the deception and will proceed only with the marriage to the Welchman as approved by Sir William.

206. light] permission.

214-215. Go...in't] The drone, or male honey bee, gathers no honey and serves only to impregnate the queen; so long as honey is being gathered in plenty drones are tolerated, but no sooner does the honey harvest show signs of being over than they are mercilessly cast out of the hive by the workers. Either Tabitha (Armin) is being sarcastic (when she says "ye do _not_ loue the hiue") or she is under some misapprehensions about apiarian protocol, implying that males _choose_ to leave the hive when there _is_ honey in it, whereas in fact they are forced to leave when there is _not_. wiue] Following Grosart, I have emended _Q._'s "winne" in order to maintain the couplet (a pattern initiated in the previous two lines) and to improve the sense; the two words might be hard to distinguish in Elizabethan manuscript.

216-218. if...mistresse] Tutch seeks to be reassured that if he is endangered in the course of his efforts to bring about the marriage of Filbon and Tabitha, she will defend him against her father's wrath.

222. bargaine] Probably refers to his arrangement to impersonate the Welshman.

222-223. Ile...you] A pun on "shift," meaning in the first case "trick, toy, deception" and in the second "exchange" (i.e., of clothes).

225-226. vse...mine] A similar remark is made in George Farquhar's _The Beaux Stratagem_ (1707), in which Aimwell poses as his own older brother and his friend Archer assumes the livery of Aimwell's servant.

227. I...debter] Through Filbon's love for Tabitha Tutch has been provided with new employment; thus he is love's debtor.

[Scene XVII]

7. poize] weight.

10. Dig] W. J. Lawrence (pp. 153-154) discusses the scene as proof of the commonness of "grave traps" on the rear stages of Elizabethan theaters.

13. beauty...lapidary] beauty made all the other precious stones seem dark (stained) by comparison.

16. vallue...price] Cunliffe gives "estimation" and "worth" as synonyms for "value," "price," and "prize." The phrase might best be paraphrased as "prize of such value."

23-24. he...Fate] he that seems most secure, least in danger of dying, sits in great pomp and solemnity ("state"), unwittingly being tended to and directed toward death by the hand of Fate.

28-29. So...red] The flames of the ceremonial candles and of his passion are still burning and flaming.

30. good mans] the priest's.

32. disgested] dispersed, dissipated.

33. word.euer] In reference to the priest's order that their marriage shall last forever.

34. his period] its conclusion.

37-38. this...guiding] this catechizing is little needed to guide humans. If the "catechizing" referred to is the marriage ceremony, the remark seems impious; perhaps the master refers to his own reminders to Toures of the "condition" of the contract.

38-39. to...confesse] you should need these reminders least of all, since you have admitted being guilty of taking the girl without her father's permission.

40-44. he...furthest] men in grief are like men at sea, for sailors flatter themselves that every storm ends; in the same way fancies ease the love-sick sorrower, telling him a calm will come, when actually it is furthest away.

45-46. weapon...sound] Love is the weapon that is salve and surgeon, because love for the departed is like a wound, but falling in love again will salve the wound.

51. I...woe] I consumed myself in tears.

52. laugh] I.e., bitterly.

54. rend] An intransitive use of the verb, meaning "to burst apart."

56. hand...out] turn to throw the dice is over.

58. winnings...friends] winnings are not our friends because they don't come to us.

59-60. wind...beake] A curious, if not original, conceit.

64. hersed] coffined, in a container for the dead. A hearse was a frame which covered the coffin and carried lighted tapers, decorations, and perhaps even short poems or epitaphs pinned to it by mourners.

65. decest] deceased.

66-67. I...rights] Toures indulges himself in a fantasy or hallucination in which he imagines he is the music that awakens Mary on her wedding morning and calls her to the rites.

72. Neuer attempted] never sexually approached, thus virginal. as...bestowed] intact, as at birth.

73. Madam...end] Armin apparently and oddly uses "madam" as a synonym for "maiden" or "virgin"; thus she was at her beginning and still deserves to take the same title at her end.

79. proue...martyr] prove to be his martyr? experience his torture?

81. tire] attire. abilliments] habiliments, garments.

82. remembrant] remindful.

84. key cold] very cold, cold as a key. Cf. same phrase at XII.85, and in Shakespeare's Richard III (I.ii.5) Lady Anne mourns Henry VI as a "Poor key-cold figure of a holy King!"

90. blewnesse] I can find no parallel for Armin's use of "blue" for what must have been dark gray.

96-97. Although the couplet could belong to the Master, as Q. indicates, expressing his fear that he may have to leave the dallying Toures behind, it seems more likely that Toures himself is offering a final lament that a man should live and be forced to leave behind the love of his soul.

[Scene XVIII]

1. Scillie] The Scilly Islands are a group belonging to the British Crown, lying at the entrance to the English Channel, about twenty-five miles west of Land's End. Their

number is variously reckoned from forty to one hundred forty; only five, however, are inhabited; the rest are mere rocks, and owing to reefs and shoals, navigation there is hazardous during the rough weather.

4. prospectiuely] as through a perspective glass, an optical instrument for looking through or viewing objects with; a spy-glass, telescope, _etc_. In Greene's _Friar Bacon and Friar Bungay_ Edward uses a "glasse perspective" in scene vi to see, from Bacon's cell at Brasenose College, what is happening at Fresingfield.

5-8. The governor describes his problem, saying that since the islands are surrounded by warring kingdoms, the islanders ought to have fear, but armed by "foresight" (which is probably a pun referring to anticipatory caution and a clear view of approaching enemies), they are able to offer solid resistance.

5. danger...string] Danger is personified as holding and releasing the string of a bow, thus propelling the arrow.

7. resist] resistance.

8. brags] boasts.

12-14. Standing in the Scilly Islands, facing France, one would see Ireland to the right, France and Jersey ("Garsie") ahead, and Britain on the left.

15. Ilands...hostilitie] The governor may refer to the tragic relations between Ireland and England or to the pirates' use of Jersey as a sanctuary. R. B. Sharpe (p. 225) says that during the latter part of Elizabeth's

reign Spain traded on Irish hostility to England and established a military force in Kinsale. On October 8, 1601, Sir Francis Godolphin, then in charge of the defense of the Scilly Islands, wrote to Sir Robert Cecil, "'I needs must write of the present dangerous estate of the isles of Scilly under my charge, being the fairest inn in the direct way between Spain and Ireland.'" See also pp. 17-18.

16. splendious] splendid. <u>OED</u> lists Armin's as the first usage.

16-17. Which...frailtie] The enemy islands fluctuate in their relative might; they wax and wane like the sunshine.

18-19. An obscure couplet, perhaps best paraphrased: "We, being neighbored by all, must strengthen ourselves, while acting as if we frolic fearlessly, not even seeing the danger."

26. decaied] rotted (in the grave).

28. subscribd] submitted.

31. haild] haled, pulled, drawn, or hauled with force of violence.

34-35. her...will] she is governed by her own will.

47-48. our...heape] our sudden coming scared away those who piled this heap, so that they had to make a hasty ("new") ending.

50-51. what...it] The gentleman suggests alternative courses: should we dig it up? should we leave it? Then, in line 52, he offers a reason for rejecting the second course.

53. purpose] proposition (i.e., the first one). make one] do it.

57-60. A dispute over the use of tobacco raged in England, the most notable writings in the controversy being King James's *A Counter-Blaste to Tobacco* (1604) and John Deacon's *Tobacco Tortured* (1616). men...nostrels] men sell their land and spend the money on tobacco, thus their land is going up in smoke and out their nostrils. In *Bartholomew Fair* (II.vi.34-50), *Everyman In His Humour* (III.v.69-170), and *Everyman Out Of His Humour* (IV.iii.88-98) Jonson ridicules extremists on both sides of the dispute. spared] done without or used frugally.

66.1. *she sits vp*] The absurdity of Mary's sprightly recovery is made more patent by comparing it with the more credible, if still clumsy, equivalent scene (III.ii) in *Pericles, Prince of Tyre*, in which Thaisa, Pericles' wife, is also recovered from a ship-wrecked coffin; Thaisa is gradually brought back to consciousness by the physician, Cerimon. One would like to believe that Armin is burlesquing such romantic motifs, but Mary's speech, though preposterously self-possessed under the circumstances, seems to be delivered in deadly earnest. Both the authorship and date of composition of *Pericles* are too uncertain to afford solid basis for speculation on cross-influences.

72. Amaze not] Don't be amazed or astonished.

73. earthly] pale or lifeless.

75. chance...slaine] She believes her chance for a happy

married life is slain (i.e., destroyed).

80-81. returne...paine] Her sorrow as a deprived lover leads her to ask for Death's return. wanton] capricious.

83. time...comfort] situation calls for immediate rest.

87. dying...miserie] A peculiarly inverted word order for "story of your dying and misery."

[Scene XIX]

0.2. like...another] each in the former disguise of the other.

5-7. beleeue...himselfe] accept unsuspectingly your desire for haste, as he formerly heard Sir William grant approval of the wedding.

8. me alone] me go alone. follow...sonne] you follow, son.

12. stroken] struck.

13. He] I.e., Humil.

20-22. Grosart says, "clearly the whole of this belongs to Tutch, none to Tabitha." He does not explain his reasoning, but it is apparently based on the reference to "these two" rather than "we two," which would be more natural if Tabitha is speaking. But Tabitha has not left the scene yet, and the last sentence of the speech is an exit line ("I am gone"), which would be appropriate to Tabitha's role but would be impossible for Tutch since he speaks the next line.

23-24. you...mine] Filbon must now speak in the Welsh

tongue and Tutch must imitate Filbon in the role of servant. counterfeit] I.e., rehearse the dialect.

[Scene XX]

1. oth] Presumably Humil, in his disguise as an apothecary, has sworn to kill Lady Vergir.

4. Be...sorrow] Pretend to be killed with dark clouds of sorrow.

4-5. tis...gloue] Incomprehensible, but apparently metaphorical for, "the device is guaranteed to work."

7-8. My...thine] Sir William, of course, does not recognize Humil and is here deceiving the "stranger" by promising him a daughter whom he has just delegated to the "Welshman."

11. Hides] _Q._'s "Sites" makes no sense; "hides" would mean "overshadows."

14. Shal she] If she shall. noble] Funk and Wagnalls' _Standard College Dictionary_ gives "chemically inert" as one current definition; the word probably had some technical meaning in Armin's time, but I can find no similar usage.

15-16. my...state] _Q._ prints a comma after "hate," which could indicate that the word is the last of the series of direct objects of "cause" (line 14). By removing the comma, I read "hate" as the subject of "shall...kennell," so that Sir William means his hate shall confine or conceal ("kennell") itself nastily in the respectability of rank ("pride of state").

24-25. paint...front] Sir William wants her to make

herself attractive with cosmetics and the smiles of feigned happiness. front] face.

27. bloud-creasing spring] Grosart suggests "bloud-creating." Hereford and Simpson (IX, 392) quote from Sir Thomas Elyot's Castel of Helth: "Bloudde increaseth in Sprynge tyme, frome the .viii. Idus of February, unto the .viii Idus of May." The curious part about the passage is that Sir William says, in effect, "Be like the summer, which makes people happy with its spring." Why not just say "Be like the spring"?

29. sit...state] To "sit in state" means to sit "with great pomp and solemnity, with a great train," but OED does not list "sit to state."

33. Musike seuerall] music consisting of different elements or parts, of diverse origin or composition.

38. lay...to't] set your strongest purpose or determination to the accomplishment of it.

40. To...businesse] The phrase may belong syntactically to the preceding line (i.e., "which I sent for to aid you in this business") or it may be a final imperative to the Lady (i.e., "Get to this business!").

40-41. pray...consumption] The ambiguous words here are "ye" and "consumption." It is probably simplest to assume that "ye" is plural and that "consumption" is a malapropism for "consummation"; however, "ye" could refer to Humil and "consumption" could refer to the Lady's destruction or "ye" could refer to the Lady and "consumption" to the feast.

47. I...those] I.e., one of those who extravagantly and slavishly provide amusement for knaves. No doubt Sir William would be a more gracious host if the celebration reflected his inward state. he] James.

49. appoint] OED, for an entry dated 1601, offers a definition which seems to fit the context: "to declare, in exercise of an authority conferred for that purpose, the destination of specific property." Sir William may be inviting Humil to determine either the Lady's destination or the precise sum and method of payment to be paid him from Sir William's purse (see line 50). fit] Cunliffe cites passages in which the word means "to supply or provide a person with something"; therefore Sir William may mean, "she will provide you (with a victim)."

51-52. What...of] What we are sometimes wasteful of, we may dispose of uncontrolledly, since it is our own.

52-54. tis...death] it is my love (i.e., the Lady), whom it was my destiny to marry, who has joined the horn of a cuckold to my brow and drawn me to seek the deaths of those who betrayed me.

57. cost] outlay of money, expenses, to be provided by Sir William.

68. Made...intelligence] made known or clear by my accurate information.

69-70. who...bed] When Humil obeyed Sir William's command to exile himself, he was convinced that he had falsely slandered his innocent mother. We are not told why he has changed his mind. This passage is obscure because it is not clear whether James was literally masked so that Humil "knew not who was in bed," or whether he means, metaphorically, that the other three cunningly disguised the truth and "muffled" (blinded) him. The latter is more probable.

74. subtill...truth] Though we have the phrase "to strain a point" (i.e., twist the truth), the dictionaries offer no justification for Armin's use of "strain" to mean "deception." subtill straine] deceptive song.

83. Thou...owne] It is no sin to keep our own husbands, even if by trickery.

84. O...Fairies] Hamlet, on discovering that his mother and uncle have betrayed his father, exclaims, "O, my prophetic soul! My uncle!" (I.v.40). Armin's humiliated Hamlet, on discovering that his mother did not betray his father, exclaims, "O you prophetique Fairies." (See p. 77.)

85. concaues] hollows, cavities.

86. your] Since he is responding to his mother's statement and might naturally have wanted to avoid her sight (either from a sense of shame for her "guilt" or from a sense of guilt for having falsely accused her), the pronoun could refer to the Lady, but he refers to her in the third person in line 89 and is probably still talking to himself here, so that "your" refers to the "prophetique Fairies," whom he seems to conceive of as being like the Eumenides, avengers of unavenged crimes.

87-88. But...businesse] There are several difficulties in this passage. Q. places a comma after "thinking"; this might allow the following interpretation: "after thinking a while, I was blinded to (forgot) the truth (that his mother had sinned) and thought ahead ("forethought") to what might happen" (perhaps he considered what he might do to reconcile himself with her, if he thought her innocent, or of what Sir William might do to avenge himself on her if she were, despite Sir William's denials, guilty). The ambiguities do not disappear if we drop the comma after "thinking." When he left, he seemed to believe that his mother was innocent; therefore, when he says "thinking truth was blinded," he may mean that he came to the decision that what he had reported had been correct and that the truth was being concealed ("blinded"), in which case "some following businesse" might refer to the consequences of either his own or Sir William's desire for vengeance. The same confusion about his attitude and intentions toward his mother at his return persists in the phrase "comming as one disguised to save her life," which could mean either that he wore the disguise so that he could save her life from Sir William's vengeance or that he came as one who would save her life (an apothecary, healer) when he actually intended to take it and receive a reward from Sir William. I believe that the most logical interpretation is that after he left, he trusted his own eyes more than Sir William's words and decided that he, like Orestes, must avenge his honor by killing his mother, and that he came in order to kill her. This interpretation is supported by line 90, where he says he is "dam'd for that fact"; he would not now, knowing his mother to be innocent, consider himself damned for wanting to save her, but he would for wanting to kill her. On the other hand, his mother's question in line 91 would seem to indicate that she made the opposite interpretation. "My life?" she asks, as if she is surprised that it is in jeopardy. We might expect her to ask, "what do you mean disguised?" if she had been struck by the implication that he meant her harm.

95-96. I...brought] I that brought your alleged offense to light must be the pardon brought to your trial ("iudgement").

101. flourish] Q. prints "perish," which makes no sense but was probably transferred from four lines below (XXI.1), where it also ends the line.

[Scene XXI]

5. Per...fidem] By the faith of gods and men.

9-13. The passage is very obscure and perhaps corrupt, as is suggested by the fact that the verse is mis-aligned and two words ("keept" and "quickens") are misprinted. A possible paraphrase is: "If kept, secrets give offense to those who are uninformed, and that is the situation now, for it may be that I shall lose my position. But there's a useful device ("friend") which witty repartee and circumlocution ("turning") call avoiding the issue, being noncommittal ("detraction"). That path (i.e., pretending not to be involved in the marriage) provides some hope because its cunning turns a crime to advantage.

14-15. Filbon assures Henry that they will vouch for him when he tells Sir William that he had been deceived and did not know whom he was marrying.

16-17. Tabitha offers to be his protector ("buckler"); he asks, dubiously, if she can protect herself.

18-19. Tabitha likens the marriage to a fencing match; a "venny" is a fencing bout, so an "after venny" would be the sequel, in this case the meeting with Sir William.

20-23. In a variant on the consolatory cliche to parents of newlyweds, Sir Rafe assures Tabitha that she has not lost a father but gained one.

22. his] Toures's.

28. constering] construing, making a grammatical analysis of. It is probably foolish to strain the ingenuity in attempts to make sense of the playful use of grammatical terms in this and the next five lines. For similar but wittier dialogue see _The Merry Wives of Windsor_ (IV.i.13-85).

30. Tutch says, "your father will cry out when he learns that Filbon has won you with his Welch."

36. earnest blow] ceremonial marriage kiss?

38. it...me] Auditor could mean either "I hope I am not the one to undo ('cancell') it" or "I hope it is not the cause of my undoing."

44. liberall...honour] the burden which honor requires

of a man to be generous ("liberall").

45. Triumphs] processions, ceremonies.

48. Which...quoted] who are named in a roster.

49-52. bribes...businesse] purchases or seduces ("bribes") grace and thus bestows it upon the gathering ("assembly") and promises to further the congeniality of the festivities ("businesse"). Or perhaps "bribes" is a misprint for "prides."

57. Singled] separated.

67. thou...keie] a bawdy conceit. Sir John Harrington writes (p. 312):

> Of a Lady that Left open her Cabbinett
> A vertuose Lady sitting in a muse,
> As many times fayr vertuous Ladies use,
> Leaned her Elbow on one knee full harde,
> The other distaunt from it halfe a yearde.
> Her knight, to tawnt her by a privy token,
> Said, "Wife, awake, your Cabbinett stands open."
> She rose and smylld and soft doth saye,
> "Then lock it if yow list: you keepe the kaye."

73. _Hei...nullos_] Alas for me what no one (_nullus_) [would do].

74. _pauca_] Normally "few," but here, as elsewhere, it may mean "briefly," "in short."

76-77. was...hum a] Grosart notes that "cragge de pen" refers to the judge's scratch of the pen which writes out the sentence, after which the hangman will call to him and silence him. The "da hum a" is, accompanied by gestures, his imitation of the sound or act of hanging.

79. Ile...ye] An allusion to Kyd's _Spanish Tragedy_ (IV. i.70); the statement means "I'll provide what you need."

79-80. hic & ubique] McGinn (p. 157) says the phrase is an allusion to Hamlet (I.i.141 and I.v.156).

[Scene XXII]

5. pointing stock] laughing stock.

6-7. In keeping with the birth-growth image initiated in lines 3 and 4, Sir William personifies rumor as a gossip (a sponsor at a baptism), concluding that the story of his cuckoldry will be christened with its death; by killing the Lady and James he will nip the story in the bud.

9. bountie] hospitality. niggard] be stingy with.

17-18. hast...proofe] have you prepared matters so that our murderous purposes will succeed?

23. couer] spread the cloth for a meal.

25. Blessed...fall] This is the blessed beginning of the end for my sorrows.

27.1. gallant] gorgeous or showy in appearance. braue] This word was a general epithet of admiration, like "worthy," "fine," and "good." In some contexts it means "finely-dressed," as in Heywood's Apology for Actors (1612): "One man is ragged and another brave" (cited OED).

29. luxurie] lasciviousness, lust.

30. quaint] fine, elegant in dress. Perhaps also bawdy.

32. How...woman] That is, "how can you be ashamed and still be a woman?" The assumption is that shame and womanhood are incompatible states.

33. blaze] emblazon, display. affections] desires,

feelings.

34. thy...deede] Sir William is bitterly ironic.

38. sensuable] able to be observed by the senses, visible. She claims she will blush.

43. I...remembrance] I have forgotten (your offense); I do not remember it. Or, perhaps, I am not the offended man you remember; he is dead.

53. glisters] glitters. nothing] Used adverbially. His beams give a splendor that is not at all proud but darkened by fear and hidden in a cloud.

56. darling...heart] Sir William's sardonic jealousy is at work here.

57. Euen...thing] As you say, have it your own way, but I wasn't even thinking of that.

58-59. It is not clear whether James is consoling himself with the thought that Sir William's courtly toils will not be rewarded because James will have the Lady and the last laugh, or whether he is admonishing himself that he is busy working while Sir William escorts his wife.

60-63. Humil has evidently overheard his father muttering to himself and has interpreted the grumbling as a protest; he seeks to console his father by reminding him that Sir William is merely playing at ardor ("flame"), since he knows that his Lady will not respond to him, and, anyway, the two of them will soon act to deprive ("furnish to disfurnish") him of the Lady ("what he yet enioies").

66. vitriall boales] vitreous, glassy bowls.

67. Nest...nest] a nest of goblets or bowls is made up of a large one containing many smaller ones of gradually diminishing sizes, which fit into each other.

68. tend...diet] await the request for some alternative in the menu.

69. Sirrha...trow] Humil mimics Sir William. fit] be equal to. trow] believe.

71. At hand] Humil pretends to shake hands, as if greeting a guest.

74. indored] Evidently an archaic form of "endeared," but I can find no authority for it.

75-76. were...water] would be superfluous.

77-79. your...command] A witty compliment; the gods themselves do not command a more select attendance at their bacchanals.

80. Mary] the exclamation "Marry!" an oath on the Virgin; here apparently having the force of "well," or "however," or "admittedly," since Sir William goes on to say that the nectar and ambrosia, normally present at the gods' "Bacchinels" are wanting. It is also possible that "Ambrotia" is not, with Nectar, part of a compound subject of "wants," but, instead, the subject of "smiles" (line 81).

85. suite of entertaine] set of rooms for entertainment.

88. except] accept.

95. Your...frugall] You are generous ("free"), yet frugal.

96. make...of] take advantage of.

97. But...loue] Obscure and cryptic, but perhaps "but

value her (i.e., 'curtesie's') kindness as the best sort of love."

99. Rent-free] without obligation.

100. If...receptacle] If you feel at home here.

101-102. Landlord...loue] The lines are very elliptical; Sir William and Armin are avoiding verbs, subjects, and connective expressions, while managing to be wordy at the same time. The lines can be paraphrased: "I am the landlord and shall soundly prove it by declaring fines forgiven; I release you from my debt; my love for you is freely given." As in VII.55 (see note) there are implications that guests at such celebrations frequently were asked to pay for what they took; Sir William seems to be taking and receiving a great deal of praise for his generosity in not demanding payment.

103. tenants] Again, the assumption of a landlord-tenant relationship, though jocular, implies that these guests would ordinarily be in his debt. Perhaps petty knights then, like graduate students today, held dutch-treat parties.

104. my...it] my duty requires me to offer it (i.e., welcome).

105. frolicke] An odd word to use in connection with sedentary activities, since it generally refers to playful merriment and capers requiring rapid movement. It probably means here simply "make merry," but Hereford and Simpson (X, 239n) report that a "frolick" was "an erotic or satiric

couplet wrapped around a sweetmeat. A dish was placed on the table after supper, and the guests picked them out and sent them to one another as seemed appropriate."

109. her] bale's.

110. I] Aye. But possibly a misprint for "In."

110-112. Sir William seems to be muttering to himself, thinking of the Lady's incipient death and of the mystery ("morall") and enigma of her ironic situation.

113. fal too] fall to, begin.

115. In yours] Elliptical. In your partnership, i.e., in her rank as your wife--she is among the best socially. See line 114.

116. periority] superiority.

121. censure] judge or think.

122. chalenge] See page 44 for discussion of Armin's unconventional use of this word, which here seems to mean "offer."

123. his...lends] the one who provides ("lends") the goods.

126. cockrel right] A cockerel is a young cock; "right" is an adjective modifying "cockrel," but I have been unable to determine if it is merely a general word of approbation or a cant term of more specific meaning.

128. If...owne] If my boldness may dare to match ("chal-enge") yours.

130. I...giues] Probably, "I confidently ('lightly') give the fulfillment ('performance') of my promise." The

abnormal word order may be dictated by metrical considerations.

131. Heart...boote] Willingly of heart as well. cods me] A mild oath, like "Gods me."

132-145. Skink...Lord] Throughout this passage the serving of drinks is treated in the imagery of gunnery. The wife is asked to discharge the shot (wine), but, since she has only one glass to serve, she must give it to one "principall," who will represent all. The <u>common</u> shot, which will go to all the rest as well, is a glance from her "pearsing eye," which all request. Skink] pour out or draw beer or wine.

135. vnder daunt] The word does not appear in any of the dictionaries and is apparently a neologism (see pp. 42-43). If "they" in lines 134 and 135 refers to the Lady's eyes, "vnder daunt" would mean "obligation": "if your eyes have no bullets, they avoid ('scapė') the obligation (to look at each guest) which courtesy demands." I think it more likely that "they" refers to the guests, who will, if un-hit by her "bullets" (i.e., glances), escape courtesy's "vnder daunt" (intimidation? wound?).

136. They...dies] Tilley (C57) gives, "Who was killed by a cannon was cursed in his mother's belly."

137. May...blest] The kind of shot (i.e., either wine or her glance) that the Lady is "firing" is a blessing, not a curse.

138. other] others.

143-144. mongst...voice] Obscure, but perhaps, "Among so many you are free to choose one who is of the highest importance and who acts as a voice to each of us."

145-148. She claims that by choosing their leader, the Earl, she is choosing the rest; he is their representative; just as when the king nods he is understood to be greeting all of his subjects though his eye settles on only one.

152. Pray...memories] This makes no sense to me.

155. vnlook't...welcome] your visit being a pleasant surprise (unlooked for), you are all the more welcome.

159. affect...ignorant] are fond of this fool.

166. plentifull] yielding plenty; generous.

167. Faith...me] Sir William, who has been good-naturedly mocking himself for being a miser, may suddenly shift his tone and murmur this last obscure line in recognition of the disparity between his apparent genial hospitality and his murderous intentions.

169. suck-egge] silly fellow; cf. line X.23.

180. gal'd] galled; chafed.

182. Geneua psalme] a psalm as rendered in the Geneva Bible (1560), very popular in Puritan homes.

186-187. Nurse...bedfellow] The remark provides a striking bit of dramatic irony, which Tabitha capitalizes on, but it seems contrived and unjustified.

204. fronts] places on the forehead. wreath] A cornucopian wreath was a symbol or horn of cuckoldry, because of Latin <u>cornus</u>, horn.

206. Such...followes] Such dying gasps would follow as a result of your crime.

206-207. lamps...Nemmisis] I can find no mythological references to either the lamps or the spottedness of Nemesis.

207-208. let...selfe] Q. is incoherent and may be corrupt; sense could be restored by either of two possible changes in word order: "let fall the/ Light" or "let the light/ Fall." Further evidence of a corrupt text is that Q. lines the remainder of the speech as prose. The lines may also be the fustian and saturnine mutterings of a man who does not want to be understood.

214. you...me] you shall excuse or relieve me from my promise to leave at your command. vnles with] because of.

219. promise] The promise to leave was given in XV.241-246.

226. queasie] sickish.

227. mother] A "fit of the mother" was an Elizabethan phrase for hysteria, perhaps accompanied by suffocation.

228. No...husband] She puns sardonically: it's not the "mother" that causes my pain but my husband.

231. calme] qualm.

233. Excellent fit] That is most fitting.

236. shift] trick, subterfuge.

236-237. where...be] i.e., alone with Tabitha.

237. back't] supported, defended.

240. by...daughter] Elliptical for "by telling of the

coming of thy daughter"?

241. indored] endeared; see also XXI.74.

244. ingraft...unknowne] engraft (join) us with unknown children.

245. yonkers] Nares gives, "A young person, frequently in the sense of a dupe or person thoughtless through inexperience."

255. Conicatcht] deceived. and so] and by that means.

257. Yes...right] Sarcastic: "Oh, undoubtedly ('questionlesse') you are abused, and I suppose everything has gone all right for me."

258. I to affirme] Unclear as it stands, but "I" could be "aye," and "to" could be either "do" or "too"; any combination of these would be preferable to _Q_.'s version.

259-260. When...promise] The syntax is not clear, but the sense is that he has fulfilled Sir William's requirements (given in VIII.78-79): "when you are from yourself a woman, she is yours in marriage." challendge] demand (fulfillment of).

261. Iohn...now] The title of a ballad preserved in Chappell's _Old English Popular Music_ (p. 268). The same song is referred to in Heywood's _A Woman Killed With Kindness_ (ii.33).

262. quondam] former.

264-265. I...English] Grosart paraphrases: "I counterfeited Welch that I might join these two who conster (i.e., speak) English."

266. What...recald] What, are you in a funk, gazing off? Can't you be snapped back to reality?

267-268. No...Welcome] Sir William begins by protesting against the delivery of more unsettling news then resigns himself to having it all at once.

269. doombe] judgment.

271. For...daughter] In exchange for the life you recently lost in the one you had deputed to your daughter.

273-274. Pagan] Grosart claims the word means "lie," the thing Pagans are best known for. Evidently Sir William does not believe the report of Mary's death, thinking it another trick.

285-289. cause...deare] because you knew your guilt tied that clog (i.e., a block or heavy piece of wood attached to the leg or neck of a man or beast to impede motion or prevent escape) to your legs and were uncertain of her dowry ("portion"), you thought to rid yourself of that fear of my wrath and rid me of her I loved.

293. assurance] security, safety.

295. president] precedent.

296. _Doningtons_..._Grimes_] H. N. Hillebrand (p. 328) reports that "the _Acts of the Privy Council_, under date June 14, 1597, record that Alice Stoite, a young woman of Dorset, was abducted by one Dinington and others. No further particulars are given, and I have been able to trace no other likely reference to 'Donington's man Grimes' but it seems reasonably sure that the abduction of Alice Stoite

was the one meant by Sir William." See page 14 for the significance of this allusion for dating the play.

315. chalengd] For a discussion of Armin's peculiar use of this word, see page 44. Here it seems to mean "commanded."

316-317. but...contrary] Elliptical for "but Humil thought it was otherwise"?

318. thus disguised] Modifies "sonne," referring to Humil's role as an apothecary.

319. Fearing...mischiefe] Still referring to Humil, James implies that Humil returned to protect his mother from Sir William's revenge rather than to avenge himself on his mother for the shame she brought on him. See notes at XX.86 and 87-88.

326. in few] in brief.

327-328. no...property] The words "substance" and "property" are abstract and generic, but the point seems to be, "No wonder you stayed away from my bed; you had another source of income, substance, and wealth."

329. your owne] i.e., your own wife.

331. slights] sleights, cunning tricks.

332. whats...daughter] what has this to do with the more important matter of my daughter?

339-340. theres...yet] there's some youthfulness left in you yet.

340. ye will] i.e., you will forgive her mistake.

341. vndergo] endure, suffer.

348. you...you] Perhaps the text is corrupt; a more plausible line would be: "he will reckon you rightly" (i.e., he will be assured that you are palpable and not airy).

350-351. I...anger] I have a joy which bars me from ("crosses") all anger.

352-353. this...applause] this happy event gives savor to the applause (i.e., of the audience, signalling that the play is nearly over), making it more palatable.

354. welcome...word] it is appropriate that I bid my daughter welcome.

355. faine] One meaning of "to fain" is "to welcome a person."

356. apprehends with] An object is needed for the verb, presumably "me."

357. But...what] Hesitation causes ellipsis: "but...I know not what..."

357-358. in...lyes] it lies in me.

359-360. laught...Once] Armin or the compositor tries to make "at" do double duty: laughed at at once.

361. and] Doesn't seem to mean "if" here; "one whom" is omitted.

363. complement] ceremoniousness.

365. challenge...purpose] He seems to be offering them privileges ("fauour") in return for their discretion and respect in regard to his cuckoldry, but "challenge," "perswasion," and "purpose" inhibit precise paraphrase

by their vagueness.

368. prodigious to] an omen of.

374-378. you...all] you see how good luck favors us when we are at extreme disadvantage; if any bungled evil has the appearance of being of some benefit, though it is not immediately understood as to its ultimate nature, bear with it.

379. Loosing...sonne] After losing a wife, he has gained two sons.

APPENDIX A

ROBERT ARMIN AND THE VALIANT WELSHMAN

In the introductory sections on "Author," "Text," and "Parodic Intent" I indicated that my evaluation of the printer's copy of *Two Maids* and of Armin's skill and purpose as a writer hinged significantly on my belief that he wrote a second play, *The Valiant Welshman*. This second play is listed in the *Stationer's Register* under the date of February 21, 1615 (i.e., 1614): "Robert Lownes. Entered for his copie vnder the handes of Sir Georg[e] Bucke and both the wardens a play called *the valiant welshman*." The title page of the first edition reads: THE/ VALIANT WELSHMAN,/ OR/ *THE* TRVE CHRONI-/ cle History of the life and valiant/ *deedes of* CaraDOC *the Great*,/ King of Cambria, now called/ WALES.// Written by R. A. Gent..// [ornament] // LONDON,/ Imprinted by *George Purslowe* for *Robert Lownes*,/ and are to be solde at his shoppe at the/ *Little North dore of Paules*./ 1615. A second edition appeared in 1663.

Schelling,[1] Herring,[2] and Jewkes,[3] all flatly

[1]Schelling, I, 295.

[2]Robert Herring, "The Whale Has a Wide Mouth," *Life & Letters Today*, XXVI (January, 1943), 48.

[3]Jewkes, p. 223.

attribute the play to Armin. None of them argues the case, each apparently believing the initials R. A. to be sufficient evidence. For none of them is the attribution necessary to any larger argument they make. Herring states that the play had a second edition "eighteen years later,"[4] which would put it at 1633, but I have found no further record of such an edition, though he may have misread or mistranscribed the 1663 date of the known second edition. In 1905 a German scholar, Krebs, published another edition, which I have been unable to obtain, in which he rejects the theory of Armin's authorship and assigns it instead to "some young university man,"[5] a theory which Chambers[6] endorses. Schelling, without explanation, offers 1595 as the approximate date of composition, but I agree with Chambers that the play borrows from _The Alchemist_, "which proves that the play could not have been written before 1610."[7]

Grosart nowhere mentions "R. A."'s play, and Felver, who, after Grosart, has probably read Armin most thoroughly, says: "The conjecture that Armin is the author R. A. of... _The Valiant Welshman_, pub. 1615, is not very likely since all of Armin's other works mention his own connection with the theater and there is nothing characteristic of his style

[4]Herring, p. 48.

[5]Chambers, IV, 51.

[6]Chambers, IV, 51.

[7]Jewkes, p. 223, citing Chambers, IV, 51.

in the work."[8] Felver's first reason for rejecting Armin's authorship is indisputable but irrelevant since Welshman, unlike Armin's other works, was published during a time in which, as Felver himself makes clear, Armin was not connected with any theater. His second reason is both more pertinent and more problematical. Felver presumably uses the word "style" to refer to diction, sentence structure, and grammar rather than to the larger elements of play construction such as plot, tone, characterization, and parody. But even granting this restricted use of the word, one need not altogether agree that "there is nothing characteristic of [Armin's] style in the work." One must concede from the outset that Welshman is far clearer in style and character motivation, more coherent in structure, and more polished if not more interesting in every way than Two Maids. But the differences between the two are certainly not as great as those between Shakespeare's masterpieces and his other works in which scholars have been obliged to find "another hand" in order to account for their shortcomings. And if one accepts my thesis that the printer's copy for Two Maids was the author's rough foul papers, while concurring with Jewkes, as I do, that the printer's copy for Welshman was an "author's manuscript which had been prepared with a tentative performance in mind,"[9] one need not be surprised

[8] Robert Armin, Shakespeare's Fool, p. 77.

[9] Jewkes, p. 224.

that the later play, written in a concentrated span of time during the leisure of the author's retirement, would display more coherence and professional craft than the earlier play written piecemeal in the midst of a busy career. And even allowing for the more advantageous conditions under which Armin may have written the second play, is there not something Armin-esque about the absence of a main clause in this very first "sentence" of the prefatory "To the Ingenious Reader"?

> As it hath been a custome of long continuance, as well in Rome the Capital City, as in divers other renowned Cities of the world, to have the lives of Princes and worthy men, acted in their Theatres, and especially the Conquests and Victories which their own Princes and Captains had obtained, thereby to incourage their youths to follow the steps of their Ancestors; which custome even for the same purpose, is tolerated in our Age, although some peevish people seem to dislike of it: Amongst so many valiant Princes....

In the ensuing discussion I will first point to some stylistic or linguistic parallels in the plays and then go on to an account of their common use of parody, pastiche, and imitation of Shakespeare and other dramatists of the time.

As the play opens Octavian, King of Northwales and rightful heir to the throne of Wales, is challenged by the Earl of Monmouth. Octavian is supported in combat by Cadallan, Prince of March and father of Caradoc, the titular "valiant Welshman." Monmouth kills Cadallan, and Caradoc, in revenge, kills Monmouth, temporarily saving the throne for Octavian. As a reward Octavian offers Caradoc his daughter, Princess Guiniver. Caradoc's response to the offer is one of the few obscure passages in the play:

> Accept of it, great King!
> The Thracian _Orpheus_ never entertayn'd
> More ioy in sight of his _Euridice_,
> When with his silver tunes he did inchaunt
> The triple-headed dog, and reassumde 5
> His soules beatitude, from _Plutoes_ Court,
> Then your devoted servant in this gift,
> Wherein such unrespected [_sic_] joy concurs,
> That every sense daunces within his blest
> circumference,
> And cals my blisse, A Newyeeres gift from _Jove_; 10
> And not from that which reason or discourse
> Proudly from beasts doth challenge, as from a man.
> In brief, my Lord,...

The speech is clear enough up to my line 5, but the syntax of lines 6-10 is about as uncertain as anything in _Two Maids_, and the use of "challenge" (its only appearance in _Welshman_), though probably idiomatic, is similar to Armin's in _Two Maids_.

On the page following the passage just quoted, wedding preparations are begun and directions are given to "Go you into the Church, and with your holy fires/ Perfume the altars of your countrey gods." The practice of perfuming bridal accouterments is apparently peculiar to _Two Maids_ among plays of the time, since the only reference given for it in a discussion of wedding practices in _Shakespeare's England_[10] is to Armin's play, though, of course, if Armin is merely noting a common practice, there is no reason why another playwright might not observe the custom as well.

[10]Percy Macquoid, _Shakespeare's England_ (Oxford, 1916), II, 146-147.

But there are other verbal resemblances between the two plays as well: "plannet-strook" appears at C3v in Welshman and at VIII.15 in Two Maids; the compound does not appear in OED. Also at C3v (II.i) is the phrase "after times," similar to Armin's "after joy" (III.25), "after deeds" (VII.119), "after hope" (VII.132), and "after venny" (XXI.19). At II.v in Welshman appears the unusual word "disgest," while Armin uses the form "disgested" at XVII. 32. At II.ii appears the mythological allusion to the Giants who "Hurled Ossa upon Peleon, heap'd hill on hill," used by Armin at XV.89. At II.v (D4v) appears the unusual oath "s'foot," used by Armin at XVI.34 (and also, it must be admitted, in The Revenger's Tragedy, III.vi.10 and in plays by Marston). At III.ii Caradoc utters a soliloquy about as much like Hamlet's as any of those by Humil, especially in the clause "Then my Prophetique spirit tells me true," which compares with Hamlet's "O my prophetic soul" (I.v.40) and Humil's "O ye prophetick Fairies" (XX. 84). At the conclusion of IV.i the golden fleece is used as a sex symbol, as it is in Armin's II.54-56. And at IV.v Caradoc, when at a disadvantage, resorts to "policy," as do Armin's characters as VI.26, VI.58, XII.63, and XVI.142.

Perhaps more important than these verbal similarities, many of which are commonplaces, in linking the authorship of the two plays is the less demonstrable similarity of habitual parody of Shakespeare. I have argued above (pp. 70-78) that Two Maids parodies at least Hamlet and The Spanish Tragedy, if not Lear, Macbeth, Othello, and Romeo and Juliet. Welshman, by the same token, imitates the prologue and the characterization of bluff Fluellen from Henry V, the rape scene from The Rape of Lucrece, the conniving titular character from Richard III, the graveyard scene from Hamlet, and the comic pursuit of a fairy queen from both The Alchemist and Midsummer Night's Dream, not to mention the rhetoric of patriotic sentiment that runs throughout Shakespeare's chronicles.[11] I will dwell only upon the parallels which seem most interesting. Perhaps the most delightful is the imitation of Bottom's and Dapper's infatuations with fairy queens (remember that The Alchemist is the last play in which Armin is known to have performed).

Morion, the "foolish son" of Morgan (about whom I shall have more to say presently) falls in love with the Fairy Queen (II.i):

> Morion. By my troth, my stomack rumbleth at the very conceit of this Iamall love, even from the sole of my head to the crown of the foot. Surely I will have more acquaintance of that Gentlewoman; me thinks she daunceth like a Hobby-horse.

The acquaintance is renewed at II.v when Morion and his man Ratsbane prepare to meet the fairy:

> Morion. Oh the intolerable pain that I suffer for the love of the Fayry Queene! my heeles are all kybde in the very heat of affection, that runnes down into my legs: me thinkes I could eate up a whole Brokers shoppe

[11]Irving Ribner, The English History Play in the Age of Shakespeare (New York, 1965), pp. 262-264, points out the parallels to Richard III and Henry V.

at a meale, to be eased of this love.

Ratsbane. Oh Master, you would have a villainous many of pawnes in your belly. Why, you are of so weake a nature, you would hardly disgest a Servingmans Livery in your belly, without a vomit.

Morion. I assure thee, thou sayest true, tis but grosse meate. But Ratsbane, thou toldst mee of a rare fellow, that can tell misfortunes, and can conjure: prethee bring me to him. Ile give him somewhat, to helpe mee speake with the Fayry Queene.

Whose face like to a Butchers doublet lookes,
Varnisht with tallow of some beautious Oxe;
Or like the aprons of some Pie-corner Cooks,
Whose breath smels sweeter than a hunted foxe:
Whose eyes, like two great foot-balls made of lether,
Were made to heate the gods in frosty weather.

Such ludicrously deflating similes are used nowhere in Two Maids and more's the pity.

Scholars are in general agreement that Armin played the role of the first clown in the grave-digging scene in Hamlet. It is not unlikely that he may have hoped to take advantage of whatever success and fame he may have enjoyed in that part by writing a similar one for himself in Welshman. Act IV, scene iii, opens with "a company of Rusticks bearing the body of Gloster," one of the villains. The scene is too long to reproduce in full, but some snatches of it will suggest its kinship with Shakespeare's. Notice in the following lines the concern (like that in Hamlet, V.i.29-31) with the unequal treatment of corpses:

Caradoc. Whose body is that, my friends?

Clown. Tis not a body, Sir, 'tis but a carkase, sir, some Gentleman it seemes; for if hee had beene a poore man, that labours for his living, he would have found somewhat else to doe, and not have hangde himselfe.

. . . .

Clown. My masters and fellow questmen, this is the point, we are to search out the course of law, whether this man that has hangde himselfe, be accessary to his own death or no.... I put this point to you, whether every one that hangs himselfe be willing to die or not?

2nd Neighbor. I, I, sure he is willing.

Clown. I say no, for the hangman hangs himself, and yet he is not willing to die.

3rd. Neighbor. How dos the hangman hang himselfe?

Clown. I mary dos he, sir, for if he have not a man to doe his office for him, he must hang himself: ergo, every man that hangs himself is not willing to die. [Cf. Hamlet, V.i.20-22: "Argal, he that is not guilty of his own death shortens not his own life."]

1st Neighbor. He sayes very true indeed; but now sir, being dead, who shall answere the King for his subject?

Clown. Mary sir, he that hangd his subject.

2nd Neighbor. That was himself.

3rd Neighbor. No sir, I doe thinke it was the halter that hangde him.

Clown. I, in a sort, but that was se offendendo, for it may be that he meant to have broke the halter, and the halter held him out of his own defence.

Compare these latter lines to Hamlet, V.i.6-10:

1st Clown. How can that be, unless she drowned herself in her own defense?

2nd Clown. Why, 'tis found so.

1 Clown. It must be "se offendendo," it cannot be else. For here lies the point. If I drown myself wittingly, it argues an act...."

A final piece of evidence tying Armin with Welshman is the duplication of a blustering, bumptious but likeable character, a Welshman named Morgan. Armin may have played Fluellen in Henry V (though this is disputed) and he very probably played the Welshman Evans in The Merry Wives of

Windsor.[12] It is also quite possible that one of his routines for his "enterludes" was a comic imitation of Welshmen and that he would have delighted in such speeches as the one Morgan makes upon his entry in *Welshman*:

> Morgan. Hark you, my Lord Condigune; by the pones of Saint *Tavy*, you have prattled to the King a great deale of good Physick, and for this one of her good lessons and destructions, how call you it, be Cad, I know not very well, I wil fight for you with all the *George Stones*, or the *Ursa Majors* under the Sunnes. Harke you me, Kings: I pray for you now, good Kings, leave your whimbling, and your great proclamations: let death come at her, and ha can catch her, and pray God blesse her. As for Rebell *Monmouth*, I kanow very well what I will do with her. I will make Martlemas beef on her flesh, and false dice on her pones for every Conicatcher: I warrant her for case bobby and Metheglin: I will make her pate ring noone for all resurrections and rebellions.

Although the speech of the two Morgans varies in phonetic spellings (Tutch-Morgan, for instance, would have said "Harg you me"), it is similar in vocabulary and rhythm. Such malapropisms as "resurrections" in the last line above are undoubtedly intentional, as is "molestings" at XII.16 in *Two Maids*, but "delude" ($B2^v$) for "dilute" and "capituling" ($B2^v$) for "capitulating" are more like Armin's catachreses (see p. 43). One final common denominator of the two plays (and, admittedly, of many others of the period, e.g., Dekker's *Satiromastix*) is the reference to the audience's applause in the Epilogues.

The positive case for Armin's authorship, then, hinges on these things: the recurrence of some distinctive

[12]Felver, *Robert Armin, Shakespeare's Fool*, p. 49, citing T. W. Baldwin, *The Organization and Personnel of the Shakespearian Company* (Princeton, 1927), pp. 228-229.

words and some not so distinctive allusions and stylistic mannerisms; the recurrence of a bumptious Welshman; the nearly equally astounding complexity of plot threads; and, most significantly, the heavy reliance in both plays on parody, pastiche, and imitation. In pointing out the parallels in diction, syntax, characterization, and dramatic technique I have, of course, slanted the facts and in so doing perhaps have exaggerated the points of contact between the two plays. I would be among the first to agree that not one parallel (with the exception of the use of the compound "plannet-strook") exists exclusively between these two plays. Many writers parodied _Hamlet_, as many did _The Spanish Tragedy_; some no doubt imitated specifically the grave-yard scene; Welshmen appear in several plays besides those mentioned; and allusions to piling hill upon hill are commonplace. Nevertheless, if the parallels are not individually striking, they are cumulatively impressive. There are differences in the plays as well, and though some are real, others are merely apparent, and all, I think, can be explained in a manner consistent with Armin's authorship.

The most striking difference is in the almost total stylistic lucidity of the later play, which bears little or no trace of Armin's penchant for elliptical constructions or the accumulation of appositive phrases and clauses. This difference, I have suggested, may be accounted for by the demonstrably superior finished copy of _Welshman_, which even contains act and scene divisions. The same explanation can be offered for the greater metrical regularity of Welshman: a page chosen from it at random contains twenty-two decasyllabic lines in twenty-eight of verse (and four of the extrametrical lines contain the usually elided words "every," "even," "over," and "heaven"). Thus, actually better than ninety percent of the examined lines in Welshman are regular while three examined pages in Two Maids contain only thirty, forty, and sixty-five percent of decasyllabic lines (see pp. 94-95).

The next difference likely to be noticed by readers of the two plays is the greater simplicity and clarity of character-motivation in the later play. This difference can be explained in two ways: (1) the author's growing skill, and (2) the opposing demands of the genres represented; Elizabethan chronicles are typically peopled by heroes and villains; soldiers are not expected to feel the same ambivalence as jealous husbands and disgraced sons.

The fourth difference may be felt in what seem to be contrasting tones in the plays. I have argued (pp. 71 and 87) that Armin displays a skeptical, rationalistic, unsentimental mind in Two Maids; yet I have also referred in this discussion to the expression of conventional patriotic sentiments and attitudinizing heroics. This disparity could be attributed, again, to the differences in genre, but I am not sure that it really exists. There is some reason to believe that in Welshman the author's tone is ironic, mocking, or only half-serious, that he regards the "war" of the

Welsh, in which his "heroes" are defeated, with some of the same majestic disdain that Shaw felt toward the Bulgarians battling at Slivnitz. I suspect that "the valiant Welshman" may have sounded as vaguely ridiculous to Elizabethan ears as "the brave Bulgarian" did to Shavian ones.

The final difference certainly _is_ more apparent than real. At first reading _Welshman_ seems the product of a more highly cultured, educated, and even elegant if not pretentious mind than Armin displays elsewhere. But the "history" behind it is as mishandled as the "Latin" in _Two Maids_. As Irving Ribner points out:

> In a short preface addressed "To the Ingenuous [_sic_] Reader," the author of _The Valiant Welshman_ refers to the account of his hero in _Tacitus_, but the play makes no attempt to follow either this account or the fuller one in Dio Cassius. Holinshed appears to have been used, but with no concern for historical accuracy, for the play offers an account of Caradoc's adventures quite at variance from that in Holinshed. It is probable that the author began with Holinshed's general account but gave free play to his imagination and attempted unsuccessfully to repeat some of the motifs common in the more popular plays of his time.[13]

The greater "elegance," manifested in the use of elements resembling the masque and anti-masque, could be a reflection of Armin's recent experience in Jonson's play. I have already quoted the portions of the comic pursuit of the fairy queen and will here add only the stage directions from I.i.:

> _Fortune descends down from heaven to the Stage, and then she calls forth four Harpers, that by the sound of their musicke, they might awake the ancient Bardh, a_

[13]Ribner, p. 262.

> *kind of Welsh poet, who long ago was there intombed.... The Harpers play, and the Bardh riseth from his Tomb.*

The significance of *The Valiant Welshman* is that if we accept it as Armin's, we are supported in the belief that he was preeminently a parodist, a mimic (and what actor is not?), and we must excuse the unintelligibility of *Two Maids* as stemming from negligence, not ignorance.

APPENDIX B

PRESS-VARIANTS

[Copies collated: Q (J. P. Morgan Library), BM (British Museum), Bod (Bodleian Library), Dyce (Victoria and Albert Museum), DFo1 (Folger Shakespeare Library [McKee], missing two preliminary leaves), DFo2 (Folger Shakespeare Library), DFo3 (Folger Shakespeare Library [J. P. Kemble], inlaid throughout and has some letters trimmed, affecting the title-page, the running-titles, and the signatures and catchwords; also wanting C2v), DFo4 (Folger Shakespeare Library [Mitford-Brinsley Nicholson], missing the two preliminary leaves), DFo5 (Folger Shakespeare Library, missing text after G4), MH (Harvard University), CSmH (Henry E. Huntington Library). These comprise the recorded extant copies of the only early edition of _The History of the Two Maids of More-clacke_, which is the quarto of 1609.]

All press-variants occur in the outer forme of Sheet C, indicating that special but by no means total care was taken by the printer to correct its defects; since, as the chart below reveals, the Sheet exists in five different states, we can be sure that the printer stopped the press four times after beginning the run. It is curious, and probably inexplicable, that he was scrupulous enough to correct a catchword and what would have been an admissable use of italic font (_Toures_ to Toures), and yet, having made the latter correction, did not re-correct the turned "r" in "Toures" or capitalize miniscule letters which begin some speeches on the Sheet. I list the eight variants below, giving the corrected and preferred readings first (marking them [*] as opposed to the uncorrected versions, which are marked [#], lettering them sequentially. The letters and marks then appear in a chart which shows the order in which the copies were printed.

A Sig. $C2^{v}$, line 31 (my IX.30):
* loued...play...seruant,] Q, BM, Bod, DFo1, DFo2, DFo4, DFo5, missing in DFo3.
# loud...play,...seruant] Dyce, MH, CSmH.

B line 32 (my IX.30):
* nere] Q, BM, Bod, DFo1, DFo2, DFo4, DFo5.
# were] Dyce, MH, CsmH.

C line 33 (my IX.32):
* loued] Q, BM, Bod, DFo1, DFo2, DFo4, DFo5.
# loud] Dyce, MH, CSmH.

D Sig. C3, line 12 (my IX.47):
* beach,] Q, BM, Bod, Dyce, DFo1, DFo2, DFo3, DFo4, DFo5.
# beach;] MH, CSmH.

E Sig. $C4^{v}$, line 1 (my XI.42):
* Toures] Q, BM, Bod, Dyce, DFo1, DFo2, DFo4, DFo5.
# Toures] MH, CSmH, DFo3.

F Sig. $C4^{v}$, line 27 (my XI.67):
* drunkennes] Q, BM, Bod, Dyce, DFo1, DFo2, DFo4, DFo5.
# drunkennes,] MH, CSmH, DFo3.

G line 28 (my XI.68):
* appetite?] Q, BM, Bod, Dyce, DFo1, DFo2, DFo4, DFo5.
# appetite.] MH, CSmH, DFo3.

H catchword:
* S. Wil.] BM, Bod, DFo5.
# Wil] Q, MH, CSmH, Dyce, DFo1, DFo2, DFo3, DFo4.

	MH	CSmH	DFo3	Dyce	Morg	DFo1	DFo2	DFo4	DFo5	BM	Bod
A	#	#	#	#	*	*	*	*	*	*	*
B	#	#	#	#	*	*	*	*	*	*	*
C	#	#	#	#	*	*	*	*	*	*	*
D	#	#	*	*	*	*	*	*	*	*	*
E	#	#	#	*	*	*	*	*	*	*	*
F	#	#	#	*	*	*	*	*	*	*	*
H	#	#	#	#	#	#	#	#	*	*	*
	I	I	II	III	IV	IV	IV	IV	V	V	V

I am grateful to Dr. Giles E. Dawson of the Folger Library for suggesting this schematic presentation.

APPENDIX C

LIST OF CATCHWORDS

Sig.	Catchword
A	Maide.
A^{v}	Humill.
A2	We
A2^{v}	Filles
A3	Lady.
A3^{v}	Mary.
A4	Tabitha.
A4^{v}	Yet
B	Three-
B^{v}	And
B2	Yet
B2^{v}	Tabit.
B3	S. Will.
B3^{v}	With
B4	Iohn
B4^{v}	any
C	sion
C^{v}	my
C2	Enter
C2^{v}	Iames.
C3	come
C3^{v}	Toures.
C4	Tour.
C4^{v}	Wil
D	Tutch.
D^{v}	Humil.
D2	Tutch.
D2^{v}	Filbon.
D3	them
D3^{v}	In
D4	Thinke
D4^{v}	Houres
E	No
E^{v}	Yet
E2	S. Wil.
E2^{v}	The
E3	Guide
E3^{v}	This

Sig.	Catchword
E4	Wilt
E4^{v}	Enter
F	A
F^{v}	I
F2	New
F2^{v}	go
F3	Henry.
F3^{v}	Enter.
F4	Mr.
F4^{v}	And
G	But
G^{v}	New
G2	Mary.
G2^{v}	Tutch.
G3	In
G3^{v}	Lady.
G4	That
G4^{v}	Tabitha.
H	As
H^{v}	Be
H2	The
H2^{v}	Lady.
H3	For
H3^{v}	loose
H4	S. Will.
H4^{v}	Tabitha.
I	daugh-
I^{v}	When
I2	Earle
I2^{v}	FINIS

LIST OF WORKS CITED IN THE APPARATUS

Alleman, Gellert Spencer. *Matrimonial Law and the Materials of Restoration Comedy*. Philadelphia, 1942.

A.[rmin], R.[obert]. *The Valiant Welshman*. London, 1615.

Armin, Robert. *The History of the Two Maids of More-clacke*. London, 1609.

________. *The Works of Robert Armin*. Edited by Alexander B. Grosart. Manchester, 1880.

________. *Fools and Jesters: with a reprint of R. Armin's Nest of Ninnies, 1608*. Edited by J. P. Collier. London, 1845.

Aydelotte, Frank. *Elizabethan Rogues and Vagabonds*. Cambridge, 1913.

Baldwin, Thomas Whitfield. *The Organization and Personnel of the Shakespearian Company*. Princeton, 1927.

________. "Shakespeare's Jester: The Dates of *Much Ado* and *As You Like It*," *MLN*, XXXIX (1924), 447-455.

Bowers, Fredson. "An Examination of the Method of Proof Correction in *Lear*," *The Library*, 5th series, II (1948), 20-24.

Bradbrook, Millicent C. *The Growth and Structure of Elizabethan Comedy*. Berkeley, 1956.

Browne, Sir Thomas. "Pseudodoxia Epidemica," *The Works of Sir Thomas Browne*. Edited by Geoffrey Keynes. Vols. II-III. London, 1928.

Bush, Douglas. *Mythology and the Renaissance Tradition*. New York, 1963.

Chambers, Edmund K. *The Elizabethan Stage*. 4 vols. Cambridge, 1923.

Chappell, William. Popular Music of the Olden Times. London, 1859.

Collier, John Payne (ed.). Old Ballads. London, 1840.

Craig, Hardin. A New Look At Shakespeare's Quartos. Stanford, 1961

Cunliffe, Richard John. A New Shakespearean Dictionary. London, 1910.

Davies, John of Hereford. The Complete Works. Edited by A. B. Grosart. Edinburgh, 1878.

Denkinger, Emma Marshall. "Actors' Names in the Registers of St. Bodolphe Aldgate," PMLA, XLI (1926), 91-109.

Dictionary of National Biography. London, 1921-1922.

Donne, John. Poetical Works. Edited by H. J. C. Grierson. 2 vols. Oxford, 1958.

Dudley, O. H. T. "John In the Hospital," a letter in TLS, June 17, 1949, p. 317.

Earle, John. Microcosmographie. Edited by A. S. West. London, 1897.

Ellis-Fermor, Una. "Timon of Athens: An Unfinished Play," RES, XVIII (1942), 270-283.

Farmer, J. S., and Henley, W. E. (ed.). Slang and Its Analogues. 7 vols. London, 1890-1904.

Felver, Charles S. Robert Armin, Shakespeare's Fool. Kent, Ohio, 1961.

________. "William Shakespeare and Robert Armin His Fool: A Working Partnership." Unpublished doctoral dissertation, University of Michigan, 1955.

________. "Robert Armin's Fragment of a Bawdy Ballad of 'Mary Ambree,'" N&Q, ns, VII (1960), 14-16.

________. "Shakespeare's Source for Touchstone," Shakespeare Quarterly, VII (1956), 135-137.

Gray, Austin K. "Robert Armin, The Fool," PMLA, XLII (1927), 673-685.

Greg, W. W. The Editorial Problem in Shakespeare. Oxford, 1954.

Greg, W. W. The Shakespeare First Folio. Oxford, 1955.

Harrington, Sir John. The Letters and Epigrams of Sir John Harrington. Edited by N. E. McClure. Philadelphia, 1930.

Herbert, George. The Poems of George Herbert. Edited by A. Waugh. Oxford, 1937.

Herring, Robert. "The Whale Has A Wide Mouth," Life & Letters Today, XXXVI (1943), 44-65.

Heywood, Thomas. A Woman Killed With Kindness. Edited by R. W. Van Fossen. London, 1961.

_______. The Royall King and the Loyall Subject. Edited by K. W. Tibbals. Philadelphia, 1906.

Hibbard, George Richard. Thomas Nashe. Cambridge, Mass., 1962.

Hillebrand, Harold Newcombe. "The Children of the King's Revels at Whitefriar," JEGP, XXI (1922), 318-334.

Holzknecht, Karl. Outlines of Tudor and Stuart Plays. New York, 1947.

Hotson, Leslie. Shakespeare's Motley. Oxford, 1952.

Jewkes, Wilfred T. Act Division in Elizabethan and Jacobean Plays. Hamden, Conn., 1958.

Jonson, Ben. Ben Jonson. Edited by Hereford and Simpson. 11 vols. Oxford, 1925.

Judges, Arthur Valentine. The Elizabethan Underworld. London, 1930.

Kirschbaum, Leo. Shakespeare and the Stationers. Athens, Ohio, 1955.

Kokeritz, Helge. Shakespeare's Pronunciation. New Haven, 1953.

Lawrence, William John. "Early Stage Traps," Pre-Restoration Stage Studies. Cambridge, Mass., 1927.

Lewis, John D. "Thomas Heywood's The Fair Maid of the West and Its Audience." Unpublished doctoral dissertation, University of Kansas.

Lyly, John. Works. Edited by R. W. Bond. 3 vols. Oxford, 1902.

McGinn, Donald J. _Shakespeare's Influence on the Drama of His Age_. New Brunswick, N. J., 1938.

McKenzie, D. F. "A List of Printers' Apprentices, 1605-1640," _SB_, XIII (1960), 109-141.

McKerrow, Ronald B. "A Suggestion Regarding Shakespeare's Manuscripts," _RES_, XI (1935), 459-465.

Murry, John Middleton. "Notes on Shakespeare," _The New Adelphi_, ns. (March, 1928), pp. 251-253.

Nares, Robert. _A Glossary_. 2 vols. London, 1876.

Nashe, Thomas. _The Works of Thomas Nashe_. Edited by R. B. McKerrow. 2 vols. London, 1904.

New York Times, August 29, 1953.

O'Connor, Frank [pseud. Michael O'Donovan]. _Shakespeare's Progress_. New York, 1960.

Oxford English Dictionary. New York, 1893.

Painter, William. _The Palace of Pleasure_. London, 1890.

Partridge, Eric. _A Dictionary of Slang and Unconventional English_. New York, 1961.

________. _Shakespeare's Bawdy_. London, 1955.

Percy, Bishop Thomas. _Reliques of English Poetry_. 4 vols. Edinburgh, 1858.

Plomer, Henry. _A Short History of English Printing: 1476-1900_. London, 1916.

Polti, Georges. _The Thirty-Six Dramatic Situations_. Boston, 1944.

Schelling, Felix. _Elizabethan Drama, 1558-1642_. New York, 1908.

Shakespeare, William. _As You Like It_. Edited by G. L. Kittredge. New York, 1939.

________. _As You Like It_. Edited by Albert Gilman. New York, 1963.

________. _Hamlet The First Quarto_. Edited by Albert Weiner. Great Neck, N. Y., 1962.

________. _I. King Henry IV_. Edited by A. R. Humphreys, London, 1960.

Shakespeare, William. Macbeth. Edited by Kenneth Muir. Cambridge, Mass., 1952.

________. The Complete Works. Edited by G. B. Harrison. New York, 1948.

Shakespeare's England: An Account of the Life and Manners of His Age. 2 vols. Oxford, 1916.

Sharpe, R. B. The Real War of the Theaters. Boston, 1935.

Smith, John Hazel. "The Composition of the Quarto of Much Ado About Nothing," SB, XVI (1963), 9-26.

Spurgeon, Caroline. Shakespeare's Imagery. Cambridge, 1935.

Sternfield, Frederick W. Music in Shakespearian Tragedy. New York, 1963.

Stow, John. A Survey of London. Oxford, 1908.

Sugden, Edward Holdsworth. A Topographical Dictionary to the Works of Shakespeare & His Fellow Dramatists. Manchester, 1925.

Tarleton, Richard. Tarleton's Jests and News Out of Purgatory. Edited by James O. Halliwell-Phillips. London, 1844.

Thompson, Stith. Motif-Index of Folk Literature. 6 vols. Bloomington, Ind., 1955.

Tilley, Morris P. A Dictionary of the Proverbs in England in the 16th and 17th Centuries. Ann Arbor, 1950.

Tourneur, Cyril. The Revenger's Tragedy. Edited by R. A. Foakes. Cambridge, Mass., 1966.

Turner, Robert K. "The Printing of A King and No King Q1," SB, XVIII (1965), 255-259.

Vyvyan, Clara Coltman. The Scilly Isles. London, 1953.

Williams, Philip. "The Compositor of the 'Pied Bull' Lear," SB, I (1949), 59-68.

Wolfe, Edwin 2nd. "'If Shadows Be a Picture's Excellence': An Experiment in Critical Bibliography," PMLA, LXIII (1948), 831-857.

Wright, Louis B. Middle Class Culture in Elizabethan England. New York, 1935.

Wright, Thomas. _Dictionary of Obsolete and Provincial English_. 2 vols. London, 1869.